UNDER THE SABERS

UNDER THE SABERS

✯ ✯ ✯

THE UNWRITTEN CODE
OF ARMY WIVES

✯ ✯ ✯

TANYA BIANK

ST. MARTIN'S PRESS ⚜ NEW YORK

www.stmartins.com

Library of Congress Cataloging-in-Publication Data

Biank, Tanya.
    Under the Sabers : The Unwritten Code of Army Wives
       p. cm.
    ISBN 0-312-33350-1
    EAN 978-0-312-33350-8
    1. United States. Army—Military life. 2. Army spouses—North Carolina—Fayette-
ville. 3. Fort Bragg (N.C.)—Social life and customs. 4. War casualties—United States—
Psychological aspects. 5. Murder—Case studies. I. Title.

U766.B53 2006
355.1'086'5509756373—dc22

                                                                              2005050404

First Edition: February 2006

10 9 8 7 6 5 4 3 2 1

For an Army wife close to my heart,

my mother, Patricia,

and for the families of

the United States Armed Forces

NOTE TO READERS

All of the principal individuals described in this work are identified by their real names; however, in a few instances, the names and identifying characteristics of others have been changed.

CONTENTS

PROLOGUE

This is a story about Army life, but it was death—murder, actually—that was the impetus for me to write this book.

In the summer of 2002 I was a military reporter for the *Fayetteville Observer* in Fayetteville, North Carolina, the town outside Fort Bragg. The post is home to some of the Army's most elite soldiers—paratroopers, Green Berets, and Delta Force commandos. With a density of high-performing people who thrive on adrenaline, Fort Bragg is an electrifying place to serve, a fact not missed by visiting dignitaries, government officials, and other VIPs who often note the special quality of the place. Yet that summer, in the span of just six weeks, four Fort Bragg soldiers killed their wives; then two of the men committed suicide, and a third would hang himself in jail eight months later. In a fifth case an officer's wife was charged with killing her husband.

It was compelling, headline-grabbing material, and I reported on those stories as well as the bigger picture that united them. As I dug deeper and deeper, I realized that there was a broader tale I wanted to tell, a story that was buried in the commotion of one tragic, overexposed summer in Fayetteville. Even without sensational murders, the lives of Army wives are the stuff of drama. These women play roles that are bound by convention in circumstances that are sometimes precarious, frequently close-knit, and too often heartrending. Yet what life is really like for Army wives has never been closely examined.

To tell a story about the Army lifestyle, it helps to have been a part of it. I grew up an Army brat, moving from post to post. My father, now a retired colonel, served thirty years in the military. Though I had gone away to college and traveled and worked overseas, eventually I realized, a bit grudgingly, that my blood would always be tinged Army green. It raised eyebrows when I became the first female reporter at the *Fay-*

etteville Observer to cover Fort Bragg, but I didn't give it a second thought. I felt just as comfortable talking with generals in their red-carpeted offices about training policies and deployments as I did chatting with privates in the field about why they preferred chewing one brand of tobacco over others.

Long before "embedded media" became a common term, I was flying on C-130 airborne operations, joining helicopter search-and-rescue missions, and trudging through mud with infantrymen in foreign countries. I always strove to show the human side—perhaps because the Army had touched my personal life—of an organization known for uniformity and conformity. It helped that my background gave me credibility. I could rely on the "I'm from your world, too," factor. Plus I liked the place.

I had arrived in Fayetteville early in the spring of 1995 just as the dogwoods were blooming. Despite their fragile beauty, however, this was no genteel southern town. Fort Bragg is one of the largest military installations in the country and the base for 42,000 mostly airborne soldiers. If there is a trouble spot somewhere in the world, chances are good that Fort Bragg troops are in the mix.

There's a sense of real purpose here—a bona fide war mission and a long and proud history of belonging to something greater than oneself. Even the streets and neighborhoods are named after World War II battle campaigns: Normandy Drive, Ardennes Street, Bastogne Gables, Nijmegen, Corregidor Courts, Luzon, Bataan, and Salerno. Soon, no doubt, the campaigns of Afghanistan and Iraq will start cropping up on street signs, too.

Within this environment a whole community—with arcane traditions and a well-defined military caste system—thrives. The senior officers' families live in the prettiest part of post near the parade field in century-old homes, all within walking distance of the golf course and the officers club pool and tennis courts. The most junior of enlisted couples live in dowdy duplexes known as ghettos—though Fort Bragg is finally tearing these down—where nineteen-year-old brides sit on steps strewn with toys, watching their children ride tricycles on the sidewalk. They have to drive to get to their pool. And every day a bugle call to reveille and a cannon jolt at 6:30 A.M. remind you of where you are and why.

Over the last decade I became part of the community and friends with the soldiers' families, who were my neighbors or whom I met at church. I got to know and love the veterans, the "old-timers." And I realized that Fayetteville's greatest asset was its people, a hodgepodge of races, religions, and ethnic groups, both haves and have-nots, who live in one of the most integrated communities in the country. As one black Vietnam vet, who had been severely wounded in combat, once told me, "If you have to die next to each other, living together isn't so hard."

For me the third week in July 2002 started off routinely enough—if writing about an AWOL soldier who claimed he had amnesia is routine. My days were generally spent juggling writing assignments and interviews that covered everything from war training to Army wives' craft shows. By Friday afternoon, July 19, I was working on a mind-numbing account of the integration of the Army's battle theories and doctrine with digital technology.

Then news of a murder hit the newsroom. A man had just led detectives to the spot where he had buried his wife, whom he had strangled three weeks earlier. A few hours later the same detectives were investigating the murder-suicide of a married couple across town. During the weekend facts surrounding both cases slowly trickled in. The husbands were soldiers. This was my beat.

I felt as if a tornado had rumbled through my stomach. There were now four dead wives in six weeks—out of the ordinary even in Fayetteville, jaded as it was by decades of violence and bad news. After all, this was a town that had had its share of extraordinary news stories over the years—including Jeffrey MacDonald's 1970 murders of his wife and daughters, a case made infamous in *Fatal Vision*.

People had barely noticed when, a month earlier, on June 11, Sergeant First Class Rigoberto Nieves, a Green Beret just two days back from Afghanistan, had shot his wife, Teresa, in the head before killing himself. The Friday after their deaths, I attended a cocktail party filled with high-ranking Fort Bragg officers and their wives. Over gin and tonic and scotch and water, the conversation focused on Italian handbags and summer sandals, new duty assignments, summer vacation plans, Osama bin Laden, and Fayetteville's drought.

A few weeks after that, on Tuesday, July 9, I'd been driving from Washington, D.C.—where I'd covered a White House Medal of Honor ceremony posthumously honoring an American prisoner of war in Vietnam—when the second murder took place. Sergeant Cedric Griffin visited the Fayetteville home of his estranged wife, Marilyn. Following an argument, he stabbed her seventy times before setting her body on fire. As grotesque and unsettling as Marilyn Griffin's murder was, it didn't really shock me either. Nor did it garner much more than a day's worth of media attention and a shake of the head by people in town.

Now the body count had risen again, and no one was making any connection.

On the following morning, I walked into the newsroom, headed to my boss's cubicle, stepped over a pile of yellowing newspapers, sat down in the chair parked behind his desk, and stared at an assortment of neckties in various colors draped over the top of his cubicle. Mike Adams, the deputy managing editor, was a short man with a penchant for cutting his own hair. He had a quick, off-color wit, the kind that kept reporters in stitches. He also had a low threshold for bullshit, from his reporters or from the public.

"What's up?" He had swung around in his chair and was studying my face, as was his habit. But he already knew.

"We gotta do something," I said.

"Start looking for patterns," Mike said. "Find out how many of these guys have been deployed to Afghanistan. Figure out how much time you're going to need. What's Fort Bragg saying?"

Not much. That I knew before I even made my first phone call. This was not a story Fort Bragg would want to have publicized. The Army liked to deal with its dirty laundry behind closed doors without civilians or the media poking around. It didn't take long for me to discover that three of the killers had served in Special Operations and had been deployed to Afghanistan. Although Fort Bragg would never admit it, I was sure one of the men was in Delta Force. I had met him myself.

As I worked on the story, events had turned even more bizarre by the next day: Police suspected an Army wife of shooting her husband to death as he slept.

I kept at it. From the beginning I was interested in more than just the who, what, where, and when of these deaths. I started looking at couples whose history of fights and affairs turned into wife beating or worse after long separations. I investigated why wives, fearful of the repercussions from their spouses and the Army, didn't report abusive husbands. I talked with couples who knew they could benefit from counseling but stayed away, fearing it wouldn't be kept confidential and would ruin the husband's career. And I talked with husbands and wives about the importance of appearances—keeping the kitchen clean and the lawn mowed and maintaining the facade that there were no problems in the bedroom.

When my first story ran on Friday, July 26, one of my colleagues stopped me as I walked into the newsroom that morning following an interview I had at Womack Army Medical Center.

"Where have you been?" he asked. "We've been bombarded with calls from around the world."

I looked at him sarcastically. "The *world*?"

"Yeah, you're all over the news and the wires." I walked to my desk with coffee in one hand and a notebook and papers in the other and felt the eyes of other reporters on me. *What was going on?* It took a moment for everything to sink in as I saw all the e-mails and phone messages. Within hours, reporters and news crews had flown into town, and Fort Bragg officials had held a news conference to deal with the onslaught of calls it was receiving. I even started getting phone calls at home from Army wives concerned for their own safety. The calls unnerved me, because in many cases the women weren't interested in publishing their stories; they wanted help. I began to keep a women's hotline number in my Rolodex at work as well as on my nightstand.

The murders and what might have caused them were big news for weeks. Then, eventually, the headlines faded, and the stories bounced from the front page to the inside sections. All that had been left unsaid ate away at me. What about the rest of the story? The events that were played out daily behind the Army's gates, in the neighborhoods and early morning unit formations, at the military balls and the wives' coffee groups and children's playgroups, on the parade fields and in the bedrooms?

We often hear about the sacrifices soldiers make for their nation, but we rarely hear about their spouses' struggles. Army wives are bound by an unwritten code. They are expected to endure hardships with graciousness and tragedies with heads held high. Despite America's fascination with the military since 9/11 and the war in Iraq, the media generally focuses only on the families' tearful good-byes and tearful reunions. Or, in the case of the spouse murders, their deaths. The reality is far more complex and riveting.

I originally planned to write an oral history featuring nine women, but the project eventually evolved into the story of Army wives told through the lives of four women who reach a crisis point in their lives at Fort Bragg. The women are from different backgrounds and social classes; their husbands various ranks. Their stories evolve during the period from December 2000 through the summer of 2002, a year and a half that encompassed both a peacetime Army and one at war.

Finding the right mix of women with critical life turns was no easy task. Though their stories are individual, the four women in this book are emblematic. Their character traits and experiences are things all Army wives can recognize or identify with. You cannot tell the Army wife story by focusing only on a sergeant's wife or a colonel's. Though there are common threads, their roles, and therefore their day-to-day encounters, are too diverse.

Each of the four women is vastly different from the others in looks, personality, and lifestyle, yet their stories are intertwined. They experience love, hardship, betrayal, tragedy, and success, all in a world steeped in tradition, with a rigid decorum and pecking order, where perfection is expected. Each comes to a crossroads that forces her to forge her own path. Not all succeed. Was the Army accountable for their fate? Ultimately the reader will have to decide.

The women I chose are not the usual subjects profiled by out-of-town writers on a deadline. By that I mean wives who are already in the public arena, whether they are on-the-fringe Army wives speaking out at antiwar rallies or carefully screened women trotted out by the Army public affairs officers for the press hounds who "want to talk to Army wives."

I met the women the same way you would meet people in your own community, over time, through personal introductions, by chance, as well as from contacts made long before I ever decided to write a book.

I shared with them my own experiences along with my vision for this project. I wasn't going to press anyone into a cookie-cutter version of some idealized type. Stereotyping people, often based solely on rank and position, is already too ingrained within Army culture. Although some of my characters may seem at first glance to fit a general stereotype—the officer's wife who volunteers and "does lunch" or the uneducated young enlisted wife and mother who can barely make ends meet—their stories unfold in unique ways. The women shared with me extremely intimate details about their marriages, their frustrations and insecurities, their disappointments, and their darkest pain, all the human vulnerabilities that must often be tucked away for the good of the Army and their husbands' careers. The Army's motto speaks for itself: Mission First, People Always.

I met Rita Odom, the wife of Specialist Brian Odom, during Christmas season 2000. I was working on a story at the time about soldiers in the 82nd Airborne Division, who were on alert over the holidays. Rita was one of a handful of women I interviewed, and I immediately liked the way she expressed herself and turned a phrase. She was comfortable in her own skin and she was smart, with a down-home appeal. I wouldn't hear from Rita again until 2002, when she sent me an e-mail to say hello and update me on her family.

Rita was a new wife and as such could provide a set of fresh eyes on the Army experience. She knew nothing about the Army when she married a soldier she had met only a few times and left behind her small Alabama town and a life of poverty and abuse. Her experiences in Fayetteville open up the raunchier side of Army life, through the friends she meets while their husbands are in the field. All the while Rita struggles to establish equal footing within her marriage, to make something of herself, and to find her own place, while around her other women are cheating on their husbands.

I have known Delores Kalinofski and her husband, Command Sergeant Major Gary Kalinofski, for seven years. I first met the sergeant major—or should I say I heard him belting out, "Good morning ladies! Are you decent?"—when I was in Albania, to cover the 2nd Battalion of the 505th Parachute Infantry Regiment. He was the unit's command sergeant major. I peeked out from my sleeping bag in my new "bedroom," a bombed-out old Soviet bunker, and saw a man standing with his hands on his hips, his feet apart, and a big grin on his face. We formed a friendship, and we stayed in touch.

I met Delores at my surprise birthday party later in the year. She had more than twenty years of Army know-how and had spent much of that time in Fayetteville. She was a devout Catholic, frugal in her spending, and always put others before herself. Delores had to face an unthinkable event during the period of this book, and the Army community responded in good ways and, sadly, shameful ones. I always knew there was more to Delores than what was on the surface. Slowly and painstakingly, she revealed pieces of herself to me that she says even her closest friends will be shocked to learn.

I was introduced to Andrea Lynne Cory, the wife of Lieutenant Colonel Rennie Cory, a few weeks before I left on an assignment to Vietnam in 2002. Her family's story had actually inspired me to go to Southeast Asia in the first place, and I chose Andrea Lynne because a life-changing experience forced her to grapple with who she is, what she wants, and how she will live the rest of her life. She is also living proof that you can be in your forties, have four children, and still be glamorous and sexy.

As a battalion commander's wife, Andrea Lynne was an integral part of Fort Bragg's inner circle and social scene. The oldest of the service branches, the Army as an institution has maintained the protocol, customs, and courtesies of a bygone era. At their best these can be an endearing salute to the past: The gracious homes, the parades and pageantry, the patriotic speeches, the uniforms and balls are all throwbacks to a simpler, more innocent time. Andrea Lynne's story opens a window onto a world very different from that of the other Army wives.

And I got to know Andrea Floyd, the wife of Sergeant First Class Brandon Floyd, through her family, who, along with friends and detectives, have helped me tell her tale. Since this book is partly about sacrifice, I thought it was important to tell the story of one woman who had paid the Army with the ultimate price, her life. I was shocked to find soldiers who thought she deserved her fate.

Not much had been reported about Andrea Floyd's life or marriage, but there were plenty of rumors swirling around. The more I researched her background and found people willing to talk, the more I uncovered a relationship with many twists and turns. My goal from the beginning was to humanize both Andrea and her husband, showing their admirable qualities as well as their faults. Their story is an extreme example of what can go wrong for an Army couple with a marriage already in serious trouble.

In August 2001 I had a chance meeting with Brandon Floyd at Fort Bragg's legendary Green Beret Club, famous for its bar fights and colorful characters. It was a late Friday afternoon, and I was working on an article, when Brandon asked me to sit down at the table he was sharing with friends. I stayed for a couple of hours. Our conversation added firsthand insights into his character. Later, through the help of those who served with Brandon, I was also able to shed some light on his off-limits world: He belonged to Delta Force, the "black operations" group at Fort Bragg that specializes in secret high-risk missions, including hostage rescues and attacks on terrorists.

The fifth character in this book is Fayetteville itself, known to many people by its nickname, Fayettenam. When I was first heading here, I told an old veteran where I was going. "Ah, Fayettenaaam," he said, as if he was recalling his favorite porno. Green Berets had branded the town with the name during Vietnam days, when thousands of draftees passing through raised hell before heading to war. Fayettenam was sin city back then, and it became synonymous with wild times and rebellion. It takes more than a cursory visit or a trip down Bragg Boulevard to get to the heart of Fayetteville.

Today, on the post itself soldiers carry on with a focus and intensity rarely found in young men. Whether they joined the Army for college money or for God and country, they come to understand their mortality each time they parachute out of an open plane door at night or are on foot patrol in a third-world country far from home. They are indoctrinated to believe that they can save the world, but they can't always save themselves. Often your own demons are the hardest enemy to defeat.

If you ask me, Army wives serve too. My mother was an Army wife, and by watching her I learned the true meaning of resilience and resourcefulness. It's not an easy life, and it deserves acknowledgment. I wrote this book as a tribute. And for those who know nothing about the Army, I hope they come away with a better understanding about life "on the inside."

Gentlemen:

I reverently pledge you: The ladies who have shared our lives from the Equator to the Arctic; the ladies who have condoned our reverses, and inspired but to applaud our successes.

May we live to make them happy, or, and the Great Day comes, so die as to make them proud.

The Army Women, God Bless Them.

—General George Smith Patton, Jr.
April 5, 1924
(A toast to "the ladies" at
a West Point dinner in Kansas City)

I cast my lot in with a soldier, and where he was, was home to me.

—Martha Summerhayes, nineteenth-century Army wife

UNDER THE SABERS

INTRODUCTION

Lieutenant Sam Pennica wished the hearse would hurry up. He was forty-nine, and after thirty years in law enforcement the smell of decomposing flesh still nauseated him. But the shock of what one human being could do to another had worn off long ago. At his feet, stuffed inside an Army-issue parachute sack, was the crumpled body of an Army wife named Jennifer Wright.

Pennica checked his watch and took a drag on a cigarette. It was 2:30 P.M. on Friday, July 19, 2002, and the temperature had just hit one hundred degrees.

The veteran cops I've known generally fall into two categories. The first are those who have become jaded from dealing day in and day out with dirtbag criminals and a mostly unappreciative public. These policemen seem like discarded bullet casings, spent shells, long separated from the fire that had inspired them to join the force in the first place. Then there are those longtime lawmen who still have the passion and smarts for crime fighting and for life in general. Pennica fell into this second category. He still had the spark, along with a ready smile, but at the moment he was pissed.

"Where the hell is he?" The coroner should already have arrived. Years of chasing criminals in North Carolina had turned Pennica's Midwestern accent into a gravelly drawl. Because of his olive-toned skin and black hair, people often mistook Pennica for a Lumbee Indian from nearby Robeson County. He grew up in a Sicilian family in Cleveland, where he attended Catholic mass every day. He became a Southern Baptist with an affinity for vinegar-based barbecue, boiled potatoes, and slaw, but his bulky frame never could adjust to the inferno of a windless, Southern July afternoon. Pennica kept his arms akimbo, occasionally swatting the mosquitoes and deerflies swarming around his head. Sweat beaded on his upper lip and seeped through his polo shirt. Acres of spindly longleaf pines, which form a buffer between Fort Bragg and Fayetteville, offered skimpy shade. In Fayetteville, where concrete and asphalt carpet everything, this was the perfect spot to bury a terrible mistake.

I knew it was a great hiding place when I saw the site myself. No one ever would have looked for a body in a gully with snakes, pine straw, and pinecones and so thick with vines and underbrush that one of Pennica's detectives, Sergeant Rick O'Briant, had to use a machete to hack a path.

Master Sergeant Bill Wright remembered the exact spot, though. He had trained for war in these woods and hunted for squirrel here. Bill Wright was thirty-six and had a head full of thick, wavy hair the color of tar that he kept neatly trimmed and combed to the side with a low side part. Despite a farm-boy face, he was a seasoned soldier, providing wise counsel to his soldiers. He was also known to be one of the nicest guys in his company.

Everyone I met who knew Bill Wright extolled his virtues: great father, husband, and NCO. Even the cops had compassion for him. It was harder, in this town at least, for me to find people who had compassion for the wife he had just murdered.

To many at Bragg it was Bill Wright who was the victim, a politically incorrect point of view that was never part of any media coverage, including my own. At the time I never asked the one unthinkable question: Did she deserve what happened to her? The question seemed absurd. Since I didn't ask it, I couldn't learn what I know now. More than a few soldiers who either knew the Wrights or had heard about the case later told me, "She got what she deserved." Or "She had it comin'." These quick-trigger outbursts (they were never said casually) always caught me off guard. To understand the root of such venom, I had to take a step back and realize that these men identified more with Bill Wright the patriot, Bill Wright the war vet and family man, than they did with his supposedly cheating wife. An unfaithful Army wife might as well be a terrorist, soldiers hate them that much. Soldiers tend to consider infidelity as a personal slight on their own manhood. When a woman cheats on a buddy, she is desecrating not only her husband but also the flag and all those in uniform. Of course none of this applies when soldiers cheat on their wives.

Rumors of Jennifer Wright's alleged affairs had been flowing through her husband's unit for a long time before her death. And in the Army rumors are as good as reality; here perceptions *are* reality. Sadly Jennifer Wright was never able to defend her reputation. In the end the "great" father had orphaned his three boys.

On Monday, July 1, Wright had reported his wife missing, telling investigators she had run off with another man. Something seemed wrong to the police. Jennifer, a thirty-two-year-old mother, who sang in the choir at Aaron Lake Baptist Church, would never have abandoned her sons. And she hadn't taken anything with her. Her purse, makeup, and money were still in the house. Detectives started looking more closely at her husband.

The morning of July 19, almost three weeks after he reported her missing, Bill Wright had failed a polygraph test at the Cumberland County Law Enforcement Center. Informed of the results, he confessed to strangling his wife twenty-one days before. He told deputies he had accused her of infidelity and killed her in a fit of rage—shattering her jaw with a baseball bat and then strangling her with her underwear. He had buried her body in the woods off Plank Road near Fort Bragg.

Sergeant Charlie Disponzio, a homicide detective, felt sorry for the guy, more than he ever had for any murderer. He saw a man who wasn't a criminal at heart, just an Army soldier who loved his kids and who'd been screwed over so much he couldn't take it anymore. He didn't condone what the man had done by any means, but he could understand how it happened.

Now Wright was staring blankly down into a gully, fifty feet off a dirt road. "It's right there." He pointed to a depression in the ground covered with fresh dirt. Pennica had decided not to shackle or handcuff the man. He didn't want Wright to change his mind about leading them to the body.

The detectives pulled out the shovels they always traveled with, and Corporal Kenny Cain, a crime-scene investigator, and Sergeant Disponzio started to dig.

"Wait," Pennica interrupted. He motioned to Bill Wright. "Take him back to the car." No telling what the guy might do. It gave Pennica the creeps just thinking about it.

Just a few inches down they found her, wrapped in a black garbage bag inside a canvas parachute bag with handles and broken zipper. The detectives opened it just enough to make sure the body was inside. A black sports bra, tied in a perfect, single overhand knot, was tight around her neck.

Sergeant Disponzio pushed the shovel handle through the bag's carrying handles, and he and Corporal Cain lifted the bag from the grave. It was lighter than Sergeant Disponzio had expected. The smell every homicide detective comes to know intimately assaulted his nostrils like a punch.

She was the third Army wife to be murdered by her husband in a matter of weeks, but Pennica hadn't thought much about that. In his business there wasn't time. To him a murder was a murder no matter who did it. Ten days earlier there had been the Griffin murder, a particularly gruesome one. Sergeant Cedric Griffin, a black cook who worked at the commissary, had stopped by the trailer home his estranged wife, Marilyn, had just rented. After an argument later in the evening, he walked into her bedroom and stabbed her seventy times before piling her bedsheets on top of her and setting them on fire. Sergeant Griffin then ran from the trailer, leaving Marilyn's two daughters, ages two and six, to fend for themselves. The girls were able to escape the fire. Why such hatred? Marilyn was threatening to go to her husband's superiors and say he'd gotten a subordinate pregnant.

A month before that, Sergeant First Class Rigoberto Nieves, a Green Beret back from Afghanistan for just two days, had shot his wife, Teresa, in the head in the couple's master bathroom before killing himself. The couple had had serious-enough marital issues that Nieves was granted leave to come home early from deployment to deal with the problems. At the funeral one of Nieves's superiors lamented to the Green Beret's mother he never would have allowed him to go home early had he known what would happen.

And now this: a wife stuffed in a garbage bag like grass clippings and buried in the woods. Three dead Army wives in six weeks. Even in Fayettenam this was a first, but not much fazed Pennica anymore. After he retired from the North Carolina State Bureau of Investigation in Greensboro, his former colleagues thought he had lost his mind when he accepted a position as the chief detective for the Cumberland County Sheriff's Department in Fayetteville in 1996. Murders, car thefts, drug busts, burglaries, bank stickups, and fast-food restaurant robberies were so common that they garnered just average publicity in the local media unless the crime was particularly dreadful or sensational. The sheriff's department had a good working relationship with Fort Bragg when it came to such things as determining jurisdiction or sharing paperwork on a case. But Fort Bragg had its own ways, with a culture and quirks that outsiders like Pennica could never quite penetrate. Although Fort Bragg was just a ten-mile drive up Bragg Boulevard from his downtown office, the post might as well have been a world away.

Wright told the detectives he'd thrown the baseball bat and the couple's bedsheets into a Dumpster in a McDonald's parking lot on Raeford Road. While Cain and O'Briant waited for the hearse, Pennica and another detective, Mike Casey, made their way back to photograph the Dumpster. As Pennica snapped pictures, Casey got out of the Crown Victoria and approached his boss: "Damn, we got a Code 3/Code 5."

Pennica stopped taking pictures. "Where?"

"I'm not sure."

Of all times for a murder-suicide. Pennica started back to his office and got on the radio with the dispatcher. Across town, on the outskirts of Stedman, a husband and wife had been found in their master bedroom, dead from gunshot wounds to the head. Pennica divided up his homicide team.

Sergeant Disponzio was on his way to McDonalds himself, to get a double burger and fries. The day's macabre turn hadn't spoiled his appetite. It was 5:07 P.M., and he was famished. There hadn't been time for lunch, and there was still work to finish. He needed to get back to his office to do paperwork, and he wanted to talk with Bill Wright again.

In the meantime, though, Disponzio heard the same dispatch as Detective Mike Casey. A second radio call from the patrol unit on the scene asked for a detective. Soon after, Pennica called Disponzio.

"I need you to go to Stedman," Pennica said, "and get control of this situation and see what we got out there."

If there was any doubt that this was a suicide, they would need a homicide detective. The burger would have to wait. Disponzio got out of the drive-through lane and headed to the scene. Disponzio was a short, well-muscled scrapper of an Italian from Brooklyn. His old street smarts and choppy accent had stayed with him and, like Pennica, he could still stomach life's dark side. At forty-seven Disponzio had black hair, and his mustache showed just a few specks of gray. Like many of the cops in Fayetteville, he had been a soldier first. His tanned forearms were covered with blurry five-dollar tattoos that hinted at his past.

As a private in 1972, a drunken Disponzio had walked into Poison John's on Bragg Boulevard, a yellow trailer with a single lightbulb hanging from a wire. He looked up at the wall and ordered himself a number 2 and a number 7, as if he were ordering two fast-food meals. Poison John sucked down a cigarette and left his tattoos on the young soldier's flesh.

Those were the days when Hay Street, in downtown Fayetteville, was wall-to-wall bars, and the nights ended with drunken fights and paddy-wagon rides back to Fort Bragg. When a new kid got to the unit, the platoon sergeant would tell the other soldiers: "Take 'em downtown, get 'em drunk, get 'em laid, break 'em in. Give 'em a big Fayetteville welcome."

Disponzio got his nose broken at the Saigon Lounge. As for the Tavern, the Pink Pussy Cat Lounge, Rick's Lounge, the Town Pump—he knew them all.

He had gone on to serve in Grenada and the Gulf War and spent sixteen of his twenty Army years stationed at Fort Bragg. During that time he'd broken thirteen bones in his legs, hips, and shoulders while parachuting from airplanes.

Still, Disponzio had only good memories and remained fiercely loyal to the military. Yes, Fayetteville had a terrible reputation within law enforcement circles. At cop conventions Fayetteville lawmen would always get the "Oh, shit" response when they mentioned where they were from, as in, "Oh, shit, we know you guys are busy down there." Disponzio thought soldiers got a bad rap, since it was the civilians who committed most of the crimes in Cumberland County.

I'd lived in Fayetteville long enough myself to know he was right. Sure, young soldiers especially get speeding tickets and get into bar fights. Some get DUIs, get busted for drugs, or have bill collectors after them. But the soldiers aren't the ones snatching purses, stealing pedigreed dogs from yards, or plotting the break-ins, bank robberies, and Chinese restaurant stickups that seem to plague the town. Are soldiers more upstanding individuals? Well, there are a lot of good kids in the Army, and some thugs, too. More likely the service is a deterrent, since soldiers stand to lose everything if they get into serious trouble. Even minor infractions, such as speeding tickets, are compiled by military police each morning into electronic reports and then accessed by leaders. Out-of-line soldiers can get busted in rank, lose months' worth of wages, or face time in the brig. A dishonorable discharge from the military is not only humiliating but it also makes it virtually impossible to get hired at a good job in the civilian workforce.

Disponzio was alert to all the criminal possibilities when he pulled into the driveway at 1617 Carl Freeman Road forty minutes later. Yellow crime-scene tape enveloped the property like tape on a mailing package. Detective Joel Morissette pulled up at the same time. A patrolman approached them: "There's two bodies in there."

A neighbor had heard arguing and shots the night before but never bothered to call authorities. The police only got involved because the woman who lived here hadn't showed up for work. When she was four hours late, the manager of Dick's Sporting Goods had his wife drive out to the house. Both of the couple's vehicles were there, but no one answered the door, so she called her husband, who summoned the sheriff.

The detectives entered the house through a side door. Nothing was out of place. In fact, the house was extremely neat. There was no forced entry, the windows were locked; nothing had been stolen or upset. He followed the patrolman upstairs into the master bedroom. On the bed he saw a woman with blond hair, her arms folded across her chest, her face turned sideways toward the headboard. To the left of her, on the floor, a man was facedown, his torso and legs twisted like those of a discarded doll. A pistol lay next to his left hip.

"Let's get some photos," Disponzio ordered. While the crime scene photographer snapped away, the detective looked around the room. Pine paneling extended partway up the wall. Framed photographs of smiling children sat on the dresser. No signs of a struggle. No evidence of violence—except for the bed.

When the crime scene technician was finished, Disponzio walked over, pulled back the sheet, and looked at the woman's head wounds. Then he checked the man's. He had a star-shaped entry wound in the middle of his forehead, an almost textbook shape for a close-range bullet wound. Disponzio peered at the bed. Head wounds bleed profusely; the sheets and mattress were soaked. At some point the man's body had slid off his wife's and onto the floor.

"Let's walk around and see what we got," Disponzio told Morissette. Downstairs in the family room they admired the gun locker. Then a framed military print on the fireplace mantel drew his attention. He walked closer to it. It was a Mogadishu print, a battle scene from that campaign, handmade, with a serial number. Another one was near it on the hearth.

He exhaled. "These prints, they mean one thing," he told Morissette. "This is a military guy. He's with Delta Force."

"Are you sure?"

"Yeah, he's somebody from the compound. We've got an operator here." Disponzio knew immediately that this was no double murder.

"There's no way a guy like this would allow his wife and himself to be killed without a helluva struggle," he said. "This has got to be handled differently, Morissette. Keep it low profile. Get Bragg on board and CID. Get a lawyer from Special Ops."

"Got it," Morissette said as he turned to walk away.

"Hey, one more thing," Disponzio said. "You ain't gonna get a lot of cooperation from his friends, but don't take it personally."

It was ten-thirty in the evening before Disponzio left the house. The pine trees blocked the moonlight as he walked down the driveway to his car. The temperature had dropped to eighty-seven degrees. He blasted his air conditioner and gathered his thoughts. Delta operators are trained to assess severe situations calmly, he knew that. What in the world had happened here?

And then it struck him. "Oh, shit, we got anotha' one."

Make that four dead Army wives in six weeks.

PART ONE

✷ ✷ ✷

INNOCENCE
CHRISTMAS 2000

CHAPTER ONE

C hristmas 2000 had been a slower news cycle—but not so slow that I didn't have to cover the cop beat well after eleven on a Sunday evening the week before the holiday. As I parked my car and ran into an adjacent parking lot, I sank deeper into my coat.

"Hi, excuse me, I'm with the *Fayetteville Observer*. Is it a man?" I yelled out to a group of policemen walking toward me with yellow crime-scene tape.

"Yeah," an officer cop answered back, as he went to cordon off the business office parking lot. It was so cold and so quiet. Who would be around here on a Sunday night? It was an odd place for a random shooting, I thought. The weekend cop beat was a rotating duty all the reporters shared and most, like myself, dreaded. The paper had been getting ready to go to press, and I was about to go home, when news of someone being shot multiple times buzzed across the scanner.

"Just confirm it's a man and find out if he's dead," the weekend editor, Steve Coffman, had called out to me as I headed to the door. "And get back here as soon as you can."

I had arrived in time to see medical personnel load a body into the back of an ambulance.

"Just one more question, and I'll leave you alone. Is he dead?" The policeman didn't answer. I knew I was like a cockroach to this guy, feeding off any morsel of information I could get.

"Please, that's all I need. I'm not asking for a name, and I swear I'll leave. Please help me, I'm on deadline. Is he dead?"

"Yes," the cop said, a little amused at my desperation. I didn't care. I'd take an amused cop over a derisive one any day, and I'd gotten what I needed.

"Thank you so much."

"Yeah. Merry Christmas."

And with that I dashed back to the newsroom. Like most of the reporters at the paper, I hated being a weekend ambulance chaser, covering fires, murders, and car wreck fatalities, and in the summer, drownings, but there never seemed to be a shortage of those things in Fayetteville, especially around the holidays.

"He's dead," I yelled, running back into the newsroom.

"Good. You've got literally three minutes, Tanya, and then I need it. Just a graph." A follow-up story the next day would give more details. The dead man turned out to be a thirty-two-year-old Air Force pilot named Marty Theer, stationed at nearby Pope Air Force Base. He had been shot multiple times by his wife's lover, Army Staff Sergeant John Diamond, who was convicted of murder at a court-martial in August 2001. A civilian jury convicted Captain Theer's wife, Michelle, for his murder and conspiracy to commit murder in December 2004. Both are serving life sentences.

It had been a bloody Sunday. That afternoon I had walked across a yard littered with beer bottles and tried to peer into a rusty trailer with broken windows, some boarded up with plywood. A man had been shot dead inside, with a bullet to the head, as he napped on the living room couch. His fourteen-year-old son was already a suspect.

I finally got home around midnight, glad that my run as "cops girl" had ended. Most Decembers were quiet times for Army news. Soldiers were on "half-days," an annual truncated schedule that allows them time off they miss out on much of the year. For me half-days meant it was difficult to get in touch with people or set up stories, and as far as training there wasn't much of that going on—until the world came unhinged nine months later. In December 2000 the attacks on the Pentagon and the Twin Towers would have seemed like an outlandish plot in a Christmas blockbuster release, and most Americans couldn't pronounce Osama bin

Laden. Terrorism, anthrax, jihad, and weapons of mass destruction were not yet part of the everyday vocabulary.

A month later eight hundred Bragg soldiers would deploy for a six-month tour to Kosovo as "peacekeepers," but for the most part this Christmas was a time when the Army spent its days training for war rather than going to war. Some soldiers were able to take leave. For those who stayed at Bragg, there were lots of holiday festivities and parties, including battalion Christmas buffets at which one of the soldiers always dressed up like Santa with a sack full of presents for the kids. Andrea Lynne Cory, wife of Lieutenant Colonel Rennie Cory, had planned her own big party, despite her husband's initial reservations.

Under a crescent moon and dark night sky, the Corys' Fort Bragg quarters at 11 South Dupont Plaza radiated with twinkling lights and candles, and their three Fraser fir trees were lavishly decorated with ornaments collected during twenty years of marriage. Garlands of greenery and handmade Victorian lace adorned the mantelpiece and windowsills. It was four days after Christmas 2000, and Andrea Lynne steadily carried a carnival green punch bowl filled with spiked eggnog from the maid's room through the kitchen, where a huge vat of glühwein, mulled red wine, was simmering on the stove. Both were popular drinks with the ladies. Andrea Lynne used the maid's quarters—an anachronism from the days when officers' families had hired help—as a keeping room for extra dishes and kitchen sundries.

Outside, guests strolled up the sidewalk and passed a wrought-iron lamp holding a Plexiglas nameplate that announced the officer of the house in black letters: LTC RM CORY JR.

Andrea Lynne placed the punch bowl on the dining room table and called to her husband, "Rennie, the door!"

It was precisely seven o'clock. Military people always showed up on time or early for social functions. Arriving late was considered rude and undisciplined.

This Christmas party was a chance for Andrea Lynne to show off her home—and her husband. Rennie Cory had finished commanding the 2nd Battalion of the 504th Parachute Infantry Regiment (the White Devils) that summer at Fort Bragg and was now spending the year in Vietnam as a detachment commander, searching for the remains of men missing from the Vietnam War. He arrived home December 4 and was on leave for a month. So many people had asked about him that Andrea Lynne thought it would be a grand idea to throw a huge party. Her guest list included everybody who was anybody—even members of the "Bragg mafia," the insiders who ran the post and handpicked officers for important positions.

That kind of networking wasn't her husband's style. Rennie was a straight-shooter. A well-built man of forty-three, who walked with a swaggering gait (the result of too many parachute jumps), he had little patience for officers who put their own desires above the needs of the Army. Though he enjoyed having friends over to the house for drinks and dinner, Rennie wasn't out to impress or make contacts with anyone who outranked him. He certainly didn't relish these big affairs. When Rennie saw the names of generals and brigade commanders on the list of invitations, he hesitated, but Andrea Lynne wasn't about to budge.

"Rennie, let me explain three things," she said. "One, everybody always asks about you, and with all the press on Clinton's visit to Vietnam, it's a great opportunity for you to update people. Two, think of all the invitations we've received. It's only right to reciprocate at least once. And three, it's my party, and I'm making a command decision."

Rennie laughed, his eyes turning into half-moons as deep creases at the outer corners arced downward. "Baby, whatever you want."

So here he was, standing in the foyer under the mistletoe-hung chandelier, greeting guests as they streamed through the door bearing flowers, boxes of candy, and bottles of wine or Gentleman Jack. Rennie was a Jack-and-Coke man, a detail not overlooked by the company commanders who had worked for him. They brought him only the best.

I met Lieutenant Colonel Cory just one time, the previous spring at the traditional Army airborne ritual called Prop Blast. He struck me as serious-minded. His face still bore the remnants of camouflage paint, partially worn off from a day that had started at 2:00 A.M. with a rucksack march, a river crossing, and a parachute jump. Although the Prop Blast activities by tradition were raucous—including a fair amount of drinking and joshing and a mock airplane jump where inevitably some boneheads wore only a parachute and a helmet—Rennie had been in a solemn mood. He had come in late from the hospital, where one of his lieutenants had been taken after being gravely injured on the morning's parachute jump.

I t's funny what you remember about people. From that night, sitting behind Rennie, I remember the deep creases that looked like a road map on the back of his neck, not an uncommon feature for a lifelong infantryman.

Rennie had a strong handshake, and as he greeted his party guests, he looked people in the eye. He often touched his men when he talked to them; now he gave them a hug and a slap on the back. He had an uncanny sense of right and wrong, and he never lied, no matter what. His temper might flare up every now and then, but he wasn't afraid of anybody and told it like it was, damn his career. Sometimes that scared Andrea Lynne. She feared he'd get into trouble, but instead he just earned respect. His men loved him.

Exactly six feet tall, Rennie wore his dark hair short on the sides and only slightly longer on top, just long enough for a side part, as was the custom of many field-grade officers in the 82nd Airborne Division. His pale skin had long ago turned ruddy from too much sun. For the party he wore Levi's and the green Irish sweater that was a Christmas gift from Andrea Lynne. The jeans were Rennie's standard outfit, no matter the occasion. Besides, this was his house.

For their part the generals and their wives were coming in at seven right on cue—so they could exit first, an unspoken courtesy that allowed lower ranks to kick back and relax later in the evening.

The Corys were a popular couple, at the center of their social set and well known to many of the officers on the post where they had spent four tours of duty—ten of Rennie's twenty years in the Army. The men respected Rennie, and the women loved to see Andrea Lynne's latest decorating projects. The couple had a reputation for throwing great parties. Before long everyone had arrived: Colonel and Mrs. Cerrone, Colonel and Mrs. Roberson, Lieutenant Colonel and Mrs. Mayville. Lieutenant Colonel Mike Ellerbe, Rennie's best friend from childhood (both were Army brats), and his wife, Lucille, the daughter of a retired two-star general, slipped in through the back door an hour late. Soon the house was filled with laughter and chatter as guests balanced wineglasses or bottles of beer and plates of food.

Lieutenant Colonel Mike Garrett came up to Andrea Lynne in the living room, where she was standing near a table of food talking with some wives, and introduced himself. Rennie had met Garrett, a new neighbor, that afternoon on the golf course and invited him and his wife, Loralei, to the party. The Corys' second oldest daughter, Caroline, seventeen, a senior in high school, had agreed to babysit for them during the party, a testament to how quickly relationships formed on Army posts.

"You are just a wonder woman," said Garrett, a good-looking black commander.

Andrea Lynne cocked her head to one side. "What do you mean?"

Garrett looked around. "All this. Your home. It's right out of a magazine. The food is fabulous, everything. And look at you, you're gorgeous!"

"Okay, what do you want?" Andrea Lynne said matching his grin with her own big smile.

"No, Andrea, this is amazing. Rennie is a lucky man."

It was true that Andrea Lynne never did the minimum when it came to food and drink. She wanted guests to feel as if they never wanted to leave her home.

Social gatherings have always been an integral part of Army life. They date back to isolated Old West outposts, where Army families lived on an austere and often hostile frontier and where they had only one another for protection and companionship. The post came to symbolize security and community. And many Army couples enjoy the military tradition of entertaining in their homes. The coffees and parties offer a chance to get to know one another despite a constant state of flux. Every month there are "hails and farewells" for officers and their spouses who are joining a unit or leaving it.

The Corys' toffee-colored, stucco Spanish Colonial Revival–style house was part of Fort Bragg's Normandy housing area, which was named, like all the streets and neighborhoods on the post, for the great battle campaigns of World War II.

Fort Bragg itself—home to the 18th Airborne Corps headquarters, the 82nd Airborne Division, the Green Berets, and the secretive Delta Force—has more than 42,000 soldiers and is mammoth, with almost four times the land area of the nation's capital. The post had been named for Braxton Bragg, an arguably inept and indecisive Confederate general who was despised by his men and had been relieved of his command but was nonetheless a Civil War hero in the Old South. All the necessities of urban life are there: a post office, hospital, schools, churches, day care, movie theater, florist, shopping, gas stations, two Class VI (liquor stores), sports bars, fast food restaurants, pools, bowling, two golf courses, gyms, fishing, parks, you name it. It is possible to stay on the post and never leave. I grew up hearing my parents and others casually refer to life on the outside. The world beyond the gates is known as precisely that—the outside— a foreign place populated by slack civilians.

At Fort Bragg I found that many of the senior officers wanted to live in Normandy, which seemed happily suspended between the present— the high-paced operation tempo that governed life on a combat-ready post—and a bygone era in which Army wives wore hats and gloves, and in which calling cards were part of their social etiquette. Normandy surrounds the Main Post Parade Field, which had been built in the shape of a chevron when "Camp Bragg" was a mule-powered field-artillery post during World War I. The trees are older than Andrea Lynne; and the houses, constructed between 1928 and 1931, belong, like old quarters on military posts everywhere, to Army tradition.

And like everything in the Army, the houses are arranged and awarded according to rank. Captains and majors live in the redbrick ranch duplexes in Lower Normandy. The quarters may be small and cramped, but there is still a waiting list to get one. The single ranches nearby are slightly bigger. You have to know someone or be willing to wait a year or two to get in. The one-story bungalows and the two-story duplexes are for lieutenant colonels. Full colonels live in two-story homes, which are upgraded for generals by adding awnings on the windows, putting an ice maker in the fridge, and maybe building a privacy fence in the backyard. Behind the quarters are small garages used in the old days to house polo ponies or Model T's. Most people use them as sheds. Rennie kept his Harley in theirs.

Rennie had lived in several Normandy homes and even helped build the quarters in Biazza Ridge as a teenager, when his father, retired Colonel Rennie Cory Sr., was stationed at the post. The duplex at 11 South

Dupont Plaza sat on the upper end of a horseshoe-shaped street that was home to officers—mostly lieutenant colonels—holding key positions. A short walk down Totten Street led to the officers' club, the pool, tennis courts, and Ryder Golf Course.

Andrea Lynne loved everything about her house—the hardwood floors, the winding staircase with its black handrail, the fireplace, the corner cabinets with glass doors in the dining room, the built-in bookcases in the living room, the high ceilings, and the deep windowsills on which she displayed treasures gathered during a lifetime in the Army. It was Andrea Lynne's dollhouse, and she decorated it in English country style with Victorian overtones.

At Christmastime she really went all out. The previous December, in 1999, the Cory home was one of twelve quarters featured on the Normandy Housing Tour of Homes, a huge annual holiday fund-raiser sponsored by the Fort Bragg Officers' Wives Club. The word on the street that night was, *You just need to go see the Cory home.*

Tonight everything was again on display. Around the lamppost Andrea Lynne had wrapped North Carolina grapevine, spray-painted white, and entwined the vines with crocheted snowflakes. The outside entrance twinkled with icicle lights and an arch of more grapevine and snowflakes. In the dining room Rennie's grandmother's silver tea set (she, too, had been an Army wife) sat on the buffet surrounded with fruit—pineapples, apples, kiwis, figs, clove-studded persimmons, filberts, and cinnamon sticks, which gave off a heavenly scent. In one corner of the dining room a mantelpiece from Georgia displayed Andrea Lynne's angel print collection. The antique went with the Corys from home to home, a wooden tribute to the military, signaling: *Home is where the Army sends us.* Poinsettias, German nutcrackers, Christmas stockings and throw pillows, a collection of Santa figurines—no space was left untouched.

Andrea Lynne looked over at her husband as he welcomed their guests. She and Rennie had made love that morning after breakfast, as they always did on the day of a party or social engagement. It was sort of a quick "Hello, I love you above all else," and a "See you at the finish line at the end of the day" ritual. For Andrea Lynne it was also a great secret to a happy marriage. She knew Rennie could get a little jealous sometimes.

The sex was her way of boosting his confidence and reassuring her husband how much she loved him.

She still loved looking at him. He had a broad forehead, framed by archless eyebrows that extended a good inch beyond his eyes, which were blue with specks of green that Andrea Lynne thought gave them a touch of sadness. His eyes were the exact same color as hers. But Rennie's eyebrows were his trademark feature and could make him look intimidating, depending on his mood.

Andrea Lynne adored seeing her husband naked. He was all man, not skinny—Rennie's weight fluctuated from 185 when he was happy to 180 when he was away from home—just right. He wasn't broad shouldered, but he made up for it in muscle, a tribute to his daily workouts. As for her husband's chest, her girlfriends joked that he had more cleavage than she did.

The sex before a party was just one of their rituals. Each morning Rennie made coffee for his wife and brought it to her bedside before kissing her good-bye. On weekends they would make love after breakfast, their kisses tasting of coffee and pancakes. And each night he'd rub Andrea Lynne's feet and shoulders. He was always touching her.

This morning, instead of cuddling and talking, it had been: *On your mark, get set, go!* They were off to orchestrate a successful party. Nothing had been left to chance, including Andrea Lynne's outfit. She wanted to look casually beautiful and sexy, and she wore a long black velvet skirt with a form-fitting baby blue velvet scoop-neck tee. Her silky black bra strap kept peeking out. She had let her shoulder-length blond hair air-dry that morning so it would stay in ringlets.

The Corys' oldest daughter, Natalie, home from college, had dressed up, too, to serve hors d'oeuvres from a silver tray. The Corys' other children were little Rennie, who had turned fifteen two days earlier and their youngest, Madelyn, age ten. Natalie, an intelligent, feminine girl with fair skin and long dark hair, liked to stay near her father. Andrea Lynne could tell Rennie enjoyed having such a beautiful daughter. He introduced her several times as his "dean's list girl." Now, in the kitchen Natalie watched like a little girl as her mother pulled trays of bubbling Gouda from the oven.

"I wish I was as pretty as Mommy," Natalie said giggling, loud enough for her mother to hear.

Rennie looped his arm around his daughter's waist and pulled her close. "You're not doing too bad." He squeezed her. "You look like your dad!"

At forty Andrea Lynne still possessed the razzle-dazzle that had turned men's eyes when she was young. She was a petite woman with sparkling eyes, a panoramic smile, and the confidence that beautiful women possessed—which could be both a blessing and a curse in the Army. Tonight, though, it was working its magic as she greeted officers and their wives.

"You look gorgeous, dahling," said Alice Maffey, as she hugged Andrea Lynne. Both had been snookered—each had been told the *other* had already agreed to do it—into serving on the PTA board, with Andrea Lynne as president and Alice as treasurer. The wife of Colonel Tom Maffey was a striking woman, tall and incredibly thin, with long blond hair. She sipped a glass of hot glühwein and moved on. The two friends never chatted much at parties. Being an officer's wife meant being onstage, working the crowd. They would talk later, when they were alone.

Andrea Lynne had her part down perfectly. She circulated constantly, giving everyone the same smile and an "I'm so glad you came!" She welcomed Command Sergeant Major Gary Kalinofski and his wife, Delores, one of the few noncommissioned officer couples at the party, then checked the CD player.

The music for the evening had been carefully planned. Andrea Lynne had chosen a Mannheim Steamroller CD as background during the formal greetings. That was followed by an assortment of Irish Christmas music and, for after the stuffed shirts were gone, some classic rock—Tom Petty, Jackson Browne, Aerosmith, John Mellencamp, Led Zeppelin, and REM. Rennie loved classic rock and often whispered lyrics in Andrea Lynne's ear. Toward the end of the party, when there were just a few couples left, Andrea Lynne would play something to heighten the romance, Sade, perhaps, or Fiona Apple and Dido.

But right now there were fifty-eight people in the house. Andrea Lynne was pleasantly surprised by the turnout. A party that big was bound to be successful. There was no room to sit—death to a party—everyone had to stand and move around. And since the bathroom was upstairs—these quarters had no lavatory on the first floor, the biggest complaint of those who lived in them—her guests got to admire more of her decorating.

The floor of the bathroom, for example, was covered in small spring-green square tiles (another frequent complaint), but Andrea Lynne had just worked with the color scheme. She covered the walls with framed photos of Rennie with the children and thought of it as a Father's Day bathroom. Everyone at the party got to see another side of her husband and commented on the pictures.

She loved displaying images of friends and family. One window ledge held photographs of Andrea Lynne's friends from past Army assignments. She liked to say that her friends were with her wherever she moved. The wall along the curving stairway had all old black-and-white photos in silver and gold and wood frames. She irreverently called it her dead people wall, even though several of the photos were of the couple and their parents as children. At the bottom of the stairs was a beautiful charcoal drawing of Rennie's mother, Patty, who had died of breast cancer when he was eight. It was the only thing he had inherited from his mother's side of the family, and Rennie adored it.

Every house Andrea Lynne lived in, she decorated from floor to ceiling, painting and wallpapering the house like a three-dimensional canvas. Some wives found her decorating excessive, but then, they didn't view themselves as artists, as Andrea Lynne did. We live here three years of our lives, Andrea Lynne told herself. We can never get those years back. Why not make them beautiful? Each corner had to be *fabulous*. She put an old-fashioned screen door on her youngest daughter's bedroom entrance, for example, and added a doormat, a battery-operated wrought-iron lamp, and a sign announcing: MADELYN'S COTTAGE. She herself made all the curtains (heavy red velvet with rich flower valances that she carried from quarters to quarters) and most of their bedspreads with her Sears sewing machine, a Christmas present from early in her marriage. Of course when moving time came around every few years, the house had to be put back the way it originally was.

As the space filled with people, Linda Jefferson, the wife of Lieutenant Colonel Dick Jefferson, a battalion commander, found Andrea Lynne and suggested a rendezvous outside with a pack of cigarettes. Whenever she saw Andrea Lynne at any function, she'd grab her to sneak a cigarette. Linda, who had short brown hair and wore glasses, was a closet smoker—and a hoot. At wives' gatherings, when it was time to say good-bye, she'd tell Andrea Lynne that she had to get home to "her Dick," and then she'd wink.

Andrea Lynne located Rennie's older sister, Stephanie, another smoker, and the three women slipped out the front door. The air was cool, cool enough for a shiver but bearable without a coat. Andrea Lynne only smoked occasionally, sometimes with her girlfriends, more frequently out of loneliness when Rennie was away. She had never smoked when she was in her twenties, when she was having babies or nursing them. And Rennie never touched a cigarette, but he encouraged her. He'd pour her a glass of wine before dinner, and on warm nights he'd ask her to come sit with him out back. "Why don't you have a drink with me? You could smoke a cig-arette." It was his way of getting her to relax and spend time with him, and it would get Andrea Lynne every time.

Smoking a cigarette now, with the sounds of the party muffled by walls and windows, Andrea Lynne reflected on just how close—and effective—a team she and Rennie had become. Army life had taught Andrea Lynne well. She felt as if she helped turn a wheel in a great military machine. As far as she was concerned, it was really the wives who ran Fort Bragg. She had a definite role to play and could play it expertly—but then she'd had years of experience. That was the only way you could learn the lessons of an Army wife; it wasn't as though the military gave you a manual to pre-pare you for the dos and don'ts of socializing, politicking, fund-raising, group dynamics, juggling—or curtain making, for that matter. Army Fam-ily Team Building (AFTB) classes aside, you had to count on your hus-band and perhaps a close friend or two to get by.

Smart women eventually shed their naïveté for military savvy, learning from their mistakes. What an officer's wife did affected her husband's ca-reer, and just as Rennie had mastered his command and risen through the ranks, Andrea Lynne, too, had had to take on increasing responsibilities and figure out how to fight her own battles and marshal her forces—the other wives. It wasn't always easy.

When Rennie was a young lieutenant in the early eighties, another lieutenant's wife had spread a rumor that Andrea Lynne had said a superior officer and his wife were prejudiced. The rumor was completely untrue, but it was picked up by a captain's wife, and Rennie got called into his superior's office and asked why his wife would make such a statement. Of course she never had, and as far as Rennie's career was concerned, that was that. But the story reached the superior's wife. One morning the woman arrived unannounced at the Corys' door. Without asking if the rumor was true, she began berating Andrea Lynne, who was still in her robe and without any makeup.

Hurt and embarrassed, Andrea Lynne stayed in seclusion for a while. They were leaving the post within the month, and since Rennie had no more problems over the incident, that was all Andrea Lynne cared about. Yet at their farewell, Andrea Lynne found herself next to the captain's wife who had helped set the rumor mill in motion. Andrea Lynne was scared about confronting a superior's spouse, but she took a deep breath and weighed in. "You don't even know me," she said calmly. "Yet you repeated hearsay. If you felt it needed to be addressed, why didn't you confirm it with me first?

"You could have made my husband's situation terrible," she went on, "all based on a lie. Please think of something you can do to make it better." And with that Andrea Lynne walked away. The experience had left its mark. In time Andrea Lynne had learned when to battle back and when to let things take their course.

A t its best the Army community has tremendous camaraderie; in a crisis no group pulls together better to take care of its own. I've witnessed it many times. Officers' wives still have to be careful. Andrea Lynne had seen it all. The women—who can be as gossipy as rival sorority girls—are always sizing one another up. They will say a wife is a snob if she is quiet, a slut if she talks to the guys, and vain if she wears fashionable clothing. If she works and doesn't participate in unit functions—well, then the word is, *She's got her own life and that marriage is not going to last.*

Much of the scrutiny is reserved for the commander's wife, and it starts even before a commander and his wife are transferred to Bragg. As soon as the news hits, the questions start flying: *How does she act? Where is she from? How many kids? Does she work? What does she look like? Is she overweight? What does she do? Thrift shop, PTA, or AFTB? Is she a*

Board Warmer? And the very first time she appears across Pike Field at the change-of-command ceremony, the rest of the wives are already guessing the bottle number her hair color comes from, wondering where she bought her dress, and assessing how she carries herself. If she wasn't smiling, why not? If she was, what does she have to smile about? Being a commander's wife is fishbowl living, and there is no escape.

These days, when any of her friends' husbands took command, Andrea Lynne gave the couples sympathy cards at their ceremonies. They would need the sense of humor. If the wife was pretty, her role was even trickier. Andrea Lynne knew that firsthand. There were no hard-and-fast rules. Your husband *might* get hired because you were pretty. Or not: One of Rennie's peers had turned down a major who was lobbying for a job because the major's wife seemed a bit too friendly and showed a little too much cleavage. "What does this major's wife have to do with his ability to do his job?" Rennie said angrily to Andrea Lynne later. "So she's friendly and pretty. When is that a bad thing?"

"Can you imagine" Andrea Lynne asked a close friend, "your husband not getting a job because you wear a low-cut blouse and show a few too many teeth to the boss?" No, if you were attractive and wore a size 4, it was best to underplay those assets and focus on the group. Find some volunteer job no one else wanted and do it well.

And learn to manage your group of wives as well as any commander. A significant number of the 750 soldiers in the battalion are married with children. The commander's wife has the responsibility, with her husband, of leading the unit's Family Readiness Group (FRG), which means keeping soldiers and spouses informed of events and issues affecting the battalion. In addition commanders' wives have to keep up with pregnancies, births, and miscarriages; the number of families in need of frozen turkeys for Thanksgiving; women who can't get their sick child a doctor's appointment; and the frantic 6:00 A.M. calls from young wives whose electricity has been turned off because their husbands didn't pay the electric bill before going into the field.

Each battalion also has its own officers' wives' coffee groups, which meet at a different house each month. The coffees are mostly social, and sometimes have a theme and some business on the agenda. The commander's wife—the leader of the coffees—introduces new wives and bids farewell to those departing, discusses upcoming events and battalion news, and passes along the men's field and jump schedules. She also has to address any concerns the ladies have.

Andrea Lynne tried to get to know each woman, find out her talents, and pull her into the group. She never let the business feel like business. Instead she'd joke with all the girls, highlighting each person at least once throughout the meeting, and introduce two or three ladies that she thought might become friends. She'd focus on the wives who were soldiers themselves, asking them about their jobs, and zero in on the new mothers when she talked about who must really be tired.

Rennie was a master at this kind of thing. She'd watched him clap some young new lieutenant on the back and tell the battalion what the guy's major in college had been, that he was the one they should ask for advice on such and such. Like him, Andrea Lynne tried never to leave anyone out, so all the women felt special, as though each one had a place.

Andrea Lynne's coffees were famous. She always brought out the china and crystal and had fun with the themes. For Valentine's Day she served aphrodisiacs: lobster chunks with Green Goddess dressing, "White Devil" eggs and caviar, shrimp cocktail, Cupid cherry-cheesecakes, chocolate-covered cherries, marinated mushrooms, sugar-frosted grapes, and pink champagne. She got the women to make Valentines for their guys, then had Rennie hand-deliver them at his next morning's meeting. The women loved it. Once, after the operations officer's wife left, they doctored the outside of her card, so that the next morning the major, in front of the staff, received a Valentine addressed to "My Stud Muffin."

The wives enjoyed the coffees at Andrea Lynne's so much that eventually they just brought food to her house and piled in till midnight. If the men were in the field, it was ladies' night out—also at Andrea Lynne's house—with music, margarita mix, dip, chips, cookies, and cake.

But it took hard work to create such a close-knit coffee group. Andrea Lynne remembered her first coffee as the commander's wife. She attended an evening pajama party and greeted the other wives wearing Caroline's footsie pajamas with her lovey (the family name for a small cotton throw) draped over her shoulder. The women drank mimosas and got down to the business of the evening: discussing a new phone number for the Robinson Health Clinic. It should have been easy. This coffee group was already well established—and the former commander's wife, Melissa Huggins, who would become Andrea Lynne's good friend, was well loved. This gathering was really about checking out Andrea Lynne—footsie PJs and all.

Most of the wives were just waiting for her lead, but one outspoken lieutenant's wife, the ringleader of a troublesome threesome, challenged everything Andrea Lynne said. Only a few weeks earlier the younger woman had caused a huge flap, because Andrea Lynne, placating some other wives, had excluded officers' girlfriends from the coffees. It seemed like a small issue, but the repercussions had spilled into Rennie's office with such force that he actually thought he'd lose his new command over it. He didn't hang any pictures in his office for a month, thinking he'd be gone.

Now here the young woman was again, challenging Andrea Lynne's authority. Such a thing would never have happened in "the old Army," in which junior officers' wives rose to their feet when the commander's lady entered the room, but that tradition, happily, had gone away with girdles and white gloves.

As Andrea Lynne began talking about using the new phone numbers to get health care at Robinson, the lieutenant's wife, a nurse, interrupted: "Andrea, everyone just calls *me* if they need to get in."

"Well, that's great," Andrea Lynne continued, "but we need to make sure we have these numbers because, you understand, these are the numbers that the soldiers are going to be using. Aaand"—here goes, Andrea Lynne thought—"it's a good idea, too. I make the time to use these numbers myself, so I can understand how long you are put on hold, how rude the appointment clerk might be, et cetera. And I can complain at command and staff, if I have to. We need to make sure our system works, you know?"

The lieutenant's wife shrugged her shoulders, got up, and started talking to some friends.

Andrea Lynne plunged ahead. "I can pick up the phone and call my husband to make something happen—and believe me, I have—but sometimes I wait in line just to see how long it takes. That way, when I hear a frustrated enlisted wife explain to me what she's been through, I can help her."

The room got quiet. The lieutenant's wife sat back down. "I know what it's like not to have your sick child taken care of in the emergency room," Andrea Lynne said. She had the wives' attention now, and she told them how, at Fort Bliss, Texas, when Rennie was away, she had had to take Madelyn to the hospital. The pediatrics section was closed, and after waiting for hours, neither her daughter nor the child of the enlisted wife behind her were even screened.

Andrea Lynne raised hell that night, and eventually the clerk at the emergency room counter was reprimanded and transferred. When Rennie got home and checked on the matter, he took the enlisted father with him to make his point.

The wives were now hanging on every word.

"I feel that it's unfair for me," Andrea Lynne said, "to take advantage of my husband's rank only for myself and not use it to benefit the troops. If I can help the White Devils, I will. If I have to work at Robinson Clinic to make sure our families get the best care, I will."

Let the lieutenant's wife resent me, she thought. It wasn't about power to Andrea Lynne, it was about what was best for the soldiers. She loved the battalion, and so did Rennie. The huge turnout at their Christmas party bore witness to that.

Back inside the house, Colonel Maffey was standing near the CD player. He spoke in serious tones, mostly about work. Andrea Lynne chatted with him but kept an eye on the dining room table, which was covered by a burgundy chintz tablecloth and laden with food from her collection of special recipes: hot crab dip, marinated cheese, pineapple meatballs, tortilla wraps, Gouda bread, hot ryes, New Orleans hot wings, and party sandwiches. She had made so much there was no way she could run out of things to eat. She surveyed the assortment of sliced breads—pumpkin, zucchini, and banana—and another tray of everyone's favorite cookie, apricot amaretto chews. There were also several tiered platters of petits fours, Russian teacakes, pound cake cookies, and homemade chocolate candies. When you give a party, go big, was Andrea Lynne's motto.

She was surprised to see that Lieutenant General Dan McNeill and his wife, Maureen, were still at the party. It was their anniversary, and Maureen, a kind, sincere woman, had originally telephoned to say they couldn't come. But her husband had called back to say they would stop by after all. Andrea Lynne had spied the general a few times from the kitchen, apparently enjoying the hors d'oeuvres. He had a full head of salt-and-pepper hair and light blue eyes in a handsome face creased by life in the Army. Andrea Lynne found him likable and charming, and she could see him smiling at the quote she had painted over the china cabinet in the otherwise formal dining room: All's well that ends in a good meal. Perhaps he is seeing us as individuals for the first time, Andrea Lynne thought. He seemed to appreciate the hospitality.

Ten months earlier, after Rennie received his orders for Vietnam, he had gone to McNeill and asked to stay on at Fort Bragg. After two grueling years in command, Rennie didn't want to leave his family for a year. Plus he had already been separated from his family for twelve months during a hardship tour in Korea. But Rennie's presence in Vietnam had been requested by name, and the general had slotted two other lieutenant colonels for the only two O-5 jobs (lieutenant colonel rank) available at Bragg. McNeill stood firm in his decision.

It was a disappointment for the Corys and others who knew them, but Rennie, as usual, set his own desires aside and concentrated on his job. For someone so attached to his family, he had tremendous fortitude. When Andrea Lynne ended up in intensive care, ill from complications of diabetes, the spring before he left, her ordeal was all the more difficult since she knew Rennie would be leaving in the summer. Andrea Lynne considered her invitation to the general a way to show she had no hard feelings. Perhaps, she thought, that was why McNeill called to accept personally.

Near the food Andrea Lynne noticed Brigadier General David Petraeus, balancing himself on crutches. He had broken his pelvis during a recreational free-fall parachute jump one weekend and ended up in intensive care himself. For a man who had once been accidentally shot in the chest by one of his own soldiers during a field exercise, the crutches were no big deal.

As she came closer, the general stiffened a bit. Andrea Lynne liked Petraeus's wife, Holly, a lot, but she didn't care much for the general. Petraeus may have been a brilliant man with a Ph.D. from Princeton, but he was too straitlaced and opinionated for Andrea Lynne's tastes. Still, that didn't keep her from her job.

"Hi, I'm so glad you could come," she said warmly.

"Thank you for inviting us," the general answered formally. "Holly sends her regrets. She really wanted to come, but she is picking up a friend at the airport as we speak."

"So you're out on the town tonight?"

He got Andrea Lynne's humor, and for a fleeting moment seemed to appreciate being treated to the same teasing as the other men. But only for a moment. Andrea Lynne quickly turned the conversation to his injury. That was her style. Flirt a little and then get serious about something. She never really gave men time to respond to her flirting. She talked to the brigadier general for only a couple of minutes, then she moved on to the McCardles.

"Hi, it's so good to see you. Thank you for coming."

CHAPTER TWO

A few minutes before midnight Command Sergeant Major Gary Kalinofski and his wife, Delores, said their good-byes and slipped out the front door of the Corys' quarters and into the fog. Nothing could affect Delores's mood. She felt as if she were floating on air. It was the Kalinofskis' twenty-first wedding anniversary; their son, who'd just joined the Army, was home for the holidays; and they'd had a wonderful time at the party.

The sergeant major had already warmed up their '96 Camry when Delores and their twelve-year-old daughter, Cherish, who'd been asleep on the Corys' couch since nine o'clock, got in. Gary Kalinofski, known as "Ski," usually avoided these kinds of officer-heavy functions, but he wanted to see his old pal, Rennie Cory. Ski considered Lieutenant Colonel Cory a charismatic leader and an easy-to-get-along-with officer. He was neither phony nor excitable, traits enlisted soldiers loathed in their commanders.

The two had served together twenty years earlier at Bragg, in Alpha Company, 2nd Battalion of the 325th Airborne Infantry Regiment, when Ski was a buck sergeant and Rennie a newly minted platoon leader. Now they had come full circle: Rennie had just finished his tour as a battalion commander in the 504th Parachute Infantry Regiment, and Ski was at the pinnacle of his career as its brigade command sergeant major. The most senior noncommissioned officer within the enlisted ranks, a command sergeant major serves as a confidant and adviser to the commander and is viewed as all-powerful by the enlisted soldiers.

Rennie and Andrea Lynne Cory had greeted the Kalinofskis when they entered the quarters.

"Delores, nice to see you," Rennie said, as he touched Delores's shoulder. Rennie Cory had asked Delores in the past to call him by his first name. She had to remind herself not to call him "sir" or "Colonel Cory."

Only officers are called "sir" in the Army, and Delores's predicament was a common one. Whether to call an NCO or an officer by his rank or his first name can be awkward for wives, even if the spouses are friends. While rank is necessary for military order and discipline, how it applies to wives in social relationships can be a somewhat gray area. Although no one would want to be labeled "rank conscious," only a foolish or inexperienced wife would discard the system. In my experience, when it comes to greetings, stature, situation, and personalities all come into play. A soldier equal in rank to one's husband or below can be called by his first name, but there are exceptions. Chances are good that a captain's wife will still refer to her husband's first sergeant exactly as her husband does, calling him "first sergeant" out of respect and not by his first name.

The Kalinofskis quickly joined the group of friends catching up. The house was abuzz with laughter and lively conversation. At fast-paced Fort Bragg there was always news about assignments, promotions, deployments, and field exercises.

Army couples who haven't seen each other in months or even years have no problem picking right back up with each other where they left off. It's expected in the Army to be close, then separated, and then sometimes reunited again at another duty station, which is often the case at Fort Bragg.

Rennie filled the sergeant major in on Vietnam, while Delores sipped red wine and talked with other wives from the brigade. At forty-five Delores had smooth, unlined skin, naturally pink cheeks, and innocent hazel eyes that gave her the appearance of a much younger woman. She rarely touched alcohol, and it took only a thimbleful to turn her nose red.

As a command sergeant major's wife, Delores had a slightly peculiar status. She wasn't one of the officers' wives, so their pecking order didn't affect her, but she often found herself at meetings and social occasions with them because of her husband's position in the unit.

Delores was neither catty nor gossipy and always excused herself from any discussion that tended in that direction. Her innocence and sunny outlook were disconcerting to some of the women, who didn't always know what to make of her. A few avoided Delores, but the kinder ones saw her optimism for what it was—genuine goodness. As the months would prove, they had no idea just how good. Delores kept her past to herself and long ago forgave those who had hurt her.

"This is a really special Christmas for us," Delores told the wives at the Corys' party. "We have our Gary Shane home from Basic." Their nineteen-year-old son, who had left for Fort Benning, Georgia, in October, had returned home for the holidays ten days earlier. She was beaming, and the other women gushed with compliments about her appearance. Her brown hair had been cut just that afternoon and arranged in a new pageboy style.

Delores stood five feet nine and a half inches, and she wore a size-8-tall stonewashed denim dress that buttoned from collar to ankles over a long-sleeved white T-shirt, black tights, and black flats—all Christmas gifts from her husband.

Ski had on his usual winter attire for semicasual parties: Dockers and a Sunday dress shirt under a black crewneck sweater embroidered with his name and regiment; he had more than a half dozen of them. Kalinofski was only a half-inch taller than his wife, and he, like her, was forty-five. His face was grizzled, punctuated with wide-set blue eyes, beneath thick gray-specked hair, shorn on the sides and cropped like a bristle brush on top. This was one face soldiers didn't want to see angry. Though he was really a teddy bear at heart, he reserved that side of his personality for his wife and daughter.

I saw Ski lose his cool just one time, in Albania, as he tried to get his driver, a not-so-bright kid, to cut through rows of backed-up Army vehicles stuck in the mud that blanketed the countryside like snow. All the yelling just made the kid mess up more. I was in the back of the Humvee trying to sink into my seat. Finally Ski got out of the vehicle wearing his full battle rattle. I thought he was going to boot the driver to the passenger's seat and drive the damn thing himself. Instead he stopped oncoming traffic and made a path for his Humvee to fit through. In the end Ski patted the kid on the back, saying, "See, son, you can do it. You'll be fine."

Ski prided himself on being in better shape than most of the privates—the Nintendo generation, as NCOs liked to call them—filling out the ranks of the 82nd Airborne Division. Ski was the best specimen of an old paratrooper on the street. He had landed unscathed in holes, on hills, and in trees. Sure, he had hurt his neck and knees, hit his head, bumped his chin and his nose a few times, and cracked his glasses, but there were no broken bones, no broken back, no lifetime disabilities or career-ending injuries.

I t really was a terrific party," Ski said as he drove the car out of Normandy and turned left onto Reilly Street. Cherish was already asleep in the backseat. "It was great to see Cory and Andrea again." Like a lot of soldiers, he generally referred to other military men by last name.

"They seem so much in love," Delores added. "Just like us." She felt like a bride all over again, as she always did on their anniversary. She squeezed her husband's hand.

He looked over at her. "You were the most beautiful woman there."

It was a second marriage for both the Kalinofskis, who had a close, loving relationship, a far cry from what Delores had known growing up. She had an uneasy relationship with her mother, and her Navy father was almost always at sea, so her grandparents, who were warmhearted people, raised her on their dairy farm in western North Carolina. In high school Delores's parents wanted her to stay with them. They were living in a trailer outside Fayetteville. By then her father had retired from the Navy. The reunion proved to be disastrous. He beat Delores, who tried her best to cover the bruises by wearing long-sleeved shirts. A neighbor reported the abuse, and the state put Delores in foster care. She was headed for an orphanage when her grandmother came and took her back to the family farm.

When she was just seventeen, Delores had fallen in love with and married a Fort Bragg soldier six years her senior. She was attracted to his bad-boy nature, which was so different from her own. She had secretly dated him since she was fourteen, and after they married, her new husband signed her high school report cards. Delores thought marriage was for-ever, but after enduring five rocky years with her husband, she left him, and at twenty-two got a job as a cocktail waitress at a rowdy Fayetteville rock-and-roll club called the Flaming Mug, on Fort Bragg Road.

"Are you sure you want to work here?" a scantily clad waitress asked Delores her first day on the job. "You look like you came from the convent."

In fact she was wearing her high school clothes.

"I desperately need the money," she told the waitress, who took De-lores under her wing and taught her how to do the bunny dip and get tips. She lived off peanuts and yogurt, along with one big free meal, a steak and potato, each night at the Flaming Mug.

One Friday night in 1977, Ski sat in Delores's section and ordered a seventy-cent can of beer. He was a staff sergeant then, a wild guy in his twenties, and he told her he hoped to see her again. The two didn't meet for a second time, though, until a Veterans Day cookout two years later. This time Ski didn't wait. He proposed after only four days, and a month and a half after that, the couple hopped into Ski's baby blue '73 Monte Carlo and drove seventy miles from Fayetteville to Dillon, South Carolina—the wedding factory capital of the Southeast—and were married under an arch of dusty artificial flowers.

Ski treated his bride to a flat orange soda and dinner at Pizza Hut. Back in Fayetteville, no hotel would take a soldier's check, so the couple spent their wedding night on the floor of a buddy's den. The next morning the sol-dier kissed his new wife good-bye and left for three weeks of field training.

Delores had always dreamed of a chapel wedding, complete with gown and guests. Ski had given her an elaborate renewal-of-vows cere-mony on their twentieth wedding anniversary at the 82nd Airborne Divi-sion Memorial Chapel on Fort Bragg.

I had been at that ceremony, and it really *was* like a wedding. Delores carried flowers and wore a full-length bridal dress and veil. Cherish was the maid of honor and Gary Shane, the best man.

"Did I do okay?" Ski had asked me later at the reception. "Boy, was I nervous!"

R emember our 'wedding' last year?" Delores now asked her husband. "Yeah, that was something, wasn't it? I'm glad you didn't expect me to top that this year," he joked. Before the party the couple had gone out for an early anniversary dinner with their kids to one of their favorite restaurants, the Olive Garden.

Ski had grown up in New Jersey, the fifth of nine children of a mechanic and a housewife. He knew nothing about the Army airborne except what he saw in war movies, but after high school he filled out an advertising card in an *Outdoor Life* magazine, and shortly afterward he got a call from an Army recruiter. He joined in 1974 and had planned on staying only long enough to fulfill his four-year enlistment, but he remained for more than half his lifetime. He loved it that much—the adrenaline and the thrill of the jump, the mission and the élan of a proud unit. Some of the best leaders and most motivated officers and NCOs were at Bragg; that was why he had stayed so many years and put himself through the breakneck pace and the pressure. Ski was a "Bragg baby." He had come as a private and was "grown" here. "Just like a fungus," he liked to say. When he was twenty-one he got married. Ski was the woman's fourth husband. After a year of marriage the relationship abruptly ended.

For two decades Delores had been Ski's center of gravity. He liked to joke that if it hadn't been for her, he'd be in jail. Instead, he was a member of the post's inner circle, the old-boy network. Ski wouldn't have considered himself a member of that group, but he was. Delores kept him grounded and focused on his job and responsibilities, all without being pushy; and as a bonus, she never complained if he went out for a few beers.

Supportive and nonjudgmental by nature, Delores carried those traits over into her life as an Army wife. She adored that job. For her it was a way of expressing pride in her husband, love for her country, and satisfaction in her own ability to carry on during the tough times when Ski was away. She had learned through experience that she could be strong and still be gentle. And Delores always depended on God and her Catholic faith to get her through the hardest of times.

Delores never spoke of the dark side of her past to the other wives. She had simply picked herself up and moved on, focusing on the family she and Ski had created.

Halfway into their twenty-five-minute drive home, Delores noticed that the fog had turned Fayetteville's roads into a blurry black-and-gray canvas. After more than twenty years of back-and-forth assignments to Bragg and Fayetteville, the Kalinofskis knew the landscape by heart. They had seen firsthand the last few cycles of transformation in what had started off as a small southern town on the Cape Fear River.

Fayetteville is really like two towns. The section just outside Bragg is where a lot of military families live—where I live, for that matter. The shopping district, the chain restaurants, and all the gaudy billboards are located here. Cross over McPherson Church Road, though, and the landscape takes a dramatic turn. Suddenly there are signs of Fayetteville's bygone gentility. In Haymount, where homes date to the 1920s and 1930s, the Old South emerges like blossoms on a magnolia tree. In that original residential area of town, where descendents of old families live, the oaks and pines are mammoth, and each spring sees a burst of pink, red, white, and yellow as camellias, azaleas, magnolias, gardenias, jonquils, and forsythia come into flower, followed by the deep purple of wild wisteria and Fayetteville's trademark dogwoods in delicate shades of pink and white.

A monument to the town's Confederate Civil War dead is here, along with something many in Fayetteville are unaware of. Behind one old manor on Hay Street are former slave quarters that were converted into small apartments for officers and their families during World War II.

In the early 1940s Fayetteville's metamorphosis from a small textile and railroad town to GI boomtown began as thousands of soldiers arrived by train for mobilization at Fort Bragg before shipping off to Europe and the Pacific. Many of the young enlistees, who needed thirteen weeks of training, didn't know which state they were headed to until they got off the train at Fort Bragg. In one year the post grew from five thousand to sixty-seven thousand soldiers by the summer of '41. Construction couldn't keep up with the population explosion, which reached more than one hundred thousand soldiers during the height of the war, an astounding figure for a town that had fewer than eighteen thousand residents before Pearl Harbor. Soldiers lived "under canvas" in tent cities on Bragg, and residents did their part for the war effort by renting out their garages and spare bedrooms to GIs and their families. Cash flowed, romance budded, and North and South blended and at times clashed. Soldiers flooded the drinking establishments downtown and danced with local girls at the USO, then went on to marry them. Entrepreneurs built businesses that catered to the military, young women took clerical jobs at Bragg, and Fayetteville's high society included Fort Bragg's senior officers at events, with invitations that were reciprocated on post.

More than twenty years later, another war buildup changed everything again, as young draftees from across the nation tramped through town with Vietnam a sure thing in their futures. This time the councilmen and local merchants sold out Fayetteville's soul, allowing strip clubs, topless bars, and brothels to multiply like bacteria in a petri dish. The 500 block of Hay Street filled with druggies, hookers, and transvestites. Nearby Gillespie Street was known as Combat Alley. Green Berets stationed at Bragg christened the town Fayettenam, and the name spread like Agent Orange.

Some days it seemed the entire community was under assault: Young men smoked dope and lost their virginity to whores downtown, mothers and wives watched Walter Cronkite announce the day's body count, and local school principals had the sorry task of pulling kids from class and telling them their fathers were dead. After the war Fayetteville lay somewhere under the carnage. What remained was Fayettenam, a constant reminder of wild times and legendary violence.

To me Fayetteville has always been like the wise guy perched on the stool at the end of the bar night after night—you know, the one with the leathery skin and the scratchy voice from a lifetime of smokes. Fayetteville is the guy you always see but never bother to get to know, because you think you've already figured his kind out. In truth it takes time to understand this town. It's a multilayered, flesh-and-blood community with war heroes and crooks, garden club socialites and strippers all in close proximity. As Ski would always tell me, "I just like it here, kiddo."

Thanks to the military, it is a mix of ethnic groups, races, and religions living together as neighbors. And thanks to the military, more than $5 billion each year is pumped into the local economy. Only a small percentage of the 121,000 inhabitants can say they have roots in Fayetteville. And that's part of the problem. Semiprofessional sports teams have never generated a strong-enough following to last long here. On game days people are at home in front of the TV rooting for their own teams. That lack of hometown pride has meant that some residents think nothing of throwing trash out of their car windows, or worse, robbing their neighbors. For a community of its size, the crime rate is surprisingly high.

Ski turned into Birch Creek, and then a few streets down turned right and into their driveway at the center of a cul-de-sac. White Christmas lights twinkled from the porch. Their house was a typical two-story, three-bedroom colonial with green siding, burgundy shutters, and beige trim. Delores had found it on Father's Day 1994 while Ski was spending six months at the Sergeants Major Academy, at Fort Bliss, Texas. They'd always dreamed of owning their own home in this part of town, but at more than $150,000, the houses in Birch Creek were out of the Kalinofskis' price range. When Delores found that a house she had fallen in love with was selling for $108,000, she called her husband in Texas and made an offer.

"Honey, just find a house you like," Ski had told her. "I'm not going to be living in it, you are." He was right. A month after they moved in, Ski left for a year's assignment in Korea.

The Kalinofskis liked living off post. There were fewer rules and regulations, no garrison soldiers patrolling like yard nazis, writing residents up when they spotted weeds growing in sidewalk cracks, oil stains in driveways, double parking, uncut grass, litter, or kids out past curfew. Off post they didn't have to attend the mandatory neighborhood meetings, which often turned into bitch sessions over whose yard needed mowing and whose guests had parked in the wrong spots.

In the early nineties the family had lived in Fort Bragg's senior NCO housing, in a duplex with a small yard and a shared carport. When Delores came home to find a written notice stuck in her storm door for having a pile of dog poop on the edge of her lawn, she had had it. The problem wasn't her own poodle but the big puppy next door. Delores couldn't stand the fact that something she or her children—or her neighbor's puppy—did would result in a citation in her husband's file.

Too many citations can result in eviction from quarters. Living on post is rent-free, and all utilities—including heat, air-conditioning, and electricity—are paid by the government. Soldiers who live off the post receive a housing allowance. In return the Army expects soldiers and families to be good stewards of government property. The strict policies prevent old couches being left on porches, broken-down clunkers parked on the street, and toys scattered in yards. Still, when soldiers patrol the neighborhoods for violations, they seem not to spend much time in Normandy, where the senior officers live.

It was past midnight when the Kalinofskis came home, but Gary Shane wasn't back yet. He had gone to a party with close friends from the neighborhood. They were all good boys, so Delores wasn't too worried, but she still wanted to wait up for him. Ski and Cherish went to bed. Though Delores was exhausted, she changed into her nightgown, put on a housecoat, and went downstairs.

Admittedly she was having a hard time with her half-empty nest. She loved having Gary Shane home. Just that morning she had cooked him breakfast and washed his clothes. He had come back on December 19, on a flight from Atlanta that had been delayed till 1:00 A.M. by snow and ice. As he walked out of the gate, Gary Shane looked every bit the soldier in his Class A's and overcoat, the green uniform authorized for official travel. The boy who'd always walked with a slouch now stood as straight as a Georgia pine. He was smiling as always, his eyes half moons, and looking a bit self-conscious about his shorn brown head. When Gary Shane bent over to hug his mother, Delores held on so long that Ski had to loosen her grip.

Since being home, Gary Shane had spent much of his time sleeping in and catching up with his friends. He had no curfew, but when he stayed out late, Delores would wait up for him.

Gary Shane got home at 1:30 A.M. As he came in the door, Delores was struck anew by her son's tall good looks. At six feet one and a half inches, he was bigger than her husband, and the morning stubble that still surprised her was thicker than her husband's, too.

Delores followed her son upstairs, and the two sat on his bed and watched *Saturday Night Live* reruns for a while. Delores wanted to hear about everything her son had done that night, the party, cruising around town, where the boys ate and what they had.

"I love you, son," Delores said a half hour later as she left Gary Shane's room. He'd be gone again in six days, and she dreaded his leaving. If only this moment could stay frozen in time.

CHAPTER THREE

I t was just after nine o'clock on Christmas Eve of 2000 when Rita Odom, disguising her disappointment, held up the Christmas present from her husband: a tomato-soup-red sweatshirt with 82nd AIRBORNE DIVISION stamped across the front. Rita hadn't expected a romantic gift but maybe something picked out with a little more effort. The sweatshirt seemed too easy, and besides, the color clashed with her hair, which Rita dyed copper-penny red.

I had met Rita for the first time just a few weeks earlier on an overcast afternoon down at the barracks where her husband worked. I was writing a story about what it was like for soldiers to be on call for a mission during the holidays. There were a lot of rules and restrictions that spilled over into family life, and the knowledge that a soldier could be pulled away at any moment to respond to some crisis on another continent gave every ring of the phone an ominous meaning. I had come to talk with Rita and some other wives about that.

Rita placed the sweatshirt across her lap. She pasted on a smile, leaned over, and kissed her husband. "I love it, sweetie," she said in a backwoods Alabama accent. "Thank you so much." But Brian Odom could tell his wife was disappointed. Brian hated the gift Rita gave him, too. She had paid five dollars for his blue plaid flannel shirt at Family Dollar. Rita knew Brian loved flannel, and the blue matched her husband's eyes. Besides he already had five red ones on his side of the closet. But Brian only wore red flannel, an eccentricity Rita hadn't yet learned about her husband of five months. I love Brian, she said to herself, but I don't know him from Adam's house cat.

Brian was an infantryman and held the rank of specialist, an important-sounding title given to junior-ranking, lesser-paid soldiers who had been in the Army just long enough to break in their boots. Brian, like all the troopers who wore the maroon beret—don't call it red—preferred the tag of paratrooper. Plunging from an airplane door at eight hundred feet into darkness with a Kevlar helmet on your head, a rifle strapped to your left side, and a seventy-pound ruck—filled with ammo, grenades, mortar rounds, water, and a vacuum-sealed pouch of vegetarian tortellini—across your thighs was an adrenaline rush. The Army couldn't make you sign up for paratrooper duty, but for volunteers willing to face their fear and say yes to a challenge, the 82nd Airborne was the place to be. That's why I loved writing about the unit.

Everyone in the 82nd jumped from airplanes, a trait that bonded the bottle washers to the graying generals. The division's artillery guns, two-and-a-half-ton trucks, and Humvees exited aircraft the same way the paratroopers did. On my first plane ride with paratroopers late one night high above Fort Bragg, I witnessed what makes these soldiers unique. As the aircraft's engines slowed down to a rumble, the doors opened. I was now standing on a steel ramp a few feet away, strapped into a harness tethered to the floor. I was close enough to see each face, each set of alert eyes, and each ramrod-straight body before it plunged into a vacuum of darkness. For me it was one of those mystical life moments, the ones you don't always share. All the things that permeate society, a person's skin color, status, age, religion, and politics didn't matter in the belly of that flying tin can. What mattered was trusting the guys around you, completing the mission, keeping everyone safe, and staying alive. Rita knew little about those details, only that her husband was gone a lot.

But the Odoms were together this holiday, virtually under house arrest. Every time the phone rang, Brian scrambled to answer it as if he were expecting a call from the president. Brian's unit, Bravo Company, 1st Battalion of the 505th Parachute Infantry Regiment, was on a two-hour recall, the DRF-1. The Division Ready Force 1 cycle—shared during the year among all the units of the 82nd—meant that if called upon, Brian and his buddies, within eighteen hours of notification, could parachute into any hot spot in the world with enough firepower, fuel, and food strapped to their bodies to sustain themselves for three days. The possibility both frightened and excited Rita. For the Odoms, this cycle just happened to fall over Christmas.

The couple sat cross-legged on their mattress, which they had dragged into the family room as a last-stand barrier to keep Rita's three sons from opening their presents before sunrise. With the boys tucked in bed, the couple sipped the one indulgence Rita allowed herself: mugs of Wal-Mart's Great Value Pack instant cappuccino.

Rita snuggled close to Brian. "Do you realize a year ago tonight was the first time we ever laid eyes on each other?"

They had met the previous Christmas Eve in Rita's hometown, Alexander City, Alabama. Alex City, as the locals called it. On that night Rita had just put her kids to bed and was wrapping a few gifts donated from Toys for Tots when the phone rang.

"Hello," Rita said, putting the phone to her ear.

"Hey, Rita, you by yourself?" said her friend Felicia.

"Yeah."

"Well, Andy's cousin's on leave from the Army, and he's visiting for Christmas. He's really cute, Rita. I'm not kidding. Why don't we bring him on by later tonight?"

At age twenty-five, with three boys and a six-dollar-an-hour job answering phones at a Ford dealership, Rita had no time for dating. Real life had deadened her desire for courtship. On her good days she paid her $325 rent on time. On bad days fast-food ketchup packets mixed with hot water served as dinner.

But at least the misery had stopped.

She had ended a stormy marriage that had taken an emotional toll on her. Life looked so much more promising when she was younger. Rita had graduated near the top of her high school class. She was given a scholarship to Central Alabama Community College and planned to transfer to Auburn. She married a man right out of high school and got his named tattooed on her left breast. He was a welder by trade and could lay tile, but the bills weren't paid, and the couple struggled to buy food. When

Rita experienced complications during her first pregnancy, she left college. Someday I'll go back, she had always told herself. But that day never came. Instead, Rita wasn't allowed to work, own a telephone, or have a driver's license.

Finally, on the first Sunday in February 1997 she came home clutching a church bulletin and found him gone. Before long her landlord came rapping on the door with an eviction notice. Rita got a job at Burger King, but she soon discovered she was pregnant with her third baby, the result of a brief fling with a friend from high school. She thought about having an abortion, but the baby's father talked her out of it.

"Take the money I give you, and get a divorce. Don't have an abortion," he told her. Now every time Rita cradled Johnathan, a happy two-year-old with blond hair and blue eyes, she cried at the thought of what she had almost done.

"Rita, are you there?"

"Yeah, Felicia, I'm sorry."

"I think Brian's the one for you. Let me bring him over. He's got a good paycheck. He might be the perfect man for you."

"Look, Felicia, I don't care if he's the one. I don't care if he's Jesus Christ himself. Don't bring him to my house."

"Come on."

Rita assumed Brian would be just another of Andy's redneck cousins. Felicia was always trying to fix Rita up with somebody in her family or her husband's. Rita's broad smile and porcelain complexion dotted with freckles attracted suitors who wanted a girl who looked more like Miss Americana than Miss America. But who would take on three little boys and a mailbox of unpaid bills? Here I am, I'm twenty-five, divorced. I've had a hysterectomy because of cancer a couple of years ago. No one is going to want me, she thought.

"No, no, don't bring him to my house," Rita told her friend.

"Well, he's got red hair, Rita."

Rita cradled the phone between her cheek and shoulder and kept her voice deadpan. "Well, bring him over then."

When Brian walked through Rita's front door after a day of hunting, he had cleaned the deer blood off his face—smearing it on after a first kill was a local custom—but he still wore his camouflage cap with "Bud Racing" stitched across the front. An inch shorter than Rita's five-foot-eight frame, he was lean and had a boyish look that appealed to Rita. She decided to have some fun.

She gave Brian a seductive look and accentuated her drawl. "Well, hello, sweetie, come on in."

Brian's eyes grew wide. What was up with this chick? He was taken aback by Rita's body language and intimidated by her forwardness.

"Take off your hat," she said.

Brian obliged, revealing a head shaved to the skull.

"Oh, God," Rita said, turning away. Andy and Felicia laughed. The twenty-two-year-old had found that shaving off his strawberry blond hair made for easier maintenance in the California desert, where he was stationed at Fort Irwin.

The four listened to Garth Brooks and played spades and smoked Marlboros past midnight, until Andy and Felicia fell asleep on the couch. Only then did Rita drop the hoochie mama routine and show Brian the real her. Rita walked outside onto her porch. She lived in an old A-frame clapboard house across from a convenience store, and she loved her porch. It was ten feet wide, the kind of porch perfect for sipping sweet tea and passing time on a summer evening, but this night was cold and bright. Rita huddled in the green sweater she'd had since she was fifteen. Maybe the air would clear her head. It seemed as if she and Brian had known each other forever, but it had only been a few hours. They had talked about growing up, hard times, and broken hearts, things you don't normally discuss with strangers. God, she liked him so much, maybe could even love him if she let herself. She felt she was handing him her heart, all taped and bandaged together.

Brian followed her outside, and the two shared some awkward pauses.

"Let me show you something," she said, as she leaned close to him. She could smell his cologne now. "See those three bright stars? They make up Orion's belt." It was the only constellation Rita knew, something she'd learned from an eighth-grade science project. What she really wanted to say was, "Just kiss me, it'll be all right." Instead, the two went back inside and talked some more. At 5:00 A.M. Brian remembered his family had no idea where he was. Rita wrote down her address and phone number, and then they hugged good-bye.

"Well, it was nice talking with you," Brian said a bit awkwardly as he headed out the door. "Merry Christmas." He didn't plan on seeing her again.

Rita closed the door and leaned her back against it. Her heart was beating so fast. Brian wasn't like anyone she had ever met. She was intrigued, too, by the Army. Soldiers were supposed to be wild and crazy, but Brian didn't even drink a beer that night. I'll bet he's got lots of girls after him, Rita thought. Put a guy in uniform in Alex City, and you'll have girls coming out of the woodwork.

For the following months Rita couldn't get Brian out of her mind, and she often asked Felicia if she had heard from him. When a letter came to Felicia and Andy, asking about Rita in passing, she scribbled a note on the back of her grocery list and had Felicia tuck it inside a package Andy was sending to Fort Irwin.

"Hey, I still remember you," Rita wrote. "You can write me or call me." Brian never bothered. At twenty-two, he was focused on the Army, and besides, he thought, if I can't throw it in the back of my truck, I don't need it.

That spring, on the last Saturday in April, Rita's phone rang. It was Felicia.

"Hey, we're having a barbecue at my place. I know it's short notice. Why don't you come on over?"

"I'm kind of tired, Felicia."

"Well, Brian's here."

"I'll be there in ten minutes."

Rita canceled a date for the evening and dropped her two older boys off at her mother's. She brought Johnathan, who was still in diapers, with her. She hoped Brian was what she remembered. Would he recognize her?

Brian wasn't there when she arrived. For an hour Rita sat on a lawn chair in the shade and swatted mosquitoes. Frustrated, she got up to leave, but then she saw him—his eyes and his smile just as she had remembered them. When Brian grinned at her, she couldn't breathe. For the rest of the evening Rita sucked down wine coolers and flirted with Brian. By nightfall they were holding hands, and her head was swimming. When she finally crashed on a bed in a spare bedroom, there was a knock on the door.

"If you're going to sleep, good night," Brian said.

"I'm not going to sleep," Rita said, propping herself up on her side. "I just don't feel well. But you can come and lie down with me if you want."

Brian stretched out on the bed and began stroking Rita's arm. Soon they were taking each other's clothes off.

"Are you sure?" Brian asked her.

"No," Rita said. He wasn't sure either, yet neither wanted to stop. It was the first time Brian had ever made love to a woman, but he didn't want Rita to know that. How would that look? A virgin in the Army? All his buddies thought he had lost it long ago, but secretly Brian had wanted to wait until he got married.

The next morning he left for Airborne School at Fort Benning, Georgia, where soldiers learn how to jump from airplanes. Before he left for the three-week course, Brian asked for Rita's phone number and address and promised to see her on weekends. As she watched Brian's truck roll away, she realized that she didn't have to be on her own in order to be free.

True to his word, every weekend Brian drove an hour and ten minutes from Fort Benning to Alexander City. By now they were sleeping together, spending every free moment as a couple. That May, Rita attended his Airborne School graduation. When Brian introduced her to his family as "my friend, Rita," he saw her face fall. She refused to look at him. Okay, it's time to end it, Brian thought. He didn't want a girlfriend anyway, especially one with three kids by two different fathers. But he couldn't stay away. During his month of leave, Brian found himself going back to Alex City and Rita.

He was just like part of the family, Rita thought. She wasn't the only one who thought so. One evening during the second week of his leave, Brian sat on Rita's couch, and her four-year-old son, Alan, asked, "Are you my daddy?" Heartsick, Rita covered her face and started to cry.

"No, no, I'm not," Brian said. He knew he had to make a decision. Either he was in this for the long haul, or he had to call it quits.

On June 20 Brian left before dawn for his new duty assignment at Fort Bragg. In Brian's mind only real soldiers went to Bragg. That was the reason he had gone to Airborne School. He didn't want to be a soldier fifty miles from the front lines. He wanted to be in the thick of things, and that's where the guys at Bragg always were. They kissed good-bye in Rita's driveway, and she waved to him from her porch. Then she crawled back into bed and cried. *He's a soldier. He probably has lots of girls,* she thought. *What does he want with me?*

During the eight-hour drive, Brian thought only of Rita. He admired how she got by despite the odds. He never did have a whole lot of respect for people who had had a smooth ride in life. But did he want a woman with so much baggage, who had had such violent relationships? He'd dated Rita for only a month and a half. Even if they got married, she would never be able to give him children. As he drove into Fayetteville, Brian found himself at a proverbial crossroads. *Do I pass up the soul mate of a lifetime and look for someone who can give me children but who I don't feel strongly about?* As soon as he arrived at the Knights Inn, a shabby hotel on Bragg Boulevard, he called Rita from his room.

"I cried all the way to Atlanta," he said. "Between Atlanta and Fort Bragg I decided I want you to marry me."

"Well, are you asking me?"

"Yes."

"Well, ask me."

"Will you marry me?"

"Yes."

Two weeks later Brian headed south over the long July Fourth weekend and married Rita in a ceremony in her living room. Barefoot, in front of her sons and a few friends, Rita said her vows. Her electric blue nail-polished toes peeked out from under the hem of the light blue flower-print dress she often wore to work. The groom wore an Alabama Crimson Tide shirt and starched, rodeo-style Wranglers, creased down the front and cinched with a Confederate flag belt buckle the size of a slice of white bread.

The next day Brian headed back to Fort Bragg, unsure when he would be able to get Rita and the boys to Fayetteville. All he knew was that he was spending the next two months in the field and had to do sit-ups the following morning at 6:30 A.M.

By the end of August, after phone calls and tears, Brian risked a month's worth of wages and weekends cleaning latrines and left without a pass, heading to Alabama to pack up his new family. Brian was at the wheel of a seventeen-foot U-Haul, and Rita drove her husband's beloved 1987 GMC Sierra, its bumper covered with Confederate flag stickers. She discovered the broken windshield wipers and busted blinkers during a rainstorm outside Atlanta. Her hands tightened around the steering wheel, her palms were sweaty, and she could feel the moisture in her armpits. Her back and legs ached. She was afraid she'd kill herself and Jay, her oldest son, who was in the cab with her.

At one point Brian looked in his rearview mirror to see Rita nowhere in sight. He got off at the nearest exit, and ten minutes later found her on the side of the road, sitting on the bumper, crying. The traffic around Atlanta had terrified her. Rita had only had her driver's license a few months. How was she supposed to drive in the rain with no windshield wipers?

"I can't take it anymore," she told Brian. "I hate your truck, and all this traffic scares me. Just get me a hotel."

Brian ran his hand across the stubble on his head. How could she just pull off on a four-lane highway? He was furious. He couldn't afford a hotel. He had to get his ass back at Bragg in time for Monday-morning formation. The Army didn't care if she was tired. Didn't she know anything?

"I'm not going anywhere. I'm not driving anymore. I want a hotel."

What he wanted to say was, "Get back in the truck, dry your tears, suck it up, and drive." Instead, after fruitlessly looking for a hotel for a half hour, he came back and gently urged her on.

"Honey, I had no idea you were this petrified. I had no idea, but you've got to drive. Even to get to a hotel, you've got to drive, Rita. You're gonna get in front of me and drive."

By the time they stopped to get gas in Bishopville, South Carolina, two hours from Fayetteville, Brian could see that his wife was physically and emotionally whipped. He got her a room at a Holiday Inn and told her he would be back the next evening. Brian arrived at Fort Bragg at 4:00 A.M., barely in time for a few hours of sleep before PT (physical training). After work that afternoon, he drove back to get Rita. With him was his buddy Griffin. Brian introduced him to Rita by his last name, which was stitched on his uniform. That's what soldiers all called each other. It wasn't even unusual for friends not to know each other's first names. This time Griffin drove Brian's truck, and they arrived in Fayetteville just as it was getting dark.

The only thing Rita knew about Fayetteville and Fort Bragg was what most people knew about the place—the MacDonald murders. In 1970 Jeffrey MacDonald, a handsome Green Beret doctor, had killed his wife and kids here, an act that received enormous amounts of publicity for decades.

People still associate Fayetteville with the crime. It was one of the things that had fascinated me about the town. When I did a story on the thirtieth anniversary of the murders, I went over to the renovated MacDonald quarters at 544 Castle Drive and talked with the current residents—a sergeant and his family. I was taken aback when I saw all the angel pictures and figurines inside. Sometimes, the sergeant told me, late at night after his family had gone to bed, he'd see the shadowy face of a little girl peeking at him from the stairs. He had no idea what had happened in the house so many years before. The Army never told him. Instead the family learned of its notoriety when they noticed people constantly stopping by to take pictures.

While I was reporting the story, MacDonald wrote to me from prison, sending a handwritten, four-page letter on his physician's letterhead. He still proclaimed his innocence, believing that DNA evidence and the appeals process would vindicate him, and in the process chaining Fayetteville to a time it wanted desperately to forget.

Rita's first impression of Fayetteville was a blur of billboards in every size and color, and a mess of fast-food joints, pawn shops, and used-car lots. She didn't spot any of the tall buildings you'd expect in a city, just highways and an endless stream of commercial franchises. How was she ever going to get comfortable driving here? Rita knew she was a long way from Alex City, where the nearest mall was forty miles away.

Their journey ended on the west side of town in front of a chocolate-brown brick house with overgrown bushes. But Suga Circle was unlike any place Rita had ever lived. Rita's parents had divorced when she was a baby, and her father had died when she was eleven. Her mother worked in the cotton mills. Rita had grown up in a house with no heater and busted-out windows. Her whole life she'd wanted to live in a brick house. She was overjoyed.

Rita followed a worn carpet into the family room. "Look, boys, a fireplace!" She spotted the dishwasher next and started to cry. "People are going to say I'm spoiled, Brian."

He considered the house an average one, much like the place he grew up in, in Cocoa, Florida, but he knew it would be special for Rita. The house rented for $635 a month and had three bedrooms, two bathrooms, central heating and air-conditioning, and a garage-door opener. Rita had never dreamed of that.

"My little podunk self is going to live here?" she said as the boys ran from room to room. "This is like a Cinderella fairyland."

Later that night Brian took Rita and the boys to the barracks, where he still had some boxes to pick up. It was too dark for Rita to see much. Home to single, junior enlisted soldiers, the barracks smelled like an eighth-grade-boys' locker room. The odor just about knocked Rita over. In the hallway a soldier with his shirt off strummed a guitar.

"Hey, Scrotum," a soldier with a skull tattoo greeted Brian. "Scrotum!" yelled another. *Scrotum?* Then Rita got it. Odom. Scrotum.

At 4:30 A.M. Brian got up and told Rita he wouldn't be seeing her much in the coming weeks. He had to work on his Expert Infantryman's Badge, a must-have for every grunt in the 82nd Airborne Division.

Rita didn't know a soul and didn't know her way around. After several days, any romantic visions she had of marriage to a soldier were fading with every piece of furniture she lugged off the U-Haul by herself. The next four months were a polarity of accomplishment and frustration. She tried hard to be a housewife, but when she found herself staring at a daytime TV schedule, she knew she was in trouble. She talked to Brian about getting a job at Burger King, but he wouldn't hear of it. So she looked at car dealerships but never got any calls back. That was fine with Brian. He wanted her to stay home and take care of the house and the "little ones," as he called them.

"Rita, you've had it hard all your life," he said. "Now you can rest. I'm going to support you." Brian's conviction was heartfelt, but it felt odd to Rita, who had learned the hard way how to be independent, to ask for grocery money. She wanted to finish school and earn a paycheck at something other than a dead-end job. Potty training and ironing her husband's BDUs was not the life she had imagined. BDU was one of the first Army terms Rita learned; it stood for battle dress uniform, the everyday attire for soldiers at Fort Bragg. Brian, like many soldiers, was particular about how he looked in his uniform. After her first failed attempt to crease his pants properly, he picked up the iron himself.

"Okay, Rita," Brian said, standing in front of the ironing board, his legs apart. "I'm gonna show you how to do it this *ooone* time. Are you ready? It has to be this way." And with that Brian ironed a ruler-straight crease down the seam of his green-and-black camouflage-print pants. Perfect. "Got it?"

Rita pressed her lips together and tried to look serious. "Okay, honey." That was one memory she kept to herself.

Brian used so many Army acronyms that Rita often didn't know what he was talking about. His truck was his POV (privately owned vehicle), the mess hall was the DFAC (dining facility), 11 Bravo was his infantryman job, and so on. When he told her he had to be at work at 0600 and to expect him home at 1700, Rita had no clue. Brian explained military time to her, and she spent several months counting on her fingers before she learned the system without thinking about it.

At least she'd figured out how to juggle their meager finances. Brian got paid the first and the fifteenth of every month, and Rita had quickly learned to avoid Wal-Mart and grocery stores on those days. The Odoms were digging their way out of credit-card debt; they lived paycheck to paycheck. Every dollar went to bills and food. Even then they couldn't always stretch the funds to the next payday, so Rita fed her family by using "floating" or "hot" checks, as she called them. She paid by check at the grocery store on a Saturday, knowing it wouldn't be cashed before payday. This system worked well, and Brian was proud he had a wife who was so resourceful. Floating checks was such a common practice in the Army that in October 2004 the Army and Family Readiness Groups (FRGs) disseminated e-mails and flyers to soldiers' families informing them of a new law by which checks would be cleared electronically within minutes.

They'd been lucky with furniture, too. For months they sat on boxes and lawn furniture; then a soldier in Brian's unit gave the couple a dinette set and a wood-frame couch with a Western print. Its tan cushions showed a fireplace with a pot on the hearth, a deer head and rifle hung above, and a horseshoe nailed onto the mantelpiece. In front a cowboy hat teetered on the back of a rocking chair. When Brian brought it home, Rita thought it was the most godawful thing she had ever seen, but it was functional. It'll keep my butt off the floor, she said to herself.

Rita got up and made herself another mug of cappuccino. Near the window on a table stood a ten-dollar artificial Christmas tree that looked nothing like its picture on the box. It, too, came from Family Dollar.

"Rita, it's Christmas, we've gotta have a tree, at least for the kids," Brian had said despite Rita's protests. It seemed like a waste of money. In the past she had simply put her boys' gifts in the corners of her house.

"Brian, if we put an ornament on it, it'll fall over," Rita had said when they brought the tree home a few weeks earlier. Well, the tree was still standing. And the kids had gifts, mostly from Brian's parents or Fort Bragg's chaplains' programs that helped Army families in need of holiday food, clothes, and toys.

Even if she didn't love her sweatshirt, she had to admit it was amazing how Brian had walked right into an instant family and become "Daddy." The boys adored him for it.

People often told Brian how much her blond-haired sons resembled him. "Everyone tells us that," he'd respond. Strangers and acquaintances would never have imagined the family's actual path to Fayetteville, but Rita wanted to leave her past in southern Alabama. All she wanted to do now was meet other wives, make her husband happy, and be the best Army wife on Fort Bragg.

CHAPTER FOUR

I started hearing about the Delta Force compound not long after I moved to Fayetteville. The home base of what was officially the 1st Special Forces Operational Detachment, a secret unit specializing in international counterterrorism, the place generated rumors like a news rag. Supposedly there were cameras in the trees and secret underground tunnels that led to the drop zones on Fort Bragg. But that was just Fayetteville lore. For the record there are no tunnels, and the only cameras are inside the compound on tall poles. Granted, they catch every movement. Anyone who stops a vehicle outside the fence is politely told to move on. And if anyone tries to take a photo, guards firmly confiscate the film.

The secrecy goes with the territory. For years the Army never acknowledged that this unit existed. Even now, when an operator is killed, his real unit is never named. As a reporter, I could always tell, though, when a casualty was a Delta Force guy: The giveaway was his Army identification only as a Special Operations soldier. If pressed further the Army would say he was from Headquarters and Headquarters Company, United States Army Special Operations Command, which is an umbrella unit. Because of the secret nature of the organization, there is no public recognition for the men in Delta Force. But those I've met over the years carry a lot of self-pride, knowing they are the best at what they do.

Today when regular soldiers drive past the compound on their way to Sicily Drop Zone, one of them will inevitably say, "There's the Delta compound," then mockingly whisper, "Oh, but it doesn't exist, shhh." It's a multimillion-dollar facility, and people have a lot of wild ideas about why it's there. I discovered that the truth is more pragmatic than sexy. There the men can train without distraction. There are no barracks, but it has an excellent mess hall, an Olympic-size swimming pool and a climbing wall, an airliner used for hostage-rescue practice, world-class "shooting houses" for close-quarter battle, and seven outdoor firing ranges.

Just how much money goes into Delta is classified, but my sources put it this way: The government pours money into Delta as if it were a billion-dollar NFL team, ensuring that its operators have the best of the best in resources, weaponry, and equipment. Unlike the ranges on Bragg, where units had to compete for time to train, if an operator wanted to go to the range on Saturday afternoon all he had to do was show up. It was an elite training ground for an elite fighting force.

A few days after Christmas, Andrea Floyd turned on her radio and caught the middle of George Strait's *Love Without End, Amen* as she veered her blue Chevy Astro van onto McKellars Lodge Road, heading away from Fort Bragg's day-to-day garrison grind. Pike Field slipped away behind her, and she continued down the wooded two-lane highway, which crossed the northwestern portion of the military reservation. Andrea used to drive a Jeep Cherokee, but the van was perfect for carting around her three kids. She looked at the two boys in her rearview mirror. They were blond, like their mother. Strapped in the backseat were BJ, four, and Garrett, three, giggling and poking each other. Her daughter, Harlee, six, was still at school.

The song mixed with the chatter of gunfire from Range 25, where soldiers wearing Kevlar helmets and camouflage lay prone on reddish-orange dirt, using their M4 machine guns to fire at targets some three hundred meters away. The sight held the same level of interest for Andrea as a cow pasture. The *rap-rap-rap* of gunfire was a familiar sound at Fort Bragg, and she was no stranger to shooting ranges. In the early nineties she had been an Army private in Baumholder, Germany, fresh out of high school, when she met and fell in love with another soldier on a ski trip. She'd had a few boyfriends before that, but Brandon Floyd was the first man she was ever smitten with. He had charm and good looks: dark brown hair and hazel-green eyes under a prominent brow. And she liked his slight Southern accent, a remnant from his upbringing in the hills of Arkansas.

Like her husband, she had been an excellent marksman. Brandon loved to hunt, sometimes with a rifle, sometimes with a bow, always with his dogs. He had bought Andrea a bow of her own and wanted to introduce the children to his passion as well. So they now had their own BB and paintball guns. Andrea didn't mind as long as the kids were supervised. No, guns were not unfamiliar objects. Brandon kept a handgun in the glove compartment of his truck, and he had bought one for Andrea, too, for the times he was away.

It was just after Christmas, and Andrea had been running some errands after taking the kids to see the horses at the Fort Bragg Riding Stables. Someday she'd own enough land to have a couple of horses, one for her and one for Harlee. Someday . . . she thought.

Andrea passed Ranges 24 and 23, which soon gave way to longleaf pines that hugged the road. Another mile down, a chain-link fence topped with barbed wire replaced the pines, surrounding a compound of cream-colored buildings with shiny red aluminum roofs and landscaped with enough Bradford pear trees to rival a retirement community. The place had its own staff to look after the well-kept grounds. Nothing else on Fort Bragg looked like this.

Andrea passed a few men jogging along the edge of the road. Their eyes were shaded by Wiley X sunglasses, and their legs were noticeably well muscled. Concrete barriers and rust-colored steel spikes lined the fence, which was posted with warning signs, in front of a wide trench. Andrea turned her van toward the entrance of the Delta Force compound, slowing down as she approached the guardhouse.

Andrea took out her cell phone and speed-dialed Brandon's number. For her and most wives of Delta Force operators, the cell phone was a necessity, always by her side. In Brandon's line of work she never knew when or where he was going or when he was coming back. Some spouses handled the separations better than others, and many marriages didn't last as a result of them. In their case, Andrea believed the separations helped keep them together.

Andrea showed her ID to the guard. She'd called earlier to say when she would be arriving and why.

Delta wives have to get used to this, since procedures are not this meticulous in the conventional Army. There are pluses, though. Delta is extremely efficient, and wives don't have to deal with the bureaucracy or the long waits that can plague other wives trying to get something done on post.

The guard nodded, and a section of the chain-link fence lifted at an angle, like a drawbridge. Andrea drove through, and the fence lowered behind her. In front of her was another guard shack and another fence—this one she didn't have access to pass through. She parked off to the side. She was in a demilitarized zone of sorts.

"Hey, Brandon, I just pulled up to the welcome center," she said into the phone. She was there to swap vehicles with him so she could get the oil in his truck changed. She walked into the welcome center and handed over her ID, which a clerk checked against a family-member roster: "I'm here to see my husband, Sergeant First Class Floyd." They'd do the swap right there. Wives were only allowed farther inside the compound for such special occasions as organized family activities when their movement was restricted to specific areas, the unit's annual June picnic, for example. It was always a big hit with the kids. The men set up mini-parachute-jump towers, and the kids got to climb on vehicles and look at weapons.

At other times if the kids had the sniffles and needed to be seen at the clinic, or if Andrea had to update Brandon's power of attorney, she called in advance and was given an appointment time. Someone would meet her at the gate, and she would be escorted inside the second fence. At no time were wives ever left alone. Even if someone got through the second gate by mistake, he or she wouldn't be able to get into any of the buildings, which required PIN codes to gain entry.

Another driver in an SUV pulled up to the second gate and flashed the guard a photo ID badge. The guard nodded, and a section of the fence lifted again, allowing the SUV to pass through. The vehicle was now, literally, "behind the fence." That's how operators sometimes referred to the compound, when they were trying to be discreet about where they worked. Old-timers called the place "the Ranch" or "Wally World."

A few moments later a large silver truck pulled up, and a tall, lean man wearing a T-shirt and jogging shorts—despite the winter air—jumped out, leaving the truck running. "Hey, I've only got a minute," Brandon told

Andrea as he gave her a kiss on the cheek. Then he said hello to the boys, got them out of their car seats, and helped settle them into the truck. Brandon had just come from the weight room.

While the rest of Bragg officially takes lunch from 11:30 A.M. to 1:00 P.M., operators have from 10:30 A.M. to 1:00 P.M. each day to work out, eat, and take care of their personal business. Two and half hours may seem generous, but an operator's hours are unpredictable, and when they're on missions they work around the clock.

Andrea hadn't totally forgiven her husband for being such a grump during Christmas. Despite an all-expenses-paid trip to Disney World and a three-day cruise, it had been a miserable holiday for the Floyds—their worst family vacation ever. Disney World was so cold and overcast that they had to buy thirty-dollar sweatshirts for themselves and the kids, and once they got on the ship it rained a lot. Brandon was seasick, and he spent most of his time in the room, which was pretty cramped for his six foot one frame. He hadn't wanted to go on the trip to begin with, and his mood blanketed the rest of the family.

The trip had been a gift given with the best of intentions. Earlier in November, Andrea had given birth to beautiful twin girls as a surrogate mother, and the trip was a present from the twins' parents. Her family initially thought she was crazy for doing such a thing, but Andrea had been stubborn about it. "What better thing can I do than to help someone have a baby?" she asked them.

Andrea had gotten the idea the previous Christmas, when the Floyds' pastor gave a Sunday sermon that talked about each person's gifts and how they could be used to help others. What was Andrea good at? Having babies, she joked. But the sermon stuck with her, and so did the idea of birthing another couple's baby. So many couples couldn't have kids, she knew, but she was fertile and had always had smooth pregnancies with easy labors and no complications.

When Andrea set her mind on something, she followed through. She went online for information and found a nice couple from Charlotte, North Carolina, who had posted the message: "Looking for our angel to carry our baby." She set up an appointment to meet them, and by January she had begun in vitro fertilization, taking daily hormone shots so that the biological parents' egg and sperm could be implanted. It didn't work the first time, but Andrea became pregnant on the second try in February.

Brandon was proud to tell people that his wife was a surrogate mother. And having another couple's baby paid extremely well. For the first time the Floyds would be able to pay their bills—including the one for Brandon's truck—and get out of debt. They might even use some of the money as a down payment on a house. Brandon was making more money now that he was in Delta, and they could afford something better than the double-wide manufactured home they had in Cameron, a country town northwest of Fort Bragg. Andrea was happy there, but with three kids they were growing out of it. And Brandon wanted a big home. It would be nice, Andrea thought, to have enough land to ride horses and breed Labrador retrievers. Brandon had a passion for Labs. The couple kept four in their backyard, and he often worked on retrieving with his two favorites, Zoë and Ace.

For her part, having the babies and helping a family had given Andrea a sense of satisfaction she hadn't felt in a long time. After a year that had centered on her pregnancy, the babies were gone, but somehow she didn't want the feeling to disappear with them.

As Brandon got into the Chevy van, Andrea hopped into her husband's truck and drove away without any fanfare. She needed to get the oil changed, then pick up Harlee. It was Wednesday, and normally the Floyds would be attending services, but they were now having trouble finding a place of worship they liked. When Andrea became a surrogate mother, her pastor hadn't approved—though it had been his sermon that inspired her. The Floyds had ended up leaving their church over it and were looking for a new one where they felt comfortable.

Andrea remembered the flyer a pastor's wife had given her in October. A very pregnant Joanne Strickland, about to give birth to her fifth child, knocked on the Floyds' door one afternoon and found herself belly to belly with Andrea Floyd, who was extremely pregnant herself. Joanne handed Andrea a flyer about Emanuel Baptist, the new church her husband had just started in a storefront in Johnsonville, a rural community outside Cameron. Andrea still had the flyer. Maybe after things settled down they would try it out. It would be a nice way to start off the new year.

Andrea was trying to get back in shape, too. She had gained a lot of weight with the twins, and Brandon hated that. He didn't want a fat wife, he was constantly telling her. Andrea was always on one diet or another.

She couldn't help it if Brandon preferred petite women. At five foot seven, Andrea had the body of an athlete. At least she was strong and powerful.

Back at Marlington High School in Alliance, Ohio, she'd loved to compete in track. She'd spring over the hurdles and run flat out, her long blond ponytail trailing behind her, until she collapsed in a heap beyond the finish line. She had given it every last bit she had, and her track records from those days still held up.

During their seven-year marriage, she and Brandon had trained together and competed in biathlons and triathlons. Brandon had even bought her a fifteen-hundred-dollar bike.

She didn't mind working out, but she didn't like to primp. Her appearance was casual. She wore her hair long, parted on the side. If she was going out, she'd just put on a bit of mascara and blush. She was most comfortable in sweats or khakis, but that was nothing new. As a kid she'd slide into her muddy boots and go out to the barn, her favorite place, to be with her goats.

In contrast Brandon was meticulous about his appearance. He plucked his eyebrows and shaved his body hair to show off his muscle definition. Whenever Andrea caught him inspecting his body in the mirror, she wanted to hit him over the head with a frying pan. She couldn't stop him from examining his physique, even if he sometimes had a skewed version of what he looked like. Once when friends were over for a summer cookout, Brandon, wearing sixty-dollar running shorts, had expressed disgust at the sight of himself shirtless.

"Look how fat I am," he said, visibly upset. "I'm fat around the waist. Can you believe these love handles? That's it. No more beer." His friends were incredulous. The man didn't have an ounce of fat on him.

At 181 pounds, Brandon was slim and rock hard, like a cyclist. The average guy in his Delta Force unit could bench press 300 pounds and run two miles in twelve minutes; he ranked in the top three-to-five men in his squadron when it came to physical endurance. The intensity he applied to his looks was typical of everything he did. His whole group had a similar drive. Their workday was like a tough-man competition. If someone bragged he had just completed the obstacle course in nine minutes, it became a challenge to beat that time.

Brandon had been with the unit for about a year, and like his teammates he wanted to be the best shooter, parachutist, driver, all-around athlete—the best at everything. Excelling at a task was the operator's reward. Brandon took pride in knowing he could keep up with his peers day in and day out. Promotion was another powerful reward. Leadership in the unit was proof of a high level of performance, and it was what Brandon worked hard for.

Perhaps it wasn't surprising that he was always nagging at Andrea. She didn't care if the house was messy and her kids got dirty from playing and stayed that way, but Brandon couldn't tolerate it. Her husband was adamant about having things just so. The house in Heritage Village, the neighborhood where they lived, had to be spotless. Previous renters hadn't taken care of the home, which the Floyds owned, and now they spent a lot of time working on the carpet and walls.

The thirteen-hundred-square-foot house was covered in white vinyl siding, and it sat on a hill. There was a driveway but no garage, three bedrooms but no dining room. The family ate their meals at a round kitchenette set in the kitchen. The two boys shared a room with bunk beds. Harlee had her own room, with wallpaper and a bedspread that reflected her love of horses.

The decorating in the rest of the house was eclectic. Near the leather couch in the living room Andrea kept three antique suitcases stacked on each other from largest to smallest. Brandon hated them. He preferred his Army and sports awards, including pictures of himself running in triathlons, which were on the wall in the living room. He kept his trophies on the bedroom dresser. The only sporting item of Andrea's on display was the bike she hung like pop art on her bedroom wall. People always commented on it, since it was the first thing anyone noticed on entering the room.

"We bike a lot," Andrea would always explain.

The den had two recliners and a large entertainment center. The Floyds also had a top-of-the-line computerized washer and dryer. The washer alone cost fourteen hundred dollars. Andrea hadn't wanted to spend that kind of money, but Brandon wanted only the best.

A small deck overlooked the backyard—three-quarters of an acre of land—which had a shed, the dog kennels, a trampoline, and a wooden jungle gym and swing set. It was a godsend. Andrea could just look out the window, if she was babysitting, and keep an eye on everyone's kids. Brandon didn't care for a lot of kids from the neighborhood coming over, though. He didn't want the equipment ruined.

Though Heritage Village was a new subdivision and mostly treeless, the Floyds had the best-kept yard. They often worked in it together, and if Brandon was gone, Andrea had to garden feverishly to keep it up. She planted petunias in clay pots on her porch and added them, along with impatiens and snapdragons, to her flower beds. It was a lot to water and weed, and in the back of her mind she always worried that Brandon might come home a few days earlier than anticipated—that happened more than once—and the house and yard would be a wreck.

The uncertainty of his schedule was a mixed blessing. When he served with the 5th Special Forces Group at Fort Campbell, Kentucky—the Green Berets—Brandon would be deployed six months out of every year. Now that he was in Delta, his time away from home was broken up—a week here, four days there. He was rarely gone longer than a month at a time. Sometimes Brandon could tell her where he was, but usually not. Delta guys were sent all over the world, including places one wouldn't expect, such as Amsterdam, Rome, Boston, and Las Vegas. Andrea actually looked forward to the time she had to herself. She wasn't the type of wife to get caught up in Army life, and she didn't pal around with the other spouses, except for a few who were her age and had children. Growing up, she'd always had more guy friends than girls, and as a teenager she was "one of the guys." She didn't need to be around a crowd of people to be happy or to feel validated. As for the Army, she loved it when she was in it but felt a bit like a failure over the way she left.

Still, Andrea was happy for Brandon and his achievements, even if she had been around elite units long enough that she wasn't in awe of them. She thought some of the training was downright stupid, like the training exercise in which Brandon was weighted down and then thrown in a pool. He nearly drowned before he was saved by his teammates. Sure it was supposed to teach soldiers not to panic and to trust teammates with their lives, but she thought it was silly.

When he was away she enjoyed the chance to relax and catch up on things. She'd let the house go and feed the kids SpaghettiOs or hot dogs. And Brandon wouldn't be there to complain.

She *had* been looking forward to their Christmas together, particularly after Thanksgiving, when Brandon had been away. For that holiday Andrea had taken her kids home to Alliance. Her sisters and their spouses and her nieces and nephews all had a family portrait made for their mother, Penny, and Brandon had been the only husband absent. That hurt, but it was part of Army life when you were married to a Special Operations soldier. She understood that Brandon couldn't tell her what he was doing or where he was going. That was a given. But the reunions were supposed to be happy, not like the Christmas cruise. Sometimes it worried Andrea that she was enjoying the separations a little too much.

CHAPTER FIVE

Delores was already awake when the alarm clock went off at 2:30 A.M. The day she had been dreading had finally arrived. It was Thursday morning, four days into the new year, and Gary Shane was leaving on a 5:00 A.M. flight back to Fort Benning.

Delores sighed heavily, grabbed her robe, and got up to check on her son, while Ski went downstairs and switched on the coffeemaker. Gary Shane, still in pajamas, was already headed to the bathroom to take a shower. He was always good about getting up on time.

"Would you like some breakfast, son? How 'bout some bacon?"

"No, Mom, it's too early."

The boy could eat his weight in bacon. Every morning he'd been home he had asked for bacon and toast, and Delores was only too happy to prepare it. She loved taking care of him again. She had even helped him open his first checking account a few days earlier.

Ski brought up her first cup of coffee as she was getting out of the shower herself. Delores had hoped they could take Gary Shane to the airport together, but Ski needed to help get Cherish ready for her first day back at school and then get to work, too.

Delores dressed, dried her hair, and put on makeup, then checked on her son again. When she walked in, Gary Shane was leaning on one knee and looking for something he had dropped under his bed. He had a towel wrapped around his waist, and she couldn't help but notice the definition in his arms and shoulders. It was obvious that he was working out and lifting weights in his spare time. Suddenly Delores realized that Gary Shane was no longer her little boy. He was a young man in the Army, and he'd turn twenty in less than a month.

But still my son, Delores thought, my baby. She had always felt a special bond with him. He had been so sick with intestinal problems as an infant, he had to have several surgeries, but she was never more than a sneeze away. Back in those days Ski worked a second job delivering pizzas so his baby could have a crib. (Ski had never shared that detail with me, and Delores did so only as an afterthought. I know this may come as a surprise to some people, but the truth is, it's not uncommon for enlisted soldiers to work evenings or weekends at auto body shops or restaurants to support their families. Funny how the Army recruiting posters never show a soldier carrying a pizza delivery box.)

Gary Shane had grown into a quiet child and a good student. He loved music, just as she did, especially blues and Motown. When he sang, he often startled people with a big, bluesy soulful voice that contrasted with his shy behavior.

Since he'd gone to Basic, she had seen how he had changed. Gary Shane structured his time better, and he didn't drink soda or eat a lot of junk food.

When it was close to the time to leave, she checked on him again, knocking softly on his bedroom door.

"Come in."

He was in his Class A's, trying to fix the zipper on his duffel bag.

"Son, you can't pack your things in a broken bag." Ski had a new one, and she gave it to him. At least his uniform was perfect. She had it dry-cleaned for him, and made a point of telling the clerk that it was her son's.

She was so proud of him, though the Army was not what the Kalinofskis had envisioned for Gary Shane. They wanted him to go to college, an opportunity they never had at his age. And they felt that Ski's service to the country was enough for one family. Delores didn't like the idea of her boy in harm's way. Besides, the Army offered adventure but not high pay. They wanted a better life for their son.

This may seem unexpected from a couple who loved the Army life so much. The Kalinofskis wanted to make sure their boy knew what he was getting himself into by enlisting—the good *and* the bad.

"You don't get what you're worth," Delores had told Gary Shane the summer he was thinking of signing up. "You've got a brilliant mind; anything is within your reach." Yet in mid-July, when he asked her to go with him to the recruiting station in Spring Lake, she agreed to drive him.

"Please, hon', don't sign," she told him, and then sat there and cried when he did. She waited until Ski came home a month and a half later to tell him the news in person.

Ski understood Gary Shane's desire to be independent, though deep down he wished Gary Shane had talked with him more before making the decision. He had been away for two months at Fort Polk, Louisiana, when it happened. And then his son had disregarded all his advice about not joining the infantry.

Ski himself was an infantryman, and he loved the brotherhood. It was the only life he'd known since he was eighteen. The people he met and worked with couldn't be beat. But there were no marketable skills in the infantry, especially for someone like his son, who had signed up for just a few years of Army service.

When Gary Shane first left for Basic, all Ski could do was give his son some parting advice.

"It's gonna be tough. You'll miss home. Just do the best you can."

Gary Shane had only seen the Army from the outside, Ski knew, and he wasn't sure how his son would handle the pressure and stress and discipline. He even called his son's first sergeant at Benning a few times to check in on him.

"Don't worry," the first sergeant assured him. "He's doing great."

Ski had been closer to his son when Gary Shane was young. He told me they started drifting apart when Gary Shane was a teen. Ski left for Korea when his son turned thirteen. Puberty was a difficult time for the boy. He fell in with some kids Delores didn't like and started coming in at all hours of the night. He needed his dad, and Ski felt helpless so far away.

At one point Gary Shane began mouthing off to his mother, telling her to shut up, something his father would never have stood for if he was around. The year Ski was in Korea, Gary Shane started hanging out in a neighborhood known for drugs and shootings. When Delores tried to exert some parental authority, a power struggle usually ensued. In Gary Shane's mind he was the man of the house in his dad's absence; hadn't his father told him that? One time Delores blocked the front door, telling him, "I don't want you in that neighborhood!" He shoved her aside, and Delores shoved back. Gary Shane pushed her again and left. Another time he kicked her hard in the shin when she wouldn't let him leave. Once, inside a pizza restaurant, he argued with his mother about wanting to go out. It caused such a scene she had the waitress box their meals.

What happened to her mild-mannered son? Delores wondered. She had him tested twice for drugs that year. The tests came back negative both times. Ski had his brother in New Jersey and a sergeant major friend in the neighborhood talk to Gary Shane several times, but it didn't do much good. When Ski came home the following year, he sat Gary Shane down to put the fear of God in him.

"This is not how you grew up," Ski said, looking at his son from across the kitchen table. "You *cannot* hit women! I don't care what you do. You can get away with a lot. But if you touch her again—if you touch my wife—I'm going to treat you like an adult. I'm not going to warn you. I'm going to find you. Don't touch your mom."

The bad behavior stopped, and Ski thought that was the end of it. But when Gary Shane was sixteen, Ski came home late one evening after five days in the field. He was still in his uniform with camouflage paint on his face and was fixing himself some soup when Delores came downstairs. She wouldn't come close to him.

"Come here, Delores Anne. What's wrong?" Then Ski noticed the swollen black eye.

"What the hell?" His fists tightened.

"He didn't mean it," Delores said. "He didn't mean it." She had asked her son to take out the garbage. In response Gary Shane had picked up the trash can and thrown it at her. The corner caught her face.

"Delores, go upstairs," Ski said.

Delores took Cherish into her bedroom and closed the door. She heard her husband chasing Gary Shane up and down the stairs, then slapping and wrestling with the boy. Ski gave the sixteen-year-old a tough-love lesson he wouldn't soon forget. He then told his son to take a shower and go to bed.

"Do not lock your bedroom door. Leave it open." Ski then entered the master bedroom.

"This will never happen again," he told Delores. There were no more outbursts after that. In 2000, before he joined the Army, Gary Shane wrote an apology to Delores in a Mother's Day card. "I know that over the years I have put you through many things, which means that I've also put myself through many things, also. I am so sorry for what I have done. It is not right that you had to go through all that I have done to you. Despite all that I have done, you stayed strong and moved on with your life, trying to be the woman of the house. For this and everything in the past that you have done for me, I will always be thankful."

Still, there were hints that everything was not perfect. A few weeks before Gary Shane left for Basic Training he said to Delores, "Mom, I want to talk to you."

Delores was sitting at the kitchen table writing letters. She put down her pen. Her son's tone was so serious that she told Cherish to go upstairs and watch TV.

"Mom, ever since Cherish was born, Dad acts like he loves her more than he loves you or me. Please don't act like it's not true, and please, Mom, get out of the house and start doing some things for yourself. Spend some money on yourself instead of always on me and Cherish. Stand up for yourself and quit letting people walk over you and use you."

Gary Shane sounded like an adult, and for the first time she saw that her son was no longer a child. It was as if everything her son had wanted to say for a long time was coming out now, before he left home. Delores started to cry. She stood up and took Gary Shane's hand.

"Gary Shane, son, please don't underestimate the love your father has for you. Your father loves you so much, don't you know that? It's not just her, it's you, too. He loves you both the same."

How long had he been harboring these feelings? she wondered.

"I love you," she said. "I cannot tell you how much. Do you know that I love you?"

"Yes," he said.

"I loved you before I ever saw you. Please don't sell yourself short by thinking that your father loves your sister more." She held both his hands. "Please, Gary Shane, use the time you have left before you go to Basic to talk to your father."

A few weeks later, however, Gary Shane left without talking to his father about his feelings. After much deliberation Delores decided not to mention the conversation to her husband either. She didn't want to cause a rift.

By Christmas 2000, after a few months at Fort Benning, Gary Shane seemed fine. He had written a neatly penned letter home the month before telling them he was "having the best time of my life" at Basic Training and that he was learning new things each day. He talked of wanting to buy a used car after graduation, and he thanked his parents for all they had done for him.

Though he still didn't drink, smoke, or swear, and Ski knew the boy had a good heart, it was still hard for him to reach his son emotionally.

As a friend, I could sense his exasperation and sometimes desperation over his relationship with Gary Shane. Ski disciplined, encouraged, and molded young men his son's age every day, but his role as a father was far more difficult for him than that of a command sergeant major. During the holiday he made a special effort to spend time with his son. They jogged in the mornings, went to the gym, and had pizza afterward.

The day before Gary Shane had to return to Georgia, they worked out, got haircuts, ate lunch, and saw a movie, then went home and put up a storage cabinet in the bathroom.

Every time Delores heard, "Yeah, Dad, it's straight," she knew she'd miss her son all the more.

And now the moment of departure had come. Father and son hugged and said their good-byes.

"Hang in there. Keep your head up. I love you. We'll see you at your graduation."

"I love you, too, Dad."

It was 3:45 A.M., plenty of time for Delores and Gary Shane to stop for gas on the way to Fayetteville Regional Airport. She drove into the Texaco up the street and shivered as she filled up the Camry. It was dark and cold, and she felt so sad. She tried to focus on her plans for the next few months. She wanted to sign up for some adult continuing education classes—a basic math refresher course, and maybe creative writing or public speaking. Getting up in front of a crowd always scared her. Later, in January she'd take her substitute teacher exam. She was interested in subbing for phys. ed. or home economics.

Since 1995 she'd worked part-time, cleaning four houses each week. When Ski was in Korea, the extra money came in handy. Even after Ski came back, she kept cleaning houses. Delores was no stranger to work. She had grown up feeding the calves in the morning before school, gathering eggs, scooping hay, and leading cows to pasture. And besides, she liked having money she had earned herself.

As an Army wife she'd held all kinds of jobs over the years. She had babysat six infants and toddlers during weekdays in her quarters on post, had worked at several restaurants, and had been a teller at a savings and loan. When the family accompanied Ski to Germany, she took a job serving lunch in the grade-school cafeteria so that she could see Gary Shane come through the line.

And she continued to volunteer in the division any way that she could. She took part in whatever was going on at the 504th—from meetings and donut sales to car washes and hot dog sales. She and the other wives were always coming up with different ways to involve young, new, or junior enlisted wives. Early on she had learned that everyone needed to have a voice or you'd lose the group; you'd have a leader and no one else.

Delores didn't want to head things up anymore. She believed in new blood and fresh ideas. The opportunity to step into the limelight gave younger women experience and a feeling of self-worth, she felt.

"If you want my knowledge or input, call me," she'd say, though she had learned from experience there were times when she had to say no.

The more I talked to Army wives the more I discovered there is a fine line between being part of a support network for Army spouses—being there for other wives, because they are all in the unit—and being seen as "obligated" to help another woman out.

Delores knew what it was like to have more month than money, but the modern Army had built safety nets into its system to help out in those situations. Some immature wives new to the Army—and perhaps new to real life—expected other wives to go out of their way for them when their husbands were in the field for weeks at a time. That could mean anything from buying groceries to acting as babysitter or taxi service. Usually it was just a matter of immaturity and lack of planning and budgeting. A few women were just lazy or taking advantage; they knew the other wives would not let them and their children go without.

Years ago, when the Kalinofskis were stationed in Germany, Delores got a call from a twenty-year-old wife whose husband was in the field with Ski. She said her spouse hadn't left her any money for food or the electric bill. Delores took the woman shopping and paid for everything, delving into her family's emergency money. These days she handled such calls for help differently. Instead of running to a wife's rescue, Delores taught the woman how to access the post's emergency resources.

I've heard similar stories over the years from both enlisted and officers' wives who have had to rescue other wives. What bothers these women most is that their help was expected more than appreciated. How can this be? Some blame the system. One colonel's wife I know went as far as to call FRGs "adult women's hand-holding groups," saying that the system had created "monsters."

That's just one view, of course. An FRG's main function is to be the official source of unit information for soldiers' families. From what I have experienced, active FRGs do a lot of good, especially during deployments. They also hold a lot of fund-raisers, which benefit soldiers and families. That doesn't mean the system works perfectly. There's usually a she-monster in every unit, who knows how to take advantage, or a young woman who has not learned basic adult life skills. For years a wife and her children were known as "dependents" in the Army. The word was replaced a few years ago with the more politically correct term "family member," when the Army realized wives could have a lot of responsibilities, too, or perhaps the Army hoped to change a deeply ingrained mindset. Even so, the old term is still used.

Delores felt strongly that Army wives had to learn to take responsibility, or they wouldn't be able to be independent when they returned to civilian life. "Figure out how to do for yourself, because your husband is not always going to be there." That was Delores's credo. It was a lesson she knew only too well. She had often been both mother and father to her kids. Ski had missed Cherish's birth, first birthday, and first Holy Communion; he hadn't been there for Gary Shane's high school graduation, or on countless holidays, birthdays, and anniversaries. Delores paid all the bills. She didn't even know if Ski remembered how to write a check. When he was away she mowed the lawn, maintained the cars, and ran the household. Wives had no choice but to carry the entire load, just as a single mother would have to.

As she got back in the car, Delores focused on her son once again. He had offered earlier to pump the gas, but she had noticed he didn't have his coat on and told him she would do it. Suddenly she realized Gary Shane didn't have his overcoat at all and asked him where it was.

His expression turned to surprise. "It's still in my closet."

They rushed home and then sped to the airport. Delores didn't want to cry, but it was hard to fight back the lump in her throat.

"I really enjoyed having you home, son. It went by so fast," she said. "Gosh, you're all grown up. I'm so proud."

She dropped Gary Shane off in front of the Delta terminal, then hurried to park the car and ran to his gate. Passengers were already boarding.

"Are you all squared away with money?" she asked. Gary Shane was always too proud to ask for any.

"I'm fine, Mom."

She hugged and kissed him. "I hate to see you leave again." She pulled an envelope from her purse and gave it to him. "Baby, save it to read during your flight." It was a Winnie the Pooh card that read, "You're always in my heart, so I know exactly where to find you." To that sentiment Delores had added her own thoughts, ending with "Bye for now, angel. May God's peace and love be with you. Have a safe trip back to Fort Benning. Love, Your Mom xoxo."

She kissed him on the cheek. "I'll miss you. I'll be sending a package in time for your birthday. And I'll see you in March."

Gary Shane didn't have the heart to tell her he didn't want her or Ski at his graduation. He didn't want anyone to think he got special treatment because his dad was a command sergeant major, and he certainly didn't want any harassment because of it. It was bad enough that some of the guys called him "Mini Ski" and "Little CSM." He just wanted to be treated like any other soldier, to succeed on his own. But he'd worry about telling them later. First he had to make it through the rest of Basic Training.

"Don't cry, Mom. I love you, too." She'd find his belated Christmas card on the fireplace mantel when she got home.

As he walked away, he turned and smiled and waved. Delores watched his plane taxi down the runway and take off. She stayed until she could no longer see it, crying the whole time.

CHAPTER SIX

Rennie Cory rubbed his hands together in the wintry air as the engine of his black Chevy Silverado Z-71 churned to life like a waking behemoth. It was still hours from daybreak, and Rennie had the alertness that comes from adrenaline mixed with a night of restless sleep. He let the truck warm up for Andrea Lynne and returned to the kitchen for a second mug of coffee. Black was the "hoo-ah" way to guzzle a cup of java in the infantry, but Rennie drank his with cream and sugar. He'd joke to his wife that he drank it like he liked his women: warm and sweet.

It was the morning of January 10, 2001, more than a week since the party. It had been wonderful, he'd told his wife after everyone had left. "Everyone was so relaxed. For the first time someone had a gathering of different field grades merely for the sake of friendship. Nobody needed to do any politicking."

This morning the house was still and cold. Rennie walked upstairs and kissed each of his children—asleep in their beds—good-bye. In a few hours he'd be on a plane headed to Vietnam. He and Andrea Lynne had their first fight in years the day before. It had been late afternoon, and Andrea Lynne was in the kitchen cooking halfheartedly. When her son wouldn't pitch in with dinner, Andrea Lynne insisted that Rennie make the boy help. Before she knew it little Rennie was nervous and crying, and Rennie had angrily popped him on the back of the head. The flare-up was sudden, and it upset them all. Rennie didn't discipline the children often, and when he did, Andrea Lynne rarely interfered. This time she lashed out at Rennie, and they argued.

Frayed nerves from the stress that comes with not being in full control of a major life change—like the one the Corys were facing—are not unusual in the Army. So many things need to be taken care of or finalized before a deployment, and an emotional cloud hangs over everything. Misunderstandings, mundane tasks, and innocuous comments can get blown out of proportion and lead to arguments, even for couples as well grounded as the Corys.

Andrea Lynne could see that her husband and son were hurt by what happened, and suddenly she felt it was her fault. But it was no one's fault, really. Rennie's return to Southeast Asia for another six months was casting a gloom on the house that matched the overcast sky outside the kitchen window. All she wanted to do was cry and scream. She sent little Rennie to his room, and her husband went outside. Andrea Lynne stewed for a few minutes. Then she noticed the sun low in the sky, and her heart sank.

Little Rennie had just turned fifteen, and he had never driven before. She had wanted it to be his dad who took him out the first time, but this was the last day. Where had the month gone? They had so many plans. Rennie wanted to play golf with his son and get the truck serviced and ride his Harley. There were relatives to visit and friends to see. There weren't enough hours for it all. Little Rennie's first drive just slipped away. I guess it will have to be me, Andrea Lynne thought. No! she thought. No! It should be his Dad. It was almost dark, but Andrea Lynne opened the storm door and said quickly, "Take Rennie for a drive in the truck. For his first time."

"Okay," Rennie said stonily, but he looked at his wife, grateful.

Andrea Lynne went back inside and called her son from the bottom of the stairs. "Rennie!" she said firmly, to avoid getting any resistance. Before her son put on his coat, she touched his head where his dad had thumped him and rubbed it softly. "He didn't mean it," she whispered in his ear. She knew Rennie had to be feeling incredible stress to get that angry.

That night in bed, Andrea Lynne and her husband lay on their backs, barely dozing, immobile. They never slept that way, but Rennie was very serious about the coming separation. His humor was gone, and she could see him go into mission mode, as if he were disconnecting. He wasn't searching for political gain or a heroic destiny. He wasn't naïve about war or danger. For some officers, their careers came first; for Rennie, his family did. He worried that something could happen to his family without his watching over them. He would carry on like a machine, setting aside his own desires to do the job given him. Professional soldiers had a knack for doing that.

The night lights from Reilly Street streamed through the window and lit up the wall across from their bed, where Andrea Lynne had hung an Early American–style cross-stitch sampler with the words "Remember June Roses in December." The needlework was surrounded by dozens of photographs of the couple. Rennie loved that wall.

Andrea Lynne felt helpless knowing they had run out of time. She lay there numb beside him, eyes wide in the darkness, eventually sliding her left hand near his right, but she didn't take hold of it. That would have been unbearable—so much passion, too much pain. They stayed like that until the alarm went off.

Then they rose like robots. Rennie made coffee and showered. Andrea Lynne rinsed her face three times with icy water and dressed slowly. She kept on her denim-blue-and-white-plaid flannel pajama bottoms and pulled a V-neck cotton pullover on top of her white lace-edged tank. She carried her down pillow and lovey to the bottom of the stairs and saw Rennie petting Lad near the door.

This Christmas had been a sentimental one for the Corys. Andrea Lynne's stepfather had died in early December. And after two hectic years of battalion command, they were now dealing with a year-long hardship tour. It would be their last year in this beautiful house, too. Rennie was scheduled to attend the U.S. Army War College in Carlisle, Pennsylvania, the following year. Getting selected to the one-year program was important for those who wanted a shot at a brigade command or further promotion. For the Corys, there was no telling where future assignments would lead.

"It's time to go," Rennie finally said, looking up from the dog.

On the ride to Raleigh-Durham International Airport, an hour and twenty minutes away, the Corys shared the silence and eventually made small talk—the kind that avoided hurtful reality. They talked about the kids and what Andrea Lynne needed to do in the coming week. She'd be starting her first paid job, at Rhudy's Jewelry Showroom. The place was legendary in Fayetteville. It had one of the largest displays of gold, diamonds, and precious gems in the Southeast. Rhudy Phillips, the amiable owner, schmoozed with the brass and was invited to his share of ceremonies at Bragg. Signed photographs of colonels and generals—all loyal customers—lined the walls of the shop on Murchison Road.

The showroom had been there since 1961, long before the street turned into one of Fayetteville's tougher neighborhoods. But thugs and hooligans stayed away from Rhudy's, deterred by the steel bars, the gate, the cameras, the buzzer that opened the door, and the uniformed cop standing in front of racks of gold chains. For his part, Rhudy loved hiring officers' wives. They had good taste, were trustworthy, and didn't need benefits.

Andrea Lynne had decided to work part-time to pass the time and to earn some money. With their oldest in college, the extra income would come in handy. She knew that enlisted men always thought officers were rich, and, in comparison, Andrea Lynne supposed they were, but that didn't really mean anything. Sure the pensions were great, but in the meantime there were a lot of social responsibilities to pay for—dinners, golf, luncheons, coffees and balls, gowns, gifts, and decorations. And college tuition had put them over the top.

Maybe the job would be good for her psychologically, too. She had always been outgoing, yet the last six months, when Rennie was in Vietnam, she slowly began to lose steam. The Corys had been ready to give up command—though exhilarating, it was physically and emotionally draining—but Andrea Lynne had always assumed they would move on to the next thing together.

(I learned at an early age that it can be heartbreaking to assume anything in the Army. As soon as you start dreaming or making plans, Uncle Sam will go and change them. Army wives, including Andrea Lynne, all know this, too, but it was just too tempting to think about future assignments and what they could mean. That was part of the allure of Army life.)

Now Rennie would be half a world away, and she was still being pulled into the Bragg insider community through friends and wives—and that damned PTA. Andrea Lynne no longer had the responsibilities of a battalion commander's wife, but some people still came to her for information and advice, others acted as if she shouldn't be around any longer, and a few new wives probably wondered who the heck she thought she was. It was as if that black POW flag hanging from her porch symbolically clouded her sunshine.

Andrea Lynne stopped herself. That flag was a tribute to the soldiers and an important sign of support for the troops. She was so very proud of Rennie and what he was doing in Vietnam. Though he hated the separation, she knew the assignment was important to him, too. His father had served four tours of duty as a pilot in Vietnam, and even before he went to Southeast Asia himself, Rennie had felt strongly enough about POW-MIA issues to be active in Rolling Thunder—a national motorcycle group that helped educate the public. He'd ridden his Harley with them to the Vietnam Veterans Memorial Wall in Washington, D.C., over Memorial Day weekend the year before.

The conversation in the car petered out, and Andrea Lynne and Rennie were left to their thoughts. Vietnam had been part of their conversations when they were both college students at Appalachian State University in the mountains of Boone, North Carolina. The couple had met in the fall of 1979 after Andrea Lynne, a nineteen-year-old sophomore, and her best friend, Julie, pledged CAPERS (Coed Affiliates of Pershing Rifles) as a sort of a joke on their Chi-O dorm mates. Both Andrea Lynne and Julie were very antisorority, so when they saw a tiny CAPERS poster hanging by one pathetic piece of tape, Andrea Lynne said, "Now that is the sorority we are joining." The girls liked the service aspect of the group, and they decided to stick with it. As part of pledge week Andrea Lynne, well turned out in a gray angora cowl-neck sweater and matching gray cords and clogs, was gathering signatures of key people in the ROTC building.

Andrea Lynne's father had been in the military and Vietnam, and she respected the service, but in the late seventies, with Carter in office, a shortage of funding, and the attitudes of society in general, she just couldn't understand why anyone would join. She dated mostly fraternity boys or jocks, and the boys in the military science building looked like misfits to her. She dutifully collected her signatures, and frankly, she enjoyed the attention of the males who were in testosterone heaven showing off their gadgets and their survival skills.

Andrea Lynne still needed the "commando commander's" signature, and one of the students pointed her toward a guy sitting on a table who hadn't looked Andrea Lynne's way all week. This guy wasn't afraid of any-one, she could tell, and he intimidated her a bit. She dreaded approaching him, but she pranced up anyway and asked for his autograph. To Andrea Lynne's surprise, he complied.

"But I'm not the commando commander," he said. "I did that last year. I'm a senior, so I can sign right here."

As he got up, Andrea Lynne looked down at the signature and asked, "What is your name?" He looked back at her, smiling for the first time.

"Rennie—you know, like the dog, Rin Tin Tin? Rennie." And with that he walked over to the corner of the room where his two friends Larry Kusilka and Roland Johnson were casting a skeptical eye on the pretty coed. Andrea Lynne smiled at the memory of it. Little did either of them know then that after that moment he'd follow her around like Rin Tin Tin for the rest of his life.

Four months later, on Valentine's Day 1980, they eloped. When Rennie graduated that summer and was commissioned as a second lieutenant, Andrea Lynne left school and followed him to Fort Bragg.

When Rennie first joined the Army, he hadn't planned on making it a career. Though he did well in the airborne infantry and had excelled as a platoon leader in the 82nd, he wanted to work for the FBI. At the end of his three-year commitment to the Army, still in his early twenties, he took an FBI entrance test but did not score high enough on the verbal section to qualify. His esteem took a bad hit. By the time he was promoted to cap-tain, the Corys had two little girls. Looking for another job did not seem viable. Besides, people had a lot of faith in him as a career officer.

Rennie returned to the 82nd as a company commander and again stood out. After ten years he had done well enough to stay longer and had been involved with everything from antidrug operations to working with the contras. He oversaw the training of Rangers and had walked the DMZ line in Korea. He had even led a Green Beret Halo parachuting team in Central America when he was in the 7th Special Forces Group. Rennie planned to get out after twenty years, when he could draw his pension. But right when you think you may be headed for the door, the Army throws you a bone: Rennie was selected for battalion command in the 82nd.

Nevertheless, it was the assignment in Vietnam that affected Rennie the most.

"This is the first real mission I ever had," he said to Andrea Lynne after he had first arrived. Helping to heal the nation by searching for the dead and missing—sometimes just a tooth, a sliver of skull, a fragment of bone—and getting them back to their homeland, back to their families. That was the best job he ever had.

Andrea Lynne had seen him in action in October 2000. During her visit to Vietnam, a gift from her father, she got to witness her husband's preparations for the arrival of Bill Clinton, the first American president to visit postwar Vietnam. Rennie joked with his men that he needed to send Andrea Lynne home before Clinton could make a pass at her.

In fact, Clinton's November tour went off smoothly. The president actually remembered Rennie, who had escorted him in Korea years earlier. Though Rennie, like many Army officers, was a Republican—and told Clinton so—he found the Clintons to be friendly and personable. Rennie even teased Hillary about not being the first American wife to visit Vietnam: "My wife beat you to it. She just left."

Leaving Rennie in Vietnam had been one of the most painful things Andrea Lynne had ever done. She cried all night before she flew home, and the tears never stopped on the airplane. When she arrived home, there was an emotional e-mail waiting for her from Rennie: "I will not rest until I know you are safe at home. I will call to check on you. I returned to our room at the hotel after our good-bye, where I held your pillow, your scent is still there. . . . My heart breaks each time we leave each other. The pain gets harder as we grow old together. I agree, we will never part again. It is too hard. You know my love is true for you, now as always. The way I touch and look at you, listen to you, and make love to you . . . you fill my heart, each day and night. . . . I impatiently wait for the moment I wrap my arms around you and bring you close and smell your breath and kiss, holding each other as we do. . . . I LOVE YOU. . . . YOURS, RENNIE."

Now they were preparing to part again. Andrea Lynne had stayed in her pajamas because Rennie rarely allowed her to go into the airport with him. He'd always make her drive away before he went inside.

"I'd rather see you leave," he'd tell her. "That way I know you're safe." Andrea Lynne knew he could control his own tears that way, too. He always cried a little when they said good-bye.

It was still dark when the Corys arrived in Raleigh, and Rennie drove up to the drop-off lane for departures. This time Andrea Lynne insisted on watching her husband walk through the glass doors and check in at the counter. When Rennie looked back, he was surprised to see that the guard had let the car stay there. They had already kissed good-bye, but he came back to the truck and got in. They stared for a while in silence, then Andrea Lynne reached over for his arm.

"I don't want you to go," she said, but she couldn't tell him she felt afraid. You never told a soldier you had a bad feeling. Rennie pulled her to him, and they kissed, soft warm open-mouth kisses with the taste of salt from their tears. "I love you," they murmured over and over again. Every time they tried to part, they just grabbed each other tighter and kissed again. Finally Rennie opened the truck door and set his feet on the curb. His face looked lined and sad.

"Think of Hawaii," he told her, referring to the commanders' conference for his unit that would take place in April. Hawaii was the headquarters for the MIA missions. Andrea Lynne would meet Rennie there for two weeks. "I have to go," he insisted. He seemed intent, almost angry, perhaps from being put through such emotion, she thought. Then he walked away. Andrea Lynne didn't move. She just watched him until she couldn't see him anymore.

"It'll be all right, it'll be all right. I'm just getting a little too attached to that man," she joked to herself as she headed south to Fayetteville down Interstate 40. She liked to pretend she was doing him the favor of being his date. Adopting that attitude now was her way of getting through the emotion of the farewell. And when the sun finally rose, it comforted her, as if seeing the light of day could make all the pain go away.

PART TWO

✯ ✯ ✯

CRISIS
FEBRUARY 2001 TO
MARCH 2002

CHAPTER SEVEN

By the beginning of February 2001, I had just returned from an assignment in Bosnia, reporting on National Guard soldiers from Fayetteville who had been keeping a fragile peace in a region that had known little of it. This was the part of the globe that had rammed "ethnic cleansing" into the world's vocabulary. In small towns along the Croatian border, I was struck by the obvious devastation—bullet holes pocking every standing structure, young people missing a leg and hobbling along on crutches, and a noticeable absence of any men, young or old.

The American soldiers I talked to had been in the region long enough to have tired eyes and weathered skin, surprising features in young faces, yet characteristic of these deployments. Looking back, I find it strange now to have witnessed Muslims smiling and waving as they welcomed American troops carrying M 240 Bravo machine guns in the turrets of armored Humvees. It was a different time, and it wasn't the Middle East. To the south, in Kosovo, a battalion of soldiers from the 82nd Airborne Division had just arrived for six months of duty maintaining harmony between ethnic Albanians and Serbs.

Meanwhile, back in Fayetteville, whether their husbands were home, on field training, or on distant posts, wives coped with humdrum everyday life. Errands, bills, diapers, kids' colds, work shifts, college classes, and housecleaning all punctuated the days. Some women wanted a break from it all.

Shortly after 9:00 P.M. on the third Friday in February, Rita and four friends shivered in line as they waited to enter Club Metro, a nightclub on Fort Bragg Road popular for its dollar-beer nights, hard rock bands, and wet T-shirt contests. Women got in free before 10:00 P.M., a club custom in Fayetteville. Rita shoved her hands in her jeans pockets. Rita, like the other women standing in line, had left her coat in the car. She had never been to a nightclub before, and Brian would be furious if he knew. But *I'm with a bunch of married women. We have each other*, she thought. Three of the women's husbands were out on a training exercise with Brian. After six months in Fayetteville, Rita was finally getting to know some of the enlisted wives whose husbands were in Brian's squad, thanks to the FRG meetings.

She had been eager to attend the first one in October, excited that it wasn't just for wives but rather for soldiers and spouses. She saw it as time she and Brian would have together, as well as an opportunity to learn how to behave as an Army wife. It turned out that most of the information—aside from useful lists of resources on post and clinic numbers—was common sense as far as she was concerned.

The group had introduced her to other women, like Mandy, who had served in the Army and who liked to cuss. Mandy's husband had lived on Brian's hall in the barracks. She was slim, with long hair, dyed blond, and large eyes. Her father, who had been in the military, had met her mother while she was a prostitute in Germany.

"Just don't call me Mrs. Gold Bond," Mandy said after introducing herself. Mandy's husband used so much of the foot powder in his boots he had taken on the nickname.

"That's a deal," Rita said. "As long as you don't call me Mrs. Scrotum."

The two became fast friends. Rita got to meet some of the other wives that autumn at cookouts, which were popular with junior enlisted families who wanted to entertain but were on a budget. Guests usually brought their own meat and beer. Rita always looked forward to these get-togethers and welcomed the opportunity to make some friends. *We're in this together*, she thought.

And they were. Their husbands all worked the same hours and brought home the same paychecks and stinky PT clothes. They shared the same laughs and gripes, and secretly each wondered what she would do if the chaplain ever darkened her doorway with tragic news. They shared all the things that make for swift friendships on an Army post, but, as Rita would find out, some wives simply attract trouble.

On this Friday the women planned their night out much like a military operation. Tiffany, at nineteen the youngest wife in the group, was the designated driver. Later, the women would crash at Mandy's, where they had put their children to bed before they left. Donna's fiance was babysitting all seven children. Dollar-beer night always pulled a big crowd and promised as much watered-down beer as the women could stand. All Rita wanted to do was nurse one brew and dance.

That was naive on Rita's part, for this wasn't "girls' night out" in the sense of dinner and a movie and in bed by ten. Fayetteville is a GI town, after all, and the bars are filled with testosterone-pumped young men looking to get drunk, scope women, and if they're lucky, hook up. Wives who had been around awhile knew this, too.

After a bouncer with a mullet stamped the women's hands, Mandy laid out the ground rules. "What goes on here, stays here."

Uh-oh, Rita thought. What did that mean? Inside, the club resembled a black box with wood-topped metal tables bolted to the floor. Rita felt out of place in her Wal-Mart jeans, metallic blue button-down shirt, and black tennis shoes.

"Don't you want to put on something sexy?" Mandy had asked as they were getting dressed to go out.

"For who?" Rita asked.

Most of the women, including some from her own group, were wearing tank tops and tight low-riding jeans, but one black man near the bar outdid them all. He had on a powder blue, sequined miniskirt, and a white halter top that matched his electric white pageboy wig.

Rita pulled a crumpled twenty from her front pocket and bought her first Budweiser. Out on the dance floor, a swirl of heat and cigarette smoke enveloped arms, legs, torsos, and heads gyrating to the thumping of a bass and techno-colored lights. When she sat down at a table with Donna, Tiffany and Jenna were already out with partners, bumping and grinding to the "Thong Song."

Rita pulled out a cigarette and tried to hide her embarrassment. It was as if she were meeting these people for the first time. These were women Rita and her husband had socialized with. She'd been to their homes for barbecues. She had babysat their children. Now she watched as they pulled their jeans low on their hips, hiked up their tank tops, and dirty-danced with Jody.

No one really knows the origin of "Jody," but the nickname has been around for years. It's what soldiers call the civilian schleps and back-in-the-rear soldiers who court their wives and girlfriends while they themselves are slogging it out in field exercises or at war.

These women seemed only too happy to flirt with Jody. They seemed starved for attention. The women either had had no idea of what life in the Army would be like, Rita gathered, or they clung to some idealized vision.

Rita had her own fantasies when she married Brian nine months earlier. She thought her husband's job would be like playing cowboys and Indians. At the end of the day, he would come home, wipe the green camouflage paint off his face, and spend the night with her. When three days in the field turned into three weeks, or when Brian came home with feet that looked like hamburger and fell asleep in front of the meal she had spent all afternoon preparing, she had to look at her life for what it was.

I know this isn't making me happy, she told herself at the time, but there are times when you come first, and there are times when you don't. That much of Army living she had already accepted. Maybe these women couldn't deal with that. Or maybe their husbands always put the Army first, their own needs second, and their wives' a distant third.

(From what I have seen over the years, some women settle for third place. Others threaten divorce if their husbands don't leave the Army. These women fail to realize the Army often isn't the problem in their marriage. And some third-place women don't care, as long as they can be queens for a night in the bars and clubs around town.)

It was becoming clear from Rita's bar stool perch that some wives just wanted to be entertained at all costs. Maybe they started out by expecting their soldier-husbands to be the director of activities. If that was the case, you married the wrong man, Rita thought as she took a drag on her cigarette. Most of the time Joe—the average, young, enlisted soldier—wouldn't be around long enough to keep her happy, and when he was around, he'd be too exhausted.

As Rita sat at the table and sipped her beer, she could imagine a wife confronting Joe at the end of the day: "Oh, you want to have sex? I want to go out." Rita could see Joe figuring out his options: Well, I road-marched twenty miles today, my feet kind of hurt, but let's go to the Palomino and line-dance.

"Okay," he tells his wife. Rita smiled at the thought of it. Joe was such a predictable sucker.

Now she felt like one herself. How could she have been such a bad judge of character? She had assumed these women were like her, blue-collar mothers, similar in age, with E-4 husbands. Were all Army wives like this when their husbands went to the field?

Brian had told Rita stories of guys coming home to find their wives in bed with someone else or of wives going wild at the bars when their husbands deployed. One guy came back from a deployment to a depleted bank account, because his wife had partied at the clubs and bought her boyfriend expensive clothes. At the time Rita thought it was the stuff of urban legends, but now she wondered.

Rita figured some spouses were going to cheat no matter what their husbands did for a living; that's what she always told Brian. She was coming to realize that Army wives had lots of opportunities to do their husbands wrong if they wanted to.

And in the Army perception became reality. What you saw—or heard about—was what you believed. Rita thought of Brian. Oh, please don't let anyone who knows him tell him I'm here. I've got to tell him before somebody else does. She was glad to have Donna, who was an Army medic, to sit with. Both women were from small Alabama towns about fifty miles apart, so they talked about that. Rita ordered a second beer and a shot of vodka. She hadn't been drunk since the April cookout in Alabama. She'd been nervous then, and she was nervous now.

Tiffany and Jenna came back to the table giddy and sweaty. They immediately began singling out soldiers near the bar. "What do you think of that guy? Or that one? Oh, look at that guy. I'm going to ask him to dance."

A GI with a gold chain around his neck approached the table. "Hey, you want Jell-O shots?" he asked the women.

"No, thank you," Rita said.

"What's wrong with you?" scolded one of the wives when the soldier left to get their order.

Rita shook her head. "I just didn't want to give him a dollar's worth of conversation." She had come to the club to get out of the house, not to pick up guys. The twenty dollars in her pocket was enough to buy her own twenty beers if she wanted. Meanwhile her friends took the offered drinks and flirted. Sure, they wanted an escape from their drudgery, but did they have to tell these men they weren't married? If they're cheating, Rita thought, something is wrong at home.

There is nothing more humiliating for a soldier than to have his wife cheating on him. That kind of infidelity is a serious stigma. No matter how effective a soldier is with his troops, the innuendo that his wife is fooling around—*You can't even satisfy your wife; she's out with someone else*—makes him somehow less of a man and thus less of a warrior. Now, if a married soldier wants to screw around while overseas, well, that is accepted enough in some units for men to do it openly. As long as what happens on the road stays on the road, according to a saying popular among soldiers who bend their marriage vows. What some of them don't realize is that the same thing might be going on at home.

Rita looked down at her forty-dollar white gold wedding ring. Hadn't Mandy told her wedding bands didn't matter?

"Go ask that guy to dance, Rita." The women were encouraging her to approach a tall GI leaning against a pole. "You haven't danced with any guys."

"Shut up," she said. "I don't want to."

But finally Rita gave in. She walked over to the man and tapped him on the shoulder. "My girlfriends are making me ask you to dance, but I don't want to, so blow me off."

"You don't want to dance with me?" the man answered, almost hurt.

"No, I want you to shake your head and walk away."

"Come on, you want to dance?" the man asked.

"No, I don't. Now, when I ask you to dance, you say no, got it?"

"Wait, so you really don't want to dance with me?"

Finally he shook his head dramatically from side to side and moved away.

Rita returned to the table, and the women patted her on the back. When they got up to dance again, her friend Donna stayed put. "I can't believe you really asked that guy to dance."

"I didn't," Rita told her pointedly. She'd never betray Brian like that. She loved her husband. Ever since those first lonely weeks in Fayetteville, she'd told herself, Rita, you better grow a set of balls. You need to be less dependent on your husband to entertain you. Perhaps the wives in her husband's unit had reached a similar conclusion. Maybe spiting the Army and their husbands by turning into harlots on the dance floor was their way of dealing with it.

When the club closed at 2:00 A.M., the women headed to the Waffle House on Skibo Road. They were inebriated, and Rita was eager to get some food in her stomach. She sat in the backseat of Mandy's car, staring out the window and trying not to vomit.

I've always thought of the ten-mile strip connecting Fort Bragg to downtown Fayetteville as a ready-made backdrop for a low-budget movie. Motels catering to drug addicts, prostitutes, and transients share space on the strip with dirt and gravel parking lots filled with everything from move-it-yourself rental trucks to $2,500 cars for sale, the small American flag tied to each antenna not included. Soldiers come to Bragg Boulevard to get a tattoo, pawn an engagement ring, or see bare breasts. And places like Sharky's Cabaret, the House of Dolls, Mickey's, Show Girls, and Foxy Lady Bar give them plenty of opportunities. Nothing good has ever happened on the Boulevard after the sun went down. It is as if the darkness nourishes all the desires that lay dormant by day.

As Tiffany drove, Rita peered at people in other vehicles, thumping along to the sounds of their radios and sticking their cigarette tips out the tops of their windows. Where had they been tonight? Where were they going? Were they, too, escaping their daylight drudgeries? She placed her head against the back of the seat while the women laughed about their crazy behavior in the club. In the darkness the Boulevard's slanted utility poles, connected by sagging wires, looked like a string of drunks holding hands. Billboards passed off trailers as "1, 2 and 3 bedroom apartment homes," and cash-advance signs promised money before payday. As the women pulled up to the Waffle House, the mostly glass restaurant glowed like a fluorescent bulb.

Rita and Brian had taken the kids there for a Christmas Day meal, but on weekend nights the restaurant did brisk business serving drunk soldiers and their hookups. The women crowded in and found seats at the counter. Within minutes the smell of grease and the sight of bits of pancakes and bacon on the floor had Rita stumbling to the bathroom, with Donna right behind her.

"Damn, that sucks," Donna said, as Rita heaved into the toilet. She wet a paper towel and gave it to Rita to wipe off her face. "You need to drink some water."

Back in the dining room, two of the men from Club Metro, who turned out to be airmen from nearby Pope Air Force Base, sat at a table near the wives. Tiffany attracted another man's attention by lifting her shirt up slightly and revealing her backside. Rita scolded her, "That dude could be a serial killer. You can't be careless with your body. You don't know what this guy is going to do. He could follow us home."

Tiffany shot Rita a look. "It's just fun." While Tiffany and Jenna continued to flirt, Rita ordered some toast and coffee. She just wanted to sober up and stay awake, but the next thing she remembered was being poked by eight-year-old Jay, who wanted some cereal.

"Hey, Mama, time to wake up." It was 7:00 A.M.

"Okay, baby, just give Mama a minute." Rita's mouth was dry, and she was still woozy. Mandy lived in a three-bedroom house with a carport on a cul-de-sac. Rita had fallen asleep with her tennis shoes still on, in a spare bedroom. She remembered Club Metro, ashamed of her own naïveté. I don't ever want to be put in that situation again, she thought.

As Rita shuffled into the kitchen, sunlight through the sliding glass door made her head throb even more. She poured Jay a bowl of Lucky Charms.

"Don't eat the whole box." It was expensive cereal, and there were other children who were going to want some. "You got any Advil?" she asked Donna, who had just come into the kitchen.

"No, just keep drinking water, Rita."

Mandy got some blankets, and the two women curled up on her L-shaped couch and nursed their hangovers.

"Maybe we should have another drink," Mandy said.

"Uh-uh," Rita said. "I made a promise to God before I passed out I'd never drink like that again."

The morning light seemed to erase the previous night's excesses, transforming the women back into mommies and Mrs. Specialists. They knew how Rita felt about her husband—and it worried them.

"You're not going to say anything," Mandy reminded her. "Don't tell Brian. Don't tell him anything."

Brian and Rita shared everything, but if she confided in him, he would explode and tell the women's husbands. Rita didn't want that. Mandy was a good friend. Yet she wasn't worth keeping something from Brian. Rita would just have to find the right moment. As Rita rounded up her boys to leave, Mandy reminded her, "Now remember, we promised."

CHAPTER EIGHT

Andrea Lynne sat in Dr. Polhemus's office, crying. The doctor had asked about Rennie, and now she was unable to hold back the tears. Mark Polhemus was an attractive Army major in his late thirties, slight in build, with a receding hairline and vivid blue eyes. He had treated Andrea Lynne for her diabetes since her return to Bragg in 1998, and the two had become friends. It was Monday afternoon, April 2, and Andrea Lynne had gone to Womack Army Medical Center for a scheduled appointment before her trip to Hawaii to meet Rennie at his commanders' conference.

Dr. Polhemus walked around from behind his desk and sat beside her, studying her face. "What's going on?" he asked.

"Nothing!" Andrea Lynne said, realizing it sounded like something. She looked down at her hands. "Nothing. I'm fine, really I am. I just don't want to talk about Rennie." She began to cry again. Dr. Polhemus came closer and put his hand on her back. "Andrea, is there someone else?"

She stuttered and laughed, "Oh, no!"

"No, really, do you suspect that he—"

"Mark, no. Not no, but hell, no! Not Rennie, not ever. The very idea makes me laugh. The man writes me twice a day—love letters. Letters that make *me* blush. He calls every day. Especially now . . . I mean . . . if either of us would cheat, it would be me and *no!* That is not it."

Dr. Polhemus smiled. "It's not you?"

Andrea Lynne regained her humor and smiled back. "No—who has time?"

Laughing, the doctor encouraged her to talk seriously.

"I can't describe the emotion," she said. "I can't concentrate, and there's too much going on. All I know is that even speaking his name makes me cry. I feel like . . . like I'll never see my husband again."

A thought occurred to Dr. Polhemus, and he brought up Andrea Lynne's situation—being alone at Bragg, coming out of command, Rennie's obvious success, and her social responsibilities.

"Is Rennie on the fast track?" he asked.

Some officers get ahead of their peers by being workaholics or playing politics and forgetting about those closest to them, or at least that is the general perception in the military.

"No, Mark," Andrea Lynne answered quickly, almost as if it were an insult. "He's a due-course guy and a family man to boot. He's never neglected me."

Dr. Polhemus nodded. He felt he knew Andrea Lynne well enough to ask another question: "Are you getting support from your friends? The other women at Fort Bragg?"

It seemed an odd idea to Andrea Lynne, but maybe there was something to it.

"What do you mean?" she asked.

"Well, you're thin and attractive and rather charming; some women might find that threatening, especially with your husband on a yearlong deployment."

Andrea Lynne understood what the doctor was getting at. She listened as he emphasized his point. He told her she had made a big splash at the Mardi Gras Ball the previous spring wearing a figure-hugging gown.

Andrea Lynne loved that floor-length dress with its spaghetti straps, white sequins, and embroidered flowers. The night she wore it to the 82nd Airborne Division's spring formal she felt like Marilyn Monroe. But she wouldn't let Rennie see her in it until they were ready to go out. She wanted her appearance to be a surprise, and it was. The magic was always there for Rennie.

That afternoon, before Rennie came home, she drank some pineapple juice, checked her blood sugar, and went upstairs to put on Crosby, Stills & Nash. "Guinevere had golden hair . . ." always inspired her. She washed her own hair, conditioned and combed it, then bobby-pinned some curls on top and let it dry in ringlets. Completely nude, she sat back in her chair and assessed her body. Women at the gym often asked Andrea Lynne what exercises she did for her abs. Gave birth to four children and nursed them, she'd respond.

Andrea Lynne had a large round mirror at her dressing table, and unless she was cold or there were children running in and out, she often waited to dress. It was important for her to appreciate her body and be comfortable with it. There were no lights out for her when it came to sex. Rennie loved her body. He knew every inch of it. Rennie noticed the folds of her skin, the curve of her waist, the nape of her neck, and the pink of her nipples. And over the years his adoration gave her confidence as well. When you're told that you're beautiful years after the honeymoon, you believe it.

The sun was streaming in the window near her dressing table. She plucked a few stray eyebrow hairs, filed her nails and toenails, and painted them with clear sparkly polish. She went downstairs to crush some ice and then wrapped it in a washcloth and took it back to her room. Plumping two pillows for her head and two for her feet, she got into bed, settled in, covered her eyes with the ice pack and slept for an hour. When she woke, she drew a hot bath filled with blue bath salts and a drop of Chanel No. 5, and soaked, careful not to let any water touch her hair.

Midway through her marriage, Andrea Lynne had learned that men are fascinated by what Rennie called the "prep process." Rennie loved to watch her bathe, and he often came upstairs while she was in the tub. As she dried herself off, she'd caress her husband. She knew what he was thinking: She's giving me my fantasy. . . . She doesn't care if I mess up her hair. . . .

Andrea Lynne slipped on shimmer hose, nothing else, and wriggled into her dress. She applied a berry-stain lipstick to her outlined lips and rubbed on some gloss. She stepped into her shoes and grabbed her beaded purse and a short cashmere sweater with a boa collar—the Lafayette Ballroom could be so cold. Finally, at five o'clock she floated downstairs, where her husband, in his mess dress uniform, and children were waiting for her. The ball had a Mardi Gras theme, so Andrea Lynne fastened a pair of white satin devil's horns in her hair—in honor of the White Devils, her husband's battalion—and the kids took pictures. Andrea Lynne paraded around with her Mardi Gras mask, acting glamorous while Rennie smiled patiently at her antics. When the 5:30 cocktail hour loomed, her husband started getting nervous about the time. Fortunately, the officers club was just a moment's drive away.

The division formal was for officers in the rank of major and above and command sergeants major. The Corys joined the other couples upstairs in the club's Hodge Room, where Dave, the bar manager, made Rennie a Jack and Coke and poured Andrea Lynne a dry martini with two green olives. He always knew what the two of them were drinking.

"You're the most beautiful woman in the room," Rennie whispered into her ear, and that was how she felt. Everyone seemed to notice her. Even the top brass.

When she inadvertently dropped her sweater on the way down to dinner, both Major General McNeill (his rank at this time) and Lieutenant General Buck Kernan bent down to pick it up, bumping heads in the process. Finally Kernan pulled rank and presented her with the wrap as they streamed into the cavernous Lafayette Ballroom.

The crowd mingled near the round tables arrayed around the wooden dance floor under a large portrait of the French general the marquis de Lafayette, the Revolutionary War hero for whom Fayetteville was named. Lafayette had a smug, somewhat amused look on his face. By now he had presided over hundreds of galas in that space. Beneath the crystal chandeliers the tables had been draped in burgundy and white linen and set with china virtually elbow to elbow. The women shivered slightly in their bare-shouldered gowns. The temperature in the room was better suited to the dress blue and dress mess uniforms their husbands wore. As the officers and wives watched, soldiers drove golf carts—decorated by each unit—into the ballroom for a "Mardi Gras parade" and threw beaded necklaces to the crowd.

Then they all found their assigned seats, and after the call to mess, posting of the colors, the national anthem, and the invocation, conversations resumed. Suddenly, with the clanging of knives against water glasses, all movement stopped. Conversations hushed, and men and women stood for the traditional series of toasts, a litany Andrea Lynne knew almost by heart.

"I propose a toast to the commander in chief, the president of the United States," bellowed an officer at the head table in a baritone so loud one might think Bill Clinton was actually in the room.

Wineglasses were raised to the thunderous response: "To the president."

The wine was sipped, and the toasts continued.

"To the United States Army."

"To the Army."

"To America's guard of honor, the Eighty-Second Airborne Division."

"To the division."

"To the secretary of defense."

"To the secretary."

"To the chief of staff of the Army."

"To the chief."

Again and again the toasts were called out, honoring everyone but the general's dog.

"Gentlemen, seat your ladies."

The men then raised their glasses one last time.

"To the ladies."

"The ladies."

Over the years I've been to lots of Army formals myself and raised my glass for similar toasts, and I'd never thought much about them until an acquaintance who knew little about the Army said, "That's horrible! Wives should be the first to be toasted." It reminded me that normal military goings-on are seen through a different lens by those on the outside. Many Army wives think it is a gracious gesture to be acknowledged at all during these formalities. After the toasts at a recent Army formal, I had to smile when a wife leaned over to me and muttered, "They finally got to us."

That night at the Lafayette Ballroom, after dinner, songs from the 82nd Airborne Division Chorus, a video clip, and speeches, the dancing finally began. As Andrea Lynne headed across the room, a married colonel caught her by the elbow. Colonel Lance Mifton was drunk, and he looked Andrea Lynne up and down as if she were a dessert.

"You're going to dance with me later, right?" he said.

Andrea Lynne was caught off guard. "Sure, just come on out on the floor and grab me," she answered. But the colonel wouldn't let go of her arm.

"Are you horny?" he asked.

Andrea Lynne was mortified. She laughed uneasily, but the colonel motioned to the horns on her head. Andrea Lynne still was not amused; she hated that word. She turned to the colonel and moved in close. "Oh, I've never been that," she said. "Rennie never gives me a chance."

Turning abruptly, she walked away. The colonel came up behind her and whispered in her ear, "Promise me a dance?"

"You wish," she muttered and kept going.

Later that night, Major General McNeill stopped Andrea Lynne in the middle of the ballroom. "What are we going to do about Rennie going to Vietnam?" he asked. He seemed to want her take on the matter, maybe even her permission, Andrea Lynne thought.

Here's my chance, she said to herself, but her pride in Rennie and the MIA mission wouldn't allow her to take it. Besides, she already knew there were no jobs now for her husband at Fort Bragg. Across the room she could see Rennie watching her. She smiled broadly at him, put on a brave face, and answered the general, "It's an honorable mission, and we are becoming very committed to it."

She went on to tell him how much confidence she had in her husband for this assignment. Andrea Lynne's father had served twice in Vietnam, Rennie's four times. Both she and her husband ached for the men who died in that war and the families they left behind. Her comments seemed to surprise the general, who wanted to continue the conversation, but Andrea Lynne begged off when she noticed another colonel beckoning her. Withdrawing first gave her the edge, she knew, but she touched the general's arm affectionately—something she normally wouldn't do. She wanted to let him know gracefully that his offer of assistance was now beside the point.

It had been Andrea Lynne's experience that no one had ever really helped Rennie in his career, and she wasn't about to put either of them in an uncomfortable situation now. Besides, the opportunity to get her husband out of the assignment had already come and gone. Someone had to go to Vietnam. What difference would a conversation make? she thought.

Late that evening Andrea Lynne passed through the foyer—where young bachelor infantry lieutenants stood with loosened bow ties and spat tobacco juice into their beer bottles—on the way to the restroom, where she freshened her lip gloss. When she went into a stall, she suddenly felt dizzy and nauseous. Thinking she was about to vomit, she rested her head on the porcelain. *I'm going to ruin my dress. What am I doing?* A pain shot through her abdomen. *Was it food poisoning? What about the martinis?* She had ordered three, but the second was cleared when she was dancing, and she hadn't even touched the third.

Her friend April Thornal found her semiconscious, with her face on the floor. April grabbed the club director, then located Rennie. When he couldn't wake her, he got April's husband, and they quietly carried her out. April didn't want anyone to think Andrea Lynne was drunk. Oh, what rumors there would be!

By the following afternoon Andrea Lynne was in the ICU with a diagnosis of diabetic ketone acidosis. It had all been so sudden—one minute at the top of her game, the next minute weak and helpless.

When Maureen McNeill got in to see her, the general's wife was visibly upset. No one knew Andrea Lynne was this sick.

"Rennie can't go to Vietnam," Maureen said.

The best anyone could do was to transfer Rennie to Fort Irwin, California. And a move was the last thing Andrea Lynne needed, not only because of her health. For a couple with a senior in high school and a daughter in college, that kind of transfer only caused more headaches. They declined the offer.

Officers do have some choices as they follow a career path, although the needs of the Army may override personal preference. If the officer is fortunate, family considerations may play a role in whether he will go overseas alone or move to another post in the States. And sometimes those decisions will have unforeseen and lifelong consequences.

Dr. Polhemus brought Andrea Lynne back to the present. "I'm worried about you," he said. "What about the other women at the ball? Does it bother you that some of them may not like you?"

She laughed him off. "Really? I didn't feel any ill will. I wasn't the only attractive woman at that ball, for goodness sake! I have good friends on post," she insisted, "and I have no reason to be depressed that I know of. I'm moving in a good direction, I have a job I enjoy, I'm going to Hawaii, and I'll be seeing Rennie soon. I mean, I'm happy . . . really! I have everything going for me."

As Dr. Polhemus walked her out, Andrea Lynne did a few dance steps.

"It must be my biorhythms," she said. "You've known me three years. You're so used to me giving you a hard time, no wonder you think I'm depressed."

Three days after her doctor's appointment, little Rennie and Caroline got into a car accident on their way to school. Caroline was driving with her brother when another student hit them from behind. They were okay, and it hadn't been their fault, but Andrea Lynne felt a stiff jolt when she got the call that morning, as if someone were twisting a knife in her gut. Still in her pajama top, she pulled on sweatpants and headed to the school. Driving Rennie's truck made her feel as if he were carrying her along, but when she got on the All American Expressway, her calm disintegrated, and she found herself crying. What if she had to tell Rennie one of the children had been killed? The very thought raced around in her head: What if they were dead? I can feel death. Why am I so upset?

It took forever to get to the kids, but they were fine, just a little shook up. That was just as well, Andrea Lynne thought. Let them see what kind of serious damage several tons of metal can do. A few hours later she talked to Rennie about the children. He had e-mailed Caroline and complimented her for going up to the policeman and talking about the accident, taking matters into her own hands. She was just like her old man, Rennie had written. That was a big change from last summer, when Caroline was pulling typical defiant teenager stuff. Father and daughter were e-mailing more often now, and Rennie was proud of their newfound friendship.

Rennie was great with Andrea Lynne on the phone, as reassuring as always as he advised her about insurance companies. Thursday morning on Fort Bragg meant Thursday evening in Vietnam, and Rennie, surrounded by his men, was in a jovial mood. There is something about sharing a meal with comrades in a foreign land, especially one that was once an enemy. The Americans were having dinner at their usual table on the top floor of Al Fresco's. The British owner brought out mugs of beer and fresh-baked bread. The Rolling Stones played in the background, and Rennie joked with his wife long-distance. One of the men yelled hello to Andrea Lynne.

"I'm taking the guys out for their last supper," Rennie told her. "You know what we're having, the usual." Barbecued ribs, onion rings, and hot wings with mouthwatering French fries, fresh cut and fried to order. In Hanoi, of all places, they had found the best American food ever.

"We're going out in the morning. The weather's finally cleared," he added. Foggy, rainy weather could roll in quickly in the mountains of Vietnam, and it had delayed a trip to scout MIA crash sites for excavation in May. The Vietnamese government didn't allow any American planes, even commercial airliners, to fly over Vietnam, so the team had to rely on Russian-built MI-17 helicopters and Vietnamese pilots.

Rennie had already put off the trip three days because of the weather. Now Andrea Lynne asked him if he felt pressured to get going since he had the new incoming commander, Lieutenant Colonel George "Marty" Martin and a lot of other people there. Martin, a forty-year-old battalion commander in the 10th Mountain Division in New York, was due to replace Rennie in mid-July.

"I don't do anything unless it's under the best conditions; I don't have to. Why do you think we're still here?" Rennie said. He was so definitive, he put Andrea Lynne at ease. She knew better anyway. She wasn't even sure why she asked.

By Friday night Andrea Lynne was weak, shaky, and emotional, though she couldn't figure out why. Her blood sugar was normal. She wanted so much to call Rennie again, just to hear the sound of his voice. The conversation in the restaurant still echoed in her head. What is wrong with you? she scolded herself. I need to be strong.

After work she had gone up to her room and gotten in bed right away. She felt anxious and teary, which were often her symptoms of low blood sugar, so she checked it again. Again it was normal. There is just no reason for me to be like this, she told herself. She lay back and tried to rest, but it was impossible. Finally she slipped over to Rennie's side of the bed and called her daughter.

"Caroline! Come upstairs!" Andrea Lynne asked her daughter to stay and watch TV with her. "I feel so strange," she said.

"Do you want something to eat?"

"No, I'm trying to lose a few more pounds before my trip. But something's wrong. Please stay with me." She hated to scare the children, but she had been so sick recently.

Caroline rubbed her mother's arm. "It's okay, Mom."

Andrea Lynne started to cry. "I miss Daddy," she told her daughter, as tears filled her eyes. Stop just stop. You can do this. Just rest. It's almost over. That's what Rennie had said in his last e-mail. "Hold on," he wrote. "Just hold on until I can hold you."

She had written back that she thought she would never see him again. For months she had been haunted by a huge looming shadow, like a darkness in the corner of her heart. An evil thought floated into her mind: We'll never be together again. It wasn't just death she was thinking about. There was simply an absence of "us" in her life.

Am I getting weaker? she wondered. After being such a pillar of strength all these years am I now insecure? Have I been defeated by the Army, by my disease, by life, after all? Am I being punished for not taking up General McNeill's offer at the Mardi Gras ball, for sealing Rennie's fate?

"I'm afraid," she wrote her husband. He wrote right back: "It won't be long until I'm in your arms again in Hawaii. It'll only be a few weeks. Just hold on until I can hold you."

Remembering the e-mail soothed Andrea Lynne, and she nuzzled Rennie's pillow, comforted also by the warmth of her daughter's back. You'll see him soon. Just close your eyes.

The next morning Andrea Lynne awoke to her alarm buzzer sounding loudly. The clock said seven. She was late. Apparently she had slept through the alarm for an hour. That had never happened in her life. Caroline wasn't awake yet either.

There wasn't time to think about that, though, or even to wash her hair. Andrea Lynne pulled it back in a loose ponytail and quickly threw on some clothes—a denim jean skirt and a T-shirt from Caroline's alma-mater-to-be, the University of North Carolina. Caroline had just gotten accepted, so Andrea Lynne figured she had bragging rights. She had never worn an outfit like this to work before, and she felt a little underdressed. But it was a Saturday, she was in a hurry, and it was her last day of work. She was taking off for three weeks to prepare for her trip and travel to Hawaii.

She felt woozy most of the day. Even a coworker noticed, but Saturdays were busy, and there wasn't much time to rest. By midmorning she felt even worse. Her blood sugar was fine, though, so she fixated on arranging the rows of gold chains. Whenever Andrea Lynne felt overwhelmed, she cleaned or organized. It helped her focus.

"Oh, the chains will just be a mess by tomorrow," another coworker told her. But Andrea Lynne toiled away like a robot, methodically moving the jewelry into its proper place. By midafternoon she couldn't stand up, but she refused to leave. This would be her last day for weeks, and she felt a bit guilty. No one ever got that much time off at Rhudy's.

After closing, Andrea Lynne got into Rennie's truck and drove home in a daze. It seemed to take hours, though she followed the route she always took, down Murchison and then through the Fort Bragg Cemetery. Rennie had showed her the shortcut before he had gone back to Vietnam.

When she got home around 5:30, it was still light. She parked the truck on the street in front of the house and went inside, leaving the front door open, as she always did. She had told the kids to clean the house, but it was a disaster. Even the living room was messy. With Rennie gone, the kids often got out of hand, but she had been hoping they would have done something. Those little rascals have been avoiding me, she thought.

She put down her purse and assessed the room. Well, she thought, I have the rest of the weekend. Now maybe I can get my act together for the trip.

She was surprised to hear little Rennie's voice coming from the den. "Mom, you got a lot of messages today. I don't know who they're from." She walked toward the kitchen to look at the answering machine.

"Rennie, did you answer the phone?" she asked in an irritated voice.

"Yes."

"Well, who was calling me?"

"I don't know. They wouldn't say."

"Look," she said, "if you can't learn to take a message, then I do not want you answering the phone."

There were a lot of messages. Oh, great, probably the PTA, she thought. Just as she was about to check them, little Rennie called out, "Mom, Granddad Cory wants you to call him. He left you two numbers. One of them is a cell phone, and he said to call him right away."

Andrea Lynne noticed the numbers on a napkin on the stove, scrawled in her son's messy handwriting. She had asked him a thousand times not to do that. She picked up the napkin and went to dial the phone, when little Rennie called out again. This time his voice was different, lower.

"Mom—there's been a helicopter crash in Vietnam."

Andrea Lynne looked up and flew into the den.

"Well, what are you doing?" she said curtly, scolding him. "Why don't you have the news on? Your dad . . . your dad . . . he probably knew those people. Have you seen anything?" She was looking for the remote.

"Mom I *have* been watching. I'm looking." She grabbed the remote and frantically searched for CNN or Fox News or the networks, then remembered Rennie's dad.

"Rennie! Granddad Cory is worried about Daddy! Let me call him." She started to hurry back to the kitchen, almost happy to have a mission, but before she found the numbers, she heard Lad bark.

"Mom, there's four men in green suits coming up the sidewalk."

CHAPTER NINE

At 2:50 P.M. on Saturday, April 7, Rennie Cory put in his earplugs, fastened his seatbelt, and settled back as the chopper lifted off from Vinh Airfield and headed south along the coast of Vietnam. The dry season was beginning, and the weather had finally cleared after days of rain.

Since 1992, when the Joint Task Force Full Accounting was formed, the MIA teams had been scouring the coast, the rice paddies, and the mountains looking for the remains of its missing war dead. Of the more than fifty-eight thousand U.S. servicemen who had died in Vietnam, there were nineteen hundred whose bodies were never recovered. The U.S. government had made accounting for the missing its highest priority in opening relations with its former enemy, and, for their part, the communists were happy to assist the Americans—for a hefty price. Washington pumped nearly $6 million a year into the MIA program in Southeast Asia, which covered Vietnam, Cambodia, and Laos.

Rennie's team had spent the morning and part of the afternoon surveying a nearby crash site—preliminary work for recovery operations that would begin May 3—and had stopped at the airfield to refuel. While on the ground at Vinh, Rennie had decided to cancel a visit to a second site. Instead they would land at Dong Hoi Airfield, then fly on to Phu Bai Airfield and spend the night in Hue, Vietnam's ancient capital.

"We're turning this bird around and heading back to the hotel to have a beer," Rennie had radioed back. "We're calling it a day." He was decked out in black hiking boots, a large white-gray Timberland T-shirt, blue pants, a black belt, and baseball cap—typical attire for these trips. Wearing BDUs was forbidden. The Vietnamese government didn't even allow the American flag to be flown at the American compound in Hanoi.

Rennie had canceled the second visit because he didn't want to rush through the site, and he knew how the Vietnamese were about flying after a certain time of day. The pilots, who often flew by sight, were superstitious about flying over water or after dark. The MIA team was assigned Vietnam's best pilots, an experienced VIP detachment with years of experience, an excellent flying record, and a good working relationship with the Americans, but it didn't change how Rennie felt about the situation.

This was still a third-world country with treacherous terrain, and flying with Russian-trained Vietnamese on old MI-17 Russian helicopters with internal fuel tanks on board didn't give the American servicemen a big warm fuzzy feeling. Before Clinton's visit it took a couple of weeks to get the Vietnamese government to relent and allow two American Black Hawks to transport the first family around. I've since wondered why, if the MI-17s weren't good enough for the president of the United States and his family, were they good enough for American servicemen and -women?

At 3:18 the Vietnamese pilot radioed to Area Two Flight Management Center: "Twenty kilometers from Deo Ngang, altitude 1,000 meters." Then ten minutes later, "Passed Deo Ngang, altitude 1,000 meters." He went on to forecast, "Con Co 1615 hours, Phu Bai 1640 hours." They'd be landing in a little more than an hour. Noise from the chopper made conversation difficult. On board with Rennie were six other U.S. service members. Sitting next to him was Army Lieutenant Colonel Marty Martin, the easygoing South Carolinian from Hopkins. Also on board were Air Force Major Charles Lewis, of Las Cruces, New Mexico, the deputy commander; Air Force Master sergeant Steven Moser, of San Diego, a Vietnamese linguist; Air Force Technical Sergeant Robert Flynn, of Huntsville, Alabama, also a Vietnamese linguist; Navy Chief Petty Officer Pedro Gonzalez of Buckeye, Arizona, a medic with the Consolidated Divers Unit; and Army Sergeant First Class Tommy Murphy of Dawson, Georgia, a mortuary affairs team sergeant.

Accompanying them were two members of a Vietnamese agency assisting with recoveries, Nguyen Than Ha, deputy director of the Vietnamese liaison office, and Senior Colonel Tran Van Bien, deputy director for the Vietnamese Office for Seeking Missing Personnel. Bien had been fighting his whole life—first against the French, then the Americans—and he was a hero in his own country. There was no age for retirement in the Vietnamese military, so Bien continued to serve. He always wore a big smile, and during Rennie's nine months in Vietnam, Bien had come to like and trust the American. And Rennie respected Bien. The two men, former enemies, now sat across from each other.

The helicopter flew south along the coast at one thousand meters, less than a kilometer out over the water. The weather could change rapidly here, and when fog formed over the sea, the pilot moved inland. They were over the Bo Trach district of the central province of Quang Binh, about 280 miles south of Hanoi. The rice paddies below, snuggled between mountain passes, looked like a patchwork quilt from the sky. This had been the southernmost province of North Vietnam, just north of the former demilitarized zone. During the war it had been heavily bombed, and both sides lost numerous aircraft in these mountains.

At 3:34 the pilot radioed again as he prepared for a landing at Dong Hoi Airfield, "Request to descend to 500 meters and fly VFR [visual flight rules]."

"Descend to 500 meters, fly VFR, and report back when you have contact with Phu Bai," came the reply from the Area Two Flight Management Center.

The pilots could clearly see the ground, and the plane descended to five hundred meters and switched to VFR. Though the cumulus clouds were not significant, they were enough to impair visibility. What the crew didn't realize was that below the clouds a layer of thick fog had quickly rolled in and thickened. The pilots, not reading the altimeter, and thinking they were still in clouds, descended too far—to just two hundred meters.

Belted into their passenger seats, the Americans listened to their Walkmans, some rested their eyes, one read a *Maxim* magazine, and others scanned the excavation site materials. It had been a long day, and the men looked forward to showering, putting on fresh clothes, and going out for a big meal.

Rennie was going to call Andrea Lynne that evening. He'd be seeing her in ten days, and he smiled at the thought. In his room at night he often played a Counting Crows CD. He loved the song "Mr. Jones;" the "yellow-haired girl" of the lyrics reminded him of Andrea Lynne. In the briefcase next to his leg were two handcrafted diamond pavé earrings he'd had made for her. The jewelry had never left his side since he bought them, and he liked to pull them out before every briefing and tell his men, "Look what I bought my bride." He planned to give them to her in Hawaii as a birthday present. She had turned forty-one on March 6.

Meanwhile, in the cockpit, the pilots realized they had been descending for too long without being able to see the ground. They started to pull the chopper up. But it was too late.

The rear portion of the chopper's fuselage lightly grazed the peak of the mountain twenty-seven yards from the top, damaging the aircraft's tail rotor and causing the chopper to spin out of control.

At 3:39 the helicopter's engine roared as the chopper crashed into the side of Am Mountain and exploded. A tall column of smoke streamed from the site.

The crash killed most of the men on impact. One Vietnamese man, missing a leg, survived for forty-five minutes and told farmers he was with a U.S.-Vietnamese MIA team. The wreckage was strewn everywhere, and the bodies—most of them badly burned, some decapitated—were discovered by villagers collecting firewood or children tending to their water buffalo farther down the mountain. The Vietnamese took the clothes off the corpses to release their spirits. And as they had during the war years, the villagers scavenged the helicopter, taking the men's personal belongings along with parts of the chopper. But they never reached Rennie's body. It had been thrown higher up on the slopes. His skull was cracked, his spinal cord damaged, and his ribs and neck broken.

A year later I went to Vietnam to cover an MIA team. It was an assignment I had asked for. I wanted to walk the ground and breathe the air where so many young Americans had lost their lives. And I wanted to see the place that had defined Fayetteville and changed our nation. On a personal level I wanted a better understanding of my father, who was a battery commander in Vietnam, and who still can't talk easily about the war.

For more than two weeks I walked the streets of Da Nang, Nha Trang, and Hanoi, and I went into the jungles and out on the South China Sea with MIA teams as they searched for remains of men dead thirty years. My own ride with an MIA team on an MI-17 above the mountainous jungles of Vietnam was a harrowing experience, all the more because I could see so clearly the circumstances of Rennie Cory's death. Even our Vietnamese pilot seemed disoriented, and the Vietnamese on board were yelling at him before he landed at our site on the side of a mountain.

Mountain excavations were the most dangerous, I was told. Our chopper landed on the steep dirt landing zone, which had been hacked free of bamboo and other tropical vegetation by indigenous mountain people with homemade machetes. As the helicopter touched down and the rotor blades whipped up dust and debris, we jumped out and hit the ground, much, I surmised, like soldiers had done more than a quarter century earlier. The chopper took off, and for the first time in my life I felt my fragility as a human being. I pulled down my straw-brimmed hat and surveyed my surroundings. The jungle was a silent place, its lush green beauty as deceiving as an unfaithful mistress. The sun baked exposed skin in minutes, and the vivid greenery and rich soil hid poisonous snakes, stinging insects, and tarantulas. On another mountain a few hundred miles away, Rennie Cory had perished.

Back at Fort Bragg, Andrea Lynne stopped in her tracks. As she turned toward the sound of her son's voice, the living room window seemed to explode with light, as though she were witnessing a nuclear blast. Everything was in slow motion, and when she came around to face the door, she waited, not moving. The four men in uniform walked in. Colonel Jay Hood, the chief of staff of the 82nd Airborne Division, started toward her. "Andrea."

Colonel Leo Brooks, Rennie's former boss and the brigade commander of the 504th Parachute Infantry Regiment, was behind Hood, accompanied by two men she did not know. They kept coming nearer, and Andrea Lynne backed into the living room.

"Sit down, Andrea," Hood said.

I know what they are going to say, she thought. That Rennie's been hurt. She braced herself. I do not need to sit down. She perched on the ottoman of the papa chair, the one Rennie was so possessive of. She had even started a cross-stitch pillow that read, "Who's been sitting in my chair?" as a surprise for him when he returned home.

Colonel Hood sat down on her quilt-covered sofa, and Colonel Brooks sat next to him. The other two men stood in the background. She could see Colonel Hood was having difficulty. Neither man said anything.

Death notifications are one of the toughest duties an officer performs in his career, and one he never forgets. Much has changed since days when spouses and parents were notified by telegram. Sometimes a chaplain accompanies the notification officer, other times leaders from the soldier's unit will break the news—usually within twenty-four hours—along with what is known about the cause of death. I was surprised to learn how many officers' wives know that the "green-suiters" do death notifications only between 6:00 A.M. and 10:00 P.M. In the middle of the night, no news isn't necessarily good news.

"So . . . what?" she asked, impatient.

They didn't respond, except to shake their heads slightly. Whatever it was, they didn't want to tell her. Andrea Lynne inhaled.

"What is it?"

"Andrea, there's been an accident, a helicopter crash." Colonel Hood stopped to give her time to absorb his words.

She looked down at the carpet and then asked, "So . . . ?"

They didn't respond.

"Is it the worst?"

"Yes," Colonel Hood said quickly, almost with relief.

"No." She put her face in her left hand, rested her elbow on her thigh, and closed her eyes. *Where are you, Rennie? I would know.* She sought him in her thoughts. She had always been able to do that. *He would let her know.*

"Andrea, are you all right?" Colonel Hood was beside her now. Startled, Andrea Lynne stood up. "I need to go to the restroom." She'd had to go since she got home. As if escaping intruders, she walked quickly past the men and went upstairs to her bathroom. The light outside was dim now. She used the toilet, and afterward she looked in the mirror. Her hair was a mess, falling out of her loose ponytail. She had practically no makeup on. The house—oh, God, the house! Andrea Lynne was never this unprepared. How could this be happening? It was every Army wife's worst nightmare: You look horrible—the worst in a while, your house is at its dirtiest, the laundry hasn't been done. What kind of a housekeeper am I? One of your children is in Texas—and these men walk into your home without permission to tell you that your husband's dead.

She brushed her teeth. Her mouth was so dry, strangely dry. Then she gripped the sink, as if she were on a moving boat. She looked hard at herself in the mirror. It was like seeing another person, some innocent girl. She doesn't know what happened, Andrea Lynne thought. Don't let go, hold on. Isn't that what Rennie had told her? She nodded slowly and opened the door. One of the men, a major, was in her bedroom.

"What are you doing here?"

"I'm the division surgeon," he said. "You were in there an awfully long time. You have to understand, we were worried that you might do something rash."

Irritated, she went downstairs again. This time she sat on the chair; keeping the ottoman between her and them, but the conversations were a blur. She could hear people gathering in the foyer. Again she was told there had been a crash, that it had been confirmed, but Andrea Lynne wasn't really listening. She needed to gather her own evidence. Suddenly she stood up. "No . . ." She seemed to have solved some puzzle. "No. . . . Rennie would never leave me." She said it again, loudly. "Rennie would never leave me."

Then she heard crying in the den. She looked over and saw Colonel Brooks sitting on the couch with his arm draped over little Rennie's shoulder. Andrea Lynne wanted to rip it off.

"*No*, wait, Rennie," she said sternly. "Wait. *You wait!* We don't know anything yet."

Little Rennie looked at his mother and nodded slightly. Andrea Lynne was angry now. She turned to Colonel Hood. "I have to go there. I am going to Vietnam."

"No, you need to stay here, Andrea."

"No, he would come for me; if he's hurt I need to go there. I need to see him. I've been there. I know everybody. I know what to do. I have to go."

She heard voices around her: "Think of your health. . . . The flights

are too long. . . . Let us take care of it. . . . We will take care of it. . . .
You're needed here."

A group had congregated in the foyer. Andrea Lynne saw Mike and
Lucille Ellerbe. Behind them was Melissa Huggins, the wife of Lieutenant
Colonel Jim Huggins, with tears streaming down her reddened face. She
had sidestepped protocol by coming to the house this early, but she knew
Andrea Lynne would need her.

"Oh, Melissa," Andrea Lynne said. "Melissa, please."

Later, in the kitchen, she leaned close to her friend and said, "Melissa,
help me . . . the house, it's a mess. Please help me straighten it up."

"Andrea—" Melissa tried to console her.

"Melissa, I told the kids to clean today, and they didn't. All these people are coming in my house, *please!*"

"Okay. I will, I will." Melissa began loading the dishwasher and clearing the sink and counters. For a moment Andrea Lynne calmed down, but
she couldn't overcome the feeling of chaos. The house and yard had filled
with people, and the neighborhood was abuzz. But friends and relatives
had to be called. What about her other children? Mike Ellerbe told her she
needed to call Natalie, who was a freshman at Baylor University in Waco,
Texas.

"No, I can't," Andrea Lynne cried. She still didn't believe Rennie was
dead; she was sure it would be resolved. Melissa handed her the phone.
"Andrea, it's Natalie."

"No, no, I can't talk to her!" Andrea Lynne was now in the living
room. She felt a strong grip on her left shoulder. She turned. It was Lieutenant General McNeill.

"Andrea, you must tell her," he said.

She felt limp, helpless. She took the phone. "Hello?"

"Hi, Mommy!"

Andrea Lynne pushed the phone away.

"Andrea, you've got to tell her!" General McNeill said again.

She shrank and walked into the den. Somehow she found her voice.
"Natalie, they think your dad has been in a helicopter crash, and they
think he has been killed." Her daughter screamed and screamed again.

"Oh, Natalie, Natalie." Each cry cut her open. "They made me tell you. Is someone there?" Andrea Lynne dropped the phone and broke down in tears. Melissa, who had followed her, took the receiver and began to talk soothingly. Andrea Lynne told Mike to get Baylor security, get them there now, and to call the RA (residents assistant) on Natalie's floor. She was barking out orders like a commander. Mike was looking up numbers when Andrea Lynne screamed, "Why, *why* did you make me tell her like that? I thought she knew!"

General McNeill appeared at her side. "She was going to find out. It's all over the news. Someone was going to tell her. We couldn't risk that. And she needed to hear it from you, her mother."

His words struck a chord, and she gathered strength from his resolve. *He's right*, she thought. *She had to help her children survive. But the news? Why would it be on the news?*

Andrea Lynne went into the kitchen and saw the little bewildered face at the doorway to the den. There, among all the people clearing counters and cleaning up rooms, bringing in food and coffee urns, sweeping and making phone calls, was Madelyn, Andrea Lynne's smallest, looking up at her.

"Mom, is something wrong?"

Andrea Lynne froze. "No, Maddie. . . ." *She's been out playing*, she thought. *She doesn't know.* "Could you help clean up? This house is really messy, and all these people are here, and they are trying to help. But they don't know where anything goes, and I really need you to do it."

Madelyn looked at her mother strangely. "Mom, did something happen?"

In fact Madelyn had overheard some girls on the playground telling their friends a father had died, but she had no idea whom they were talking about. They only told her it was the house with the gray van parked out front. When Madelyn came home and saw the gray van, she had hidden in the backyard.

Now Andrea Lynne bent close to her and spoke in her ear. "They are telling me that something happened to Daddy. But I don't know. I just know that they are here, and I have to figure everything out."

There were shrieks in the other room. Caroline had been shopping with the Ellerbes' daughter, Kristen. She was on the couch, crying. Andrea Lynne came to sit with her. She knew she was supposed to comfort the girl, but she still didn't believe the news herself. She sat there with her arms half draped around her daughter, staring straight ahead.

Soon Rennie's father and stepmother were there. So was Alice Maffey. Jim Huggins had arrived, and he came down the stairs with linens in his hands. He had stripped Maddie's bed, which was also used for guests. He brought down garbage, too. Andrea Lynne made a joke about him looting. And for a moment the laughter eased the pain.

Neighbors and friends dropped off containers of prepared food, filling the refrigerator with dishes like the ziti and fettucine that Delores Kalinofski had left, complete with directions for reheating.

When such a tragedy strikes, it hits close to home on military posts, and there is an immediate outpouring of support and empathy. Death doesn't discriminate in the Army. These days at Bragg, wives whose husbands are deployed to Iraq have quietly formed "comfort teams" in case of a crisis.

As night fell the group settled in, like sentries taking up posts. Despite Andrea Lynne's protests, Alice insisted that she was not leaving. Natalie called back and said she was okay, the girls on the hall were with her, and family friends would arrive tomorrow to help her arrange a flight home. Andrea Lynne's father was on his way. Kristen Ellerbe was bunked out in the basement along with Caroline, and little Rennie's best friend was there, too. Maddie slept with Andrea Lynne in her bed.

Five days later, in the late afternoon, Dr. Polhemus stood near the stairs, took two Valiums from his BDU pocket, and placed them in Andrea Lynne's hand. She cocked her head and smiled. "You'd make the perfect Elvis employee," she said, but there was no arguing.

Andrea Lynne popped the two small pills and drank from the water bottle her cousin Lynne just happened to have handy. Lynne was her mother's cousin, a wealthy southerner from Savannah. Tall—almost six feet—and a young-looking sixty, with a charming laugh, she had always looked in on Andrea Lynne over the years. For the past few days she had been patrolling the door and monitoring the phone, pressing all visitors, even the green suits, into service.

Dr. Polhemus had been coming over every day after work to check on Andrea Lynne as well. Now he gave her strict instructions: Go to bed. No bath, no chores, no planning, no talking to anyone, nothing.

From her bedroom window Andrea Lynne could see Dr. Polhemus on the front lawn talking with Major Bruce Jenkins, her CAO (casualty assistance officer), who was helping with the immediate needs of the family, assisting with decisions regarding remains, benefits, and entitlement applications. The room was dark from lack of sun, or maybe it just felt dark, she thought. She left the lights off. She had no desire to brighten anything. Despite Dr. Polhemus's orders, Andrea Lynne ran a bath. If there were any chance of sleep it would only be after a long hot soak. She wanted to get in the tub and think a little. With so many people around, this was her first time alone. The significance of Rennie's death was just beginning to sink in. The third morning after the crash, she had sensed Rennie's presence while she was in bed. She had felt his love, and she knew then that he really was gone. But she still had to confront what was going to be required of her.

Military wives are identified with their husbands, and when a soldier dies, his spouse comes to symbolize a living link to him. How she reacts has an impact on others beyond the family. People watch the widow and take their lead from her.

Now everyone was looking to Andrea Lynne. She couldn't let Rennie down.

She heard the phone ring. It had been ringing off the hook for days, but this time there was a soft knock at her door.

"Andrea Lynne?" She heard a singsong Savannah accent. "It's Cousin Lynne. I think you need to take this one."

Andrea Lynne opened the door.

"I thought that you might make an exception for the president," she said as she placed the phone in Andrea Lynne's hand.

Andrea Lynne wrinkled her brow. President Bush was calling? He had been inaugurated three months ago. She took the receiver and said hello. Someone on the line said, "Hold for the president."

"Mrs. Cory? This is Bill Clinton."

She had known immediately who it was. He sounded just like he did on TV.

"I am so sorry," Clinton said. "I would have called sooner; I've been out of the country. I knew your husband."

"Yes, I know, he told me. We talked a lot about your visit."

The president told her how shocked he was about Rennie and how impressed he'd been with the work he was doing. Andrea Lynne told him about her own visit to Vietnam right before his. She'd had a hand in the planning. "If you had to sit through a water puppet show, it was all my fault."

The president laughed.

"I appreciate you taking the time to call me," she said after they had chatted a few more minutes, giving him the cue to say good-bye, but instead Clinton asked if there was anything he could do for her.

"I don't know what anyone can do for me," she said. "I'm still in shock. I didn't think anything could ever happen to Rennie."

The president listened to her talk about her husband. He seemed heartfelt in his sympathy and kept prolonging the conversation.

"If you need anything, let me know," he said finally.

"Thank you, I'll be fine." When she hung up, Andrea Lynne noticed that a half hour had passed.

Eight days after the crash, Rennie's body arrived back in the States. Major Jenkins picked Andrea Lynne up that night and drove her to Rogers & Breece Funeral Home. It was around ten o'clock, and the roads were dark and deserted.

She was in a daze. She entered the room where Rennie's casket stood, covered with the American flag. A shadow box held his medals, and a triangular glass container with a wooden frame held another flag. It looked perfect, surreal. Andrea Lynne walked over to the casket and removed the flag. Then she ran her hands over the wood, inspecting the hardware as if she had never really seen a coffin before. She tried to open it, and a funeral director stepped up and did it for her.

Inside she saw a uniform, a set of greens with the proper medals and patches laid on top of what appeared to be a body swaddled carefully in a green wool Army blanket carefully fastened with five large safety pins at the neck. She undid the pins, gingerly set them aside, and pulled the blanket open. Underneath there was a plastic bag. The funeral director murmured that Rennie's body was inside, wrapped in gauze, like a mummy.

"You won't be able to see him," he said.

"I understand," she said. She just wanted to feel him. Over the years her worst fear had been of seeing Rennie dead. Now she couldn't even do that. Is he really dead? What if they made a mistake? What if they mixed up the bodies?

As the men left the room and closed the door, she put her hands under the blanket and ran them along his entire body. It was crushed in places.

"Rennie? Do you know me?" She asked again and again in a low, ragged tone. His arms were bound, but his right arm crossed his waist. His left foot was twisted, too. How she wanted to straighten it.

She was weeping now, and she laid her head on his crushed chest. Maybe I should just rip open the gauze, she thought, but she remembered the mortician saying that she wouldn't recognize him anyway—after the accident, the autopsy, the time lapse. At last she closed the Army blanket as carefully as she imagined some soldier had originally done and placed his uniform on top. She held a solid gold Celtic cross and prayed. Then she kissed the cross and placed it in the left pocket of his uniform, closest to his heart.

She took out a picture of her in bed in Bangkok. He had taken it when he met her there before she caught the flight to Vietnam. The room had been filled with vases of flowers. And in the morning when she woke, Rennie had been standing over her. He had already been downstairs and brought her something to eat. He picked up their camera, and she pulled the covers up around her.

"No! I'm naked!"

"That's why I want a picture!" he said, but he didn't take it. Instead he pulled the covers back off, placed flowers on her chest, and kissed her. Then he stepped back and took one of the most sensual pictures she had ever seen. It was Rennie's favorite, and he told her that he kept it by his bed. Now she looked at the dreamy face in the photo and placed it carefully on his uniform. She felt like climbing into the casket next to him.

Next she pulled scissors from her purse, grabbed a long piece of her curly blond hair—the hair he loved—and cut a nine-inch hank, all the way to the nape of her neck, so close it hurt. Good, she thought. I want it to hurt. She tucked it under his coat. And she took out a sprig of the rosemary that they had planted in their garden. It stood for remembrance, she had told Rennie. That went in the casket, too. "We'll always remember," she cried.

Before she closed the coffin, she tucked her wet tissues in his other pockets. "Take some of my tears with you, Rennie."

She covered the casket with the flag and then let herself out.

"Bruce, I want to see my husband. I don't understand why I can't see him."

The mortician began explaining again why that was impossible.

"Look," Andrea Lynne said. "There has got to be a small part of him you can let me see. What about his hair? Please . . ."

In front of the Main Post Chapel, Andrea Lynne sat in the back of the limo with a black mantilla gathered around her shoulders. Her father had bought the long piece of rose-embroidered lace in Spain for her mother in 1966. An hour before she and her family had left, she heard the sound of an envelope sliding under her bedroom door. It was from Rogers & Breece, and inside, carefully gathered in a small bag tied with a peach ribbon was a small lock of Rennie's hair. She kept it in her music box. She glanced at her children. Before the wake she had bought them all Celtic crosses and asked Rennie's blessing for them. She knew they had some of her husband's strength, now those blessings would have to stand in for lost years of his counsel.

Outside the window she could see the eight pallbearers, uniformed and not, including Mike Ellerbe and Rennie's old college buddies, Roland Johnson and Larry Kusilka. Some of them knew each other well; others were meeting for the first time. As the men, four on each side, carried the flag-draped casket at waist level and began to ascend the steps of the church, the limo driver instructed Andrea Lynne and her family to exit the vehicle.

It was late afternoon on Wednesday, April 18, and the spring temperatures had fallen. Andrea Lynne covered her head with the mantilla, took little Rennie's arm, and followed behind her husband's casket.

I covered the funeral and was sitting in the balcony as she entered below. It was the first time I had ever seen Andrea Lynne Cory. She wore an elegant sleeveless black knee-length sheath edged in narrow white piping.

Like something Jackie O would have worn, said the friends who had taken her shopping. With it she had on the pavé diamond-and-gold cross Rennie had given her for her fortieth birthday the year before. On the left side of her chest she wore Rennie's POW/MIA pin from his uniform.

Natalie, Caroline, and Madelyn walked behind her. As they all entered the chapel, she could hear the elegiac music that she and her father had chosen, Samuel Barber's Adagio for Strings, which had been used in the movie *Platoon*. Inside people sat shoulder to shoulder in the pews. Those who could not find seats lined the walls or sat in the balcony. Interspersed with the military uniforms were ponytailed men dressed in motorcycle leathers, Rennie's Rolling Thunder crew.

Main Post Chapel was the most ornate of the chapels on Fort Bragg, built in 1934 in the same stucco style as the rest of Normandy. Andrea Lynne was surprised to see the large portrait of Rennie to the left of the altar. It had been taken when he assumed command of his battalion in July 1998. Though she could not seem to focus on the friends around her, she knew they were there. She could feel their eyes.

The eulogies began after the Gospel reading. Dressed in his greens, Lieutenant General McNeill was visibly shaken as he stood at the lectern. As he sipped from his water bottle, the three stars on his shoulders gleamed, and the ribbons on his chest rose and fell with his deep breaths. The circumstances made his task as an orator even more difficult.

"Rennie Cory Junior was not only a good soldier, but he was a good husband, a good father, a good son, a good brother, and a good friend. Truly he was one of America's sons, a patriot who always made time for family while caring for America's sons and daughters." McNeill spoke for several more minutes and was followed by Rennie's former battalion command sergeant major. Lieutenant Colonel Mike Ellerbe spoke next, remembering growing up with Rennie, unable to hold back tears.

"Like me, Rennie M. Cory Junior was a child of the Army," he said. "We were team leaders, company commanders, and battalion commanders together. . . . For thirty-one years we walked the same path, and I am a better man because of it."

The skirling of a bagpipe filled the chapel with the strains of "Amazing Grace." As the chaplain spoke and read from Isaiah, many listeners were lost in their own thoughts. Rennie symbolized much more than the "great warrior" who is so often praised at military funerals. I could see how his death had shaken the community and reopened old wounds.

Rennie had grown up here during some of Fayetteville's most painful times, when Vietnam metastasized like a cancer into the community's soul. The son of a Vietnam veteran who had survived four combat tours there, he joined the ROTC when it was unpopular to do so on college campuses. Rennie served as a peacetime soldier, wearing a uniform that once again represented honor and summoned respect. During the last decade, Rennie's hometown was finally beginning to come to grips with—some would call it dodging—the demons of another era. War of any kind seemed unlikely now, terrorism on U.S. soil an unlikely invention of the silver screen.

Having a local boy go off to Vietnam years later to bring peace to the national conscience and closure for families of the dead meant something profound here. Now his death catapulted Fayetteville back to a time of dashed hopes and aching sadness. Fayettenam was more than a place or a reckless way of life. It was an evil that seemed to rise from the past and claim as a casualty one more beloved son.

His death touched me, too. Later that day, while talking with Maureen McNeill, I found myself sobbing in her arms. I was embarrassed that I had lost my composure; that had never happened on assignment before. But I couldn't help it. I cried for the loss of a fine man and what it would mean to his family. I cried for the fifty-eight thousand war dead, and for those like my father who lived through their own Vietnam hell. And I cried for Fayetteville, the town I had come to love, still in the shadow of a Southeast Asian war.

As the memorial service ended with a final blessing, the mourners filed out. The weather had turned colder, and Andrea Lynne put on a short jacket of soft crushed velvet she had borrowed from Caroline. Back in the limo, Andrea Lynne could hear the Harleys roll out behind the hearse. Along the street, men saluted as the funeral procession drove by. Fort Bragg Cemetery was on a grassy knoll, surrounded by longleaf pines, its entrance marked by two enormous magnolia trees. Here in neat rows three thousand soldiers' graves were marked by identical white tombstones shaped like arched doorways. Slightly apart from the others were the graves of eight Germans who died at Bragg while they were prisoners of war during World War II.

TANYA BIANK

Andrea Lynne felt weak, like a person walking to death row, but the graveside mass soothed her. The incense, the singing, the prayers—Father Matthew Pawlikowski's blessing of the grave was all that mattered. Under the blue funeral tent, Andrea Lynne felt the presence of the other soldiers. Their grief was palpable, and their emotion was holding her up.

She stared at the ground, trying to absorb the priest's holy words. When Brigadier General Harry Axson gave her the American flag from Rennie's casket, she was void of emotion. She realized she had joined the ranks of women she thought she would only read about in newspapers. Yet the twenty-one-gun salute gave her comfort. It was a fine sound, she thought. Like the greatest Army toast from all its living soldiers for their beloved fallen comrade: *Here's to you, sir!*

The bugler played Taps, and the funeral director handed each family member a rose to place on the coffin. Andrea Lynne waited a moment, then she stood up with a shakiness that surprised her. The funeral director helped her toward the casket, and suddenly she forgot all the people, and she gazed at the polished wood. She removed her veil and laid it on the coffin, swirling it as if to impart some part of herself to Rennie. She laid the rose on top, her eyes brimming with tears. Then she leaned down and kissed the casket. Those around her gasped, but her body just would not let him go. She felt she was deserting him. Good-bye, Rennie. Leaving was the hardest thing she had ever had to do. Finally, as if pulled by a string, she rose and walked away.

CHAPTER TEN

I t was just after 5:30 on a Friday afternoon in mid-August, and the Green Beret Club on the corner of Buker and Ninth Streets was hopping. I'd been to the club numerous times over the years, sometimes to meet a source for a beer, other times with friends and their husbands who were in Special Forces, but this time I was by myself. I worked my way through the crowd of men just off duty and still in their BDUs and boots. Intermingled with them were a few women whose better days had passed. The colorful history of the club had always interested me, and I thought it was worth exploring for a story. The article never did materialize; a few weeks later I would be consumed with stories of a very different nature. My night at the club resulted in a chance meeting that would have profound meaning I couldn't have foreseen at the time.

"Hey, we've got a seat for you over here. You wanna join us?"

I turned around. It was Brandon Floyd. He was at the end of a rectangular table, his back facing an outdoor deck where patrons sweated it out at picnic tables waiting for the sun to go down. He gave me his chair and found another one. I sat down next to him and then found out why he was so accommodating. He wanted to introduce me to his single friend, a Green Beret visiting from Fort Campbell.

In front of Brandon at the wraparound bar, covered in green laminate to match the arched, wood-beamed ceiling, sat the old-timers with baseball caps cocked atop their heads. Most of them were Green Beret Vietnam vets and long retired. They sat in their favorite tan vinyl swivel bar chairs, most with an elbow resting on the bar, a cigarette between their fingers, and a bottle of beer within easy reach. Brandon pointed the men out to me and said I really needed to talk to them if I wanted to learn about the place. I could tell he had a lot of respect and reverence for those who had served before him.

I looked around. Beneath the ceiling fans cigarette smoke hung like fog. In the far corner near the dartboard and under a red Budweiser lampshade suspended from the ceiling, soldiers gathered around a single pool table and held their pool cues like shepherds' staffs.

Officially part of the post, the Green Beret Club was legendary at Fort Bragg. Long ago it was a place only for Green Berets, but these days anybody could go, although most soldiers who weren't in special operations stayed away. The bar was tamer than it used to be—brawls, property damage, pranks, and DUIs carried stiffer punishments than in the old Army days—but MPs still sat outside the club in their squad cars at closing time, and the Green Beret Club remained a place where a certain breed of man who had enough of a wild streak and the balls to do the nation's down-and-dirty work liked to carouse. The men didn't brag about their accomplishments, but they did take exception to anyone who tarnished their reputations. My favorite story about the wild times in the old days concerned a vet who retired and moved to West Virginia. When he heard that a fellow Green Beret had been bad-mouthing him, he drove to North Carolina the following day, entered the club, knocked the guy out, had a beer, and then headed back to West Virginia.

The club's location had changed several times over the years. It now sat in a white aluminum building on the southern end of Bragg. Budget cuts kept threatening the place with closure, but it always managed to hang in there like a street scrapper. Brandon hadn't been to the club in a while, he told me. When old friends from Special Forces called to say they were at Bragg for a course, they decided to get together at the old hangout.

Brandon was wearing what he had worn to work that day, a collared short-sleeved shirt and jeans. Operators rarely wore uniforms in garrison. The regulations of conventional units didn't exist in Delta, because its mission was so different. There were no unit formations at O dark thirty (in the early morning) and in most cases enlisted soldiers called their officers—except for the unit commander—by first name. Hairstyles reflected the fact that Delta operators often worked on their own or in small groups overseas, where they needed to blend in with the culture around them; that meant growing beards and wearing traditional garb. Brandon's hair was short by civilian standards—trimmed over the ear, not touching the back of the collar—but in a conventional Army unit a sergeant major would have dragged his ass to the barber. Some of his comrades had bushy mustaches, a dead giveaway for a Delta operator.

They are not supposed to attract undue attention to themselves on or off duty. In Fayetteville, where males barely out of puberty wear buzz cuts and proudly display their unit's insignia on T-shirts, baseball caps, and vehicle rear windows, Delta guys stick out like candles on a birthday cake. If asked, most say they are in Special Ops, and if that isn't enough they might try to change the subject. That itself provides the answer.

Brandon gave me what I later learned was a fake name and told me he was an instructor at Bragg's JFK Special Warfare Center and School. I had no reason not to believe him, though I found him to be an odd combination of charming and insulting. He let me know right away he didn't care for reporters or the media, but then, most military folks feel that way. He said I resembled his wife, Andrea, and he told me how they had met.

I don't reveal much about myself when I'm interviewing, unless I'm asked. Brandon asked. He gave me the impression that no matter what I said he'd pick it apart.

"You think you're too good for us, don't you?" he said at one point. No matter what I said, I couldn't win with Brandon. He seemed to have a chip on his shoulder, and for much of the evening he tried to peg me into a hole that I didn't fit into. I stayed for a couple of hours, and when I was getting ready to leave, he said one more thing: "I know you think I'm a jerk, and you've got me all figured out. But my dad was a bird colonel, I teach Sunday school, and I've get three kids and a wife, and I'm usually home with them, not out here." What struck me was the way he said it, as if he had something to prove.

Perhaps that's why he told me he was in Delta—in a roundabout way, that is. After giving me his name, he laughed. "That's not my real name," he admitted. "And I don't work at the schoolhouse, either."

"You work out past McKellar's Lodge, then?" He looked me in the eyes, then nodded yes. At that point I knew. I didn't ask him anything else about it. It wasn't something he could or would talk about.

"So what's your real name?" I asked. He wouldn't give it to me, but it wasn't hard to guess when his buddies called him "Brandon" or "Sergeant First Class Floyd."

It wasn't until a few years later, with the help of those who worked with Brandon, that I began to piece together the life he had only hinted to me about. He had been in Delta about a year when I met him, and was enjoying every minute of it.

Delta was formed in the late seventies as a counterterrorist response to airplane hijackings, and the unit's primary mission has remained hostage rescue. The soldiers who are accepted—just 10 percent make it through the grueling exams and rigorous six-month training course—have to be mature, disciplined, and highly motivated, capable of making decisions on their own. The physical demands are huge, including parachute free-falling and skiing. And being able to scuba dive or speak a foreign language doesn't hurt. Brandon spoke French from his Special Forces days.

Since operators often travel alone for extended periods of time, routinely making decisions on the ground that an officer would make in a conventional unit, they also have to be self-starters and creative thinkers. There is no margin of error for a bad decision or a lapse in judgment, no allowance for a breach of trust or embarrassment to the unit. An operator has to be a quiet professional, satisfied to know that what he has done for his country will be all the recognition he gets.

Brandon had been stationed at Fort Campbell, Kentucky, when he tried out for the elite unit. Delta Force was the pinnacle, the ultimate challenge for him, after serving with the Green Berets and the Rangers. He was an assault team member, an operator who initiates direct close contact with the enemy. That meant Brandon was a door kicker, one of the guys with a modified M4 assault weapon who went into buildings or airplanes under cover of snipers. Like the other men in Delta, he fired his weapons almost daily. Soldiers in some conventional units were more likely to fire their weapons once or twice a year.

Brandon always had a reputation for leading a cleaner life than some of his comrades. He wasn't wild and didn't get caught up in running the bars. He turned down offers to visit strip clubs on Bragg Boulevard, and he didn't seek out other women when he was on temporary duty.

He and Andrea spent a lot of time in their new church. He wasn't shy about talking about it to the men in his squadron, and he sometimes brought them along on Sundays. Brandon was always inviting people to church, to the delight of the pastor, Mark Strickland, who had a strong desire to reach out to military families.

Since January the Floyds had been attending Emanuel Baptist. They felt comfortable there and were now actively a part of the fifty-member congregation. It was what they had been searching for. Not only did they go on Sunday mornings, but they returned for evening services at six and came to the fellowship service each Wednesday evening at seven as well. During winter, despite the Delta demands on Brandon, the couple had taken on additional responsibilities. Brandon and Andrea taught Sunday school together to the eleven- to eighteen-year-olds, and he led the youth group. They brought the kids horseback riding on Fort Bragg and attempted a camping trip near a pond—until they got rained out. Brandon even filled in and preached one Sunday when the pastor was out of town.

Otherwise they didn't socialize much. There wasn't a lot of time in Delta, and besides, Andrea didn't like to go to a lot of the parties. She thought some of the wives in the squadron were snobby, though she could be standoffish herself until you got to know her.

Still, it was nice to kick back a bit now and then, especially with three old pals who were attending a course at Bragg. By now on that August evening, Brandon had been at the club for an hour and was feeling the alcohol. His cell phone rang.

"Heeello."

Andrea could tell her husband was in good humor. "Hey, I was going to fire up the grill. Will you be home soon?"

Brandon could hear one of his kids in the background. "Yeah, I'll be back in a bit. We'll be winding down soon."

"Tell the guys I said hello."

"I'll put 'em on and you can tell them yourself."

Andrea was glad it was Friday. She needed a little break. It had been a busy summer. She had taken the kids down to Myrtle Beach for the day to see her mom, who was vacationing there. And Andrea had also traveled to California to donate her eggs to a couple who couldn't have a child. It hadn't been a year since she gave birth to the twins; why not give another couple a chance to have a child, even if the baby would biologically be hers this time. So what if Brandon didn't feel comfortable with it. Andrea felt it was the right thing to do, and there was no changing her mind. She was regaining a confidence she had lost over the last few years.

Maybe that had something to do with their marriage, which had had a rocky start and many ups and downs. When Andrea first discovered she was pregnant in Germany, some of her Army supervisors encouraged her to have an abortion, but Andrea wouldn't hear of it. She was discharged and went home to Alliance to have the baby, mortified that she was unmarried and pregnant.

Meanwhile, Brandon returned to the States for knee surgery after a ski accident, and Andrea and her sister and brother-in-law drove from Ohio to visit him at Walter Reed Medical Center in Maryland. When she told Brandon she was going to have his baby, she thought he'd be thrilled. Instead the visit was a disaster. Brandon—bedridden and angry—lashed out at Andrea and accused her of sleeping around. He had fathered a baby boy when he was a senior in high school, and his parents were upset that he was now having a second child out of wedlock. They even questioned if it was his, which hurt Andrea and angered her family. Brandon had been her first real love.

Eventually the couple made up and married at the courthouse at Fort Benning, Georgia, on May 17, 1994, more than a month after Harlee was born and a day before Andrea's twenty-first birthday. Soon after that Brandon was out of the Army himself. Andrea had wanted to go home. Things between them had been so difficult, she thought maybe going back to Alliance would make life better. They settled in Andrea's hometown, and Brandon took a job making train car frames at American Steel.

He hated the work, and Andrea was unhappy, too.

It's not unusual for a soldier to realize the grass isn't always greener in the civilian job market and to reenlist. After six months Brandon did just that, and the couple moved to Fort Campbell, back to an environment in which they both felt at home. Andrea had loved the Army, and her stint as a soldier gave her a unique perspective as an Army wife.

Generally female soldiers have more in common with male soldiers—their comrades—than they do with Army wives. When they marry another soldier, it's easy for them to relate to their husbands on all things military. I've known lots of wives, like Andrea, who make the leap from soldier to Army spouse. They leave the Army for different reasons, often to raise children or pursue a different career path. Sometimes the wife remains in the Army and the husband gets out. Still, dual military couples—with both the husband and wife in the military—do exist, and the Army tries to accommodate them by giving them duty stations in the same area. It's known as "joint domicile," but it's never guaranteed. The needs of the Army always come first. Today's back-to-back war deployments to the Middle East are taking a toll on dual military couples, who find themselves geographically separated for a few years. Throw kids into the mix, and things get complicated. Each family has to decide what's best for them.

The Floyd marriage had plenty of problems even after Brandon rejoined the Army. When things weren't going well with Brandon, Andrea wished she were back home with her family. In 1996 she even filed for divorce, but Brandon desperately wanted to work things out. He had grown up as a Mormon, and divorce represented a complete failure. He believed that if he divorced, he wouldn't go to heaven.

Andrea agreed to stay together. "I don't want these kids to grow up without a father, like we did," she would tell her two sisters whenever she confided in them about her troubles with Brandon.

She could see both sides of her husband's personality. He could be playful. He'd dance to a Christina Aguilera CD, laughing and giggling with the kids. The next minute he'd be short-tempered, becoming furious if the boys were playing too rough or if something got knocked over. He was strict—it was always "yes, sir," and "yes, ma'am"—but then the boys would be in his lap. They worshipped their dad, and Harlee, who took after Andrea in so many ways, was a daddy's girl. She idolized her father, though he was gone a lot.

Andrea kept trying to find her own path. In 1999 she worked briefly at a sporting goods store, but she quit after less than a year. She wanted to be with her kids. To earn a little money she did day care, watching three or four children in addition to her own.

Managing a house full of kids was difficult when Brandon was away, and when he was there, he didn't like seeing other kids running around his house. She had recently decided to go back to work. Brandon gained satisfaction from his job. Why couldn't she have something to call her own? And soon they would need the extra income. Brandon had liked the house in which the surrogate twins lived so much, he told Andrea that's how he wanted to live. For months they had been looking for a bigger home to buy, even though Andrea knew they couldn't afford one.

This time she found a job at Dick's Sporting Goods, and just a few weeks earlier she had started job training. That was another reason the summer was so hectic. She had to drive all the way to Cary, outside Raleigh. At least when the store opened in Fayetteville in the fall, she'd be working closer to home. She was looking forward to that. Sticking her toe out into the unknown was exhilarating.

CHAPTER ELEVEN

I was at my desk in the newsroom on September 11, trying like everybody else to process what had just happened at the World Trade Center, when the wire services announced that a plane had crashed into the Pentagon. I ran up to my managing editor, Mike Arnholt, with the news. He was standing under a TV suspended from the ceiling in the center of the newsroom.

"The Pentagon was just hit," I said. "And my sister's there." He just looked at me. What could anyone say? Events were unfolding so quickly it was hard to grasp the scope of what it all meant. Maria had followed my father into the Army. Now she was somewhere in that enormous building. I called my parents, who lived in Virginia. My always-in-control father had a quaver in his voice as we tried to remember which corridor Maria worked in. When I got off the phone, I sobbed at my desk.

The Pentagon, the headquarters of the Department of Defense, has about twenty-three thousand military and civilian employees, and most officers and senior NCOs at Bragg knew someone who worked there. In the end 184 people died at the Pentagon, including some of my sister's coworkers. Later that afternoon Maria telephoned my mother to say she was safe. When I heard the news, I cried tears of relief and joy.

Meanwhile I had a story to cover. Bragg was unusually silent. Yards, parks, soccer fields, and the youth center stood empty. The gates to the 82nd Airborne Division headquarters, which were always open, were locked shut, and soldiers started laying down concertina wire and plastic barricades. Amid the feelings of profound sadness, shock, and loss, there was also a call to action. I saw soldiers move with more determination and sense of purpose.

In peacetime, soldiers like to grumble they "never get to do anything." Now they knew it was only a question of when. Fort Bragg, like U.S. military installations everywhere, tightened security to its highest level, training ceased, and soldiers came in from the field. Those on recall status readied their rucksacks and equipment.

I went home to my apartment around eleven that night, bleary eyed and emotionally drained. I opened a bottle of beer, sat in front of the TV in the dark, and cried again. I got a call early the next morning. It was Mike Adams, my editor, giving me my assignment for the day: head out to Bragg and cover the traffic mess that was backed up for miles.

September 12 was another bright and beautiful morning—Mother Nature's big lie, I thought. I left my car in the Ponderosa shopping center parking lot—I was lucky to get a space—and surveyed Yadkin Road, known to soldiers as the Yadkin 500 because reckless drivers darted in and out of traffic on its narrow lanes. Now traffic was at a standstill. Between thirty-five thousand and forty thousand cars pass through Fort Bragg during a typical twenty-four-hour period. By 10:00 A.M. vehicles were lined up like boxcars. In fact all major roads leading to Fort Bragg were at a five-mile standstill for much of the day.

Fearful that Fort Bragg could be targeted next for an attack, the brass had scrambled to man every road leading into the 160,000-acre post. Armed soldiers inspected every vehicle—interior, trunk, and engine—for explosives and went to the trouble to match every face to a driver's license. Soldiers named Muhammad received extra scrutiny. There was some comic relief, thank God. Some resourceful soldiers ditched their trucks and SUVs in parking lots and bought bicycles at the Wal-Mart on the corner of Yadkin and Skibo Roads. They made their way to Bragg on whatever they could find in stock, mostly dirt bikes, though one Green Beret pedaled past on a baby pink bicycle, his knees near his chin and the price tag flapping behind him. Despite warnings not to leave vehicles on the side of the road, doctors and emergency-room nurses at Womack Army Medical Center ditched their cars along the All American Expressway, the major highway that slices through Fort Bragg, and walked to work, only to find that the Army had towed their vehicles at the end of the day.

For those who stuck it out in traffic, the usual fifteen- or twenty-minute trip to work would take up to ten hours. I sat with some people in their cars and interviewed them. By midafternoon cars had overheated; some had run out of gas. Fast-food workers walked out and took orders from the road, and office clerks offered to sit in cars while motorists used the restroom. Meanwhile, on the post, armed soldiers guarded schools, neighborhoods, the hospital, and every road entrance into Fort Bragg.

In the weeks to come, as war loomed, I spent time with many military wives. Pregnant women wondered if their husbands would be around for the due date, and kids asked, "Will Dad be here for my birthday?" Wives also had to field questions from worried relatives. I was struck by the comments of one pregnant military wife I met. As she showed me her baby's unfinished nursery, she told me it gave her comfort knowing that her child would be born in two months. Why? I wondered. It seemed like a horrible time to be bringing a child into the world, and she had no idea if her husband would even be there. Her answer taught me a lot. In a world of uncertainty, the child was a definite, the one joyous thing she and her husband could talk about.

One day at a time, one day at a time, that's the other lesson I learned from Army wives after 9/11. Many took refuge in their daily routines, which provided a sense of normalcy and stability. In fact, everything had changed. For one wife in particular, the terrorist attacks merely underscored the changes that had already taken place in her life.

It was Monday, the first day of September, and the Corys' quarters at 11 South Dupont Plaza had stood empty for a few days. Andrea Lynne spent the last weekend of August there by herself, sweeping floors and scrubbing bathrooms, hardly stopping to eat or sleep. Now she sat alone on the hardwood floor, her back against the wall in the living room, as light streamed through the bare windows.

She looked over to the mantel, where she had lit a candle next to some dried flowers from Rennie's grave, faded red, white, and blue blooms sent by his old battalion. There was also a Mary Engelbreit card she had found while cleaning. It showed a lone person carrying a suitcase down the left fork of a path in the woods. The signpost pointing that way said "Your Life." The one on the right read: "No Longer an Option." Above the picture the card admonished in strong, tall letters: DON'T LOOK BACK. On the "No Longer an Option" side of the card Andrea Lynne had leaned an unframed photograph of herself and Rennie in their Harley clothes—one of their happiest times. She sat there in silence, which was unlike her, a woman who always sang to herself, even if no tune was playing. Inside she had a dark melancholy that no music could ease.

Throughout her marriage she'd occasionally let herself imagine what the pain would be like if she ever lost Rennie. Most Army wives have privately imagined the worst, but nothing Andrea Lynne ever conjured in her mind could have prepared her for the horror and agony of the past few months. She'd spent April dealing with the funeral and receiving visitors. All through May people continued to fill the house. It was a prelude to the yearly summer turnover, when soldiers and their families move off the post and are replaced by new ones.

Her dad stayed with her for a month, helping her buy a five-bedroom house with a three-car garage across town in the King's Grant neighborhood. After nine moves and two hardship tours, it would be the first house she'd ever owned; the Corys had always lived in government quarters or rented. She and Rennie had talked about getting their own house after retirement. By the end of May, Andrea Lynne had used the $250,000 from Rennie's Servicemen's Group Life Insurance policy to pay off their credit card and car debt and come up with a down payment. Rennie had another $250,000 in life insurance that she applied toward the rest of the house cost, and she saved what was left over. For months she couldn't bring herself to go to the new place and get it ready. Instead, every night at sundown she visited Rennie's grave.

During June and July she spent whole days in bed. Sometimes she had trouble breathing. Her heart literally hurt. For two months the women of the neighborhood cooked her meals—though Andrea Lynne had no appetite—and a friend did her laundry. Her daughters brought up her food, watched movies with her, massaged her feet and hands as she cried. Caroline read poetry to her, and Natalie read prayers. She didn't want to talk to anyone on the phone, but friends checked in on her. She saw Alice Maffey a lot. Melissa Huggins would ask her to come down for wine with the girls, and she agreed to help decorate for Jim's promotion party. Occasionally Andrea Lynne went for walks with her neighbors, and every Sunday she took the children to mass and then to brunch at the officers club.

With close friends she referred to herself as the "token widow," a comment that made them wince but somehow also broke down barriers. Everyone has a place and a role within the Army system. The question was whether Andrea Lynne wanted to play. The wives in her social circle encouraged her to continue with the luncheons, the workouts at the club, the volunteer work at the post thrift shop—things that would keep Andrea Lynne "current." She enrolled her kids at the youth center. Show my happy little face, she thought. Someday, she figured, she'd be the guest speaker at the ladies' coffees and lunches, but she wasn't ready for that.

She dragged herself to the change-of-command ceremonies and the farewell parties, where she was never alone for long. The men usually helped her find a seat, sometimes at the expense of their own wives. It got so embarrassing, that she stopped putting in an appearance. And it was just too painful: Never was she more aware that Rennie would have been home July 7.

At every event she missed her husband's face zeroing in on her. She missed standing on tiptoe to whisper in his ear. She missed seeing his reaction to long-winded speeches. She even missed singing the 82nd Airborne Division theme song—she knew every word by heart—and knowing Rennie was trying not to laugh.

Everywhere she went that summer—the hospital, the commissary, the PX, the youth center—she imagined him entering, looking for her, always looking for her and the kids. His ghost was everywhere. Andrea Lynne remembered how, the summer before Rennie left for Vietnam, they had done a pretend "pass and review" of the neighborhood. They walked hand in hand through Normandy, joking and saying good-bye to each house they passed. Andrea Lynne saluted the ones that housed a family they knew.

She had looked at her husband. "You're the best of them all, Rennie," she said and started to cry at the thought of his leaving so soon.

Rennie turned and lifted her up. "Don't cry; we're only halfway home!" He put her back down. "Do you know how much I love you? I can't do this without you. I need you to be strong."

She had never imagined she would have to be *this* strong.

Young Army widows are a rarity in peacetime, and because of the Corys' status and connections at Bragg, the post brass took a personal interest in how Andrea Lynne's affairs were administered. Typically a widow was given six months to stay in quarters if she wished; after that she would be charged the basic housing allowance. Andrea Lynne knew it would be acceptable for her to remain for a year, but the thought of that hurt too much. It was time to acknowledge that there would be no happy farewell, no "We'll see you back here one day!"

Finally, in August, she pulled herself out of bed to take Natalie back to college and start preparing for the move. A few weeks earlier Rennie's friend Roland had stopped to see her. They had sat in the kitchen, drunk a few beers, and talked and cried over old times. Before Roland left he gave her his phone numbers.

"If you need anything at all, anything, call me," he insisted.

She hugged him good-bye and never expected to see him again. She certainly never thought she would telephone.

At the end of August, as the move loomed and the packers began to tackle the garage and the upstairs, Andrea Lynne looked in Rennie's drawers and saw knives and bullet casings. She remembered Rennie had a gun, but now she couldn't find it. She panicked. There was so much stuff in the garage—boxes of Army equipment, a reloader machine, and things to make bullets with. Rennie had treasured those things; he had always been careful to pack them himself.

Suddenly she remembered Roland's phone number. Where had she put it? Everything was a mess, but she found the note in her address book. Andrea Lynne dialed his cell phone and got his gruff, deep voice on voice mail: "This is Roland. Leave a message."

"Roland? This is Andrea. Sorry to bother you. I'm moving. Actually the packers are here and, well, I don't know what to do with Rennie's stuff. . . ." her voice broke. "You know, his guns and knives. Well, he always took care of that, and I thought . . . maybe you could tell me how to pack it or transfer it. I really don't know how. That sounds stupid, but I know Rennie would trust you to handle it. I know you're at work. If you could call, I'd appreciate it. Thanks . . . bye."

She knew her voice was shaky. What am I going to do? she thought, as she sat down on one of the chairs on the patio. She couldn't bear to go back in the house. For all those years Rennie had been so protective of his guns and equipment. This move was different. She and Rennie had moved nine times as a couple. This was the first one alone. He never let her move alone, no matter what. She began to cry.

Just then she heard a man's voice.

"Andrea Lynne? Hey, I got your call."

Walking quickly around the side of the house was Roland. Like a man on a mission. Her heart almost stopped. Rennie had been looking out for her after all.

N ow, with all the boxes and furniture gone, Andrea Lynne got up and walked through the house one last time, calling up a happy memory for each room. Afterward she went back into the living room, got on her knees, and gave thanks for her life, for Rennie, for her children.

She gathered up the items from the mantel and stood for a long time in the foyer. She walked to the car, put her sentimental trinkets in the front seat, then returned to the house and removed the POW/MIA flag, its black fabric screen-printed with a man—a tear on his face.

Tears streamed down her own face as she remembered the morning Rennie first put it up, the day he left for Vietnam, and how Andrea Lynne told him it would come down the day he came home. She rolled it up lovingly.

"You'll only be down a short while." Her hands shook. "You'll fly with me again at our new home." She had never thought it would be with her forever, that she'd fly it for a man who would never return, who died for many men who would never return. She placed it in the backseat of the car, then returned one more time to the house like a soldier whose every step represented a duty to perform. She looked up at the American flag attached to the other porch column, removed it, and placed it in the car.

At last she locked the house door for the final time. Then she went down the front path and took down the nameplate, caressing it in her hands. This was the last home they would all have lived in together, she suddenly realized. There on the sidewalk, Andrea Lynne felt as if she were deserting her family. The pain, the endless pain, was unbearable. She turned and walked back to her car, each step underlining her thoughts: I lost my husband. I lost my life. I lost my home. And Bragg has lost me.

A few weeks later, on September 11, Gary Kalinofski came in from the showers after a PT run and was getting dressed in his office in the 504th's brigade headquarters, as he did every morning, when Colonel John Campbell called out down the hallway.

"Hey, Sergeant Major, come in here!" In an age of cell phones and e-mail, the Army custom of shouting to subordinates from one's desk still rendered the fastest results. Ski walked in and found the colonel glued to a small TV in his office. The men usually listened to the news as they dressed to raise their "situational awareness," Army speak for being informed.

"Man, a plane just hit the World Trade Center."

"What?!"

"Yeah, there it is."

With his hands on his hips, Ski looked at the TV screen, then back at his boss. Colonel Campbell was the clearheaded, unshakable brigade commander of the 504th Parachute Infantry Regiment, part of the 82nd Airborne Division. Almost all who had commanded the "Devils in Baggy Pants," as the 504th had been known since World War II, went on to wear stars, as would Campbell.

The brigade had just assumed Division Ready Brigade, the "first-to-go" status that rotated every six weeks among the 82nd's three infantry brigades. The division is the only one in the Army with the capability of parachuting into any hot spot in the world with guns blazing. But the division has also been used for humanitarian missions over the years, helping fight wildfires out West and providing flood- and hurricane-disaster relief in the South.

"Boss, I think we're going to New York City," Ski said.

He went back into his office and called Delores. "Honey, turn on the TV."

As the day wore on, Delores sat on her knees in front of the TV set and cried. She was overwhelmed by the thought of all those people who were dead or missing. Of all the families left behind. How many people hadn't made amends? How many had never said what should have been said? Delores thought about what it might mean for her family. Would Gary be leaving? Oh, God, what about Gary Shane? Could there be another attack?

All over the post, soldiers wanted to know the same thing. By 10:30 A.M. commanders and senior leaders were talking about courses of action in an emergency meeting with Major General John Vines, the 82nd Airborne Division commander. The 82nd trains constantly to be the first unit to respond to a crisis; its mission is to force its way into a country so that other units may follow. As the leading edge of a massive military machine, it is often the unit of choice for execution of National Security Policy. Now it went onto a heightened state of alert, and soldiers spent the rest of the day securing the division and the rest of the installation.

Fort Bragg was an "open post," meaning there were no gates or guards monitoring access. In fact there were countless ways to get on and off Fort Bragg, and controlling the tens of thousands of cars that rolled onto post each day, on several hundred miles of highways, was a nightmare. It would take twenty-four hours to get the post totally secure. Soldiers guarded barracks and blocked off side roads as well as Ardennes Street, one of the main thoroughfares in the division. They manned traffic-control points on Gruber Road. Back at the 504th soldiers formed human fences on the side streets; no cars were allowed between the barracks.

Like Americans everywhere, Bragg soldiers reacted to the attacks with astonishment and shock. But they were also pissed off. Someone came into our backyard and did *this*? And with the war planning and the commotion on post, it seemed as if the attacks had happened right in Fayetteville. Civilians might say, *Let's go kick some ass*; Bragg soldiers knew they would be the nation's heavies. Ski and his paratroopers were ready to go to hell itself if need be. You never could tell what the Pentagon would ask of you. A soldier's duty wasn't to question but to follow orders and accomplish the mission.

Delores, like the other wives, was equally aware of this.

"Honey, I can't discuss what it is," Ski told her when he called later that evening. "We can't talk about it over the phone. What's going to happen will happen, and where I go, I go. Keep watching the news. If I don't tell you, someone will."

Delores worried, too, about Gary Shane, who was now stationed in upstate New York, with the 10th Mountain Division at Fort Drum. They had found out in May that he was scheduled for six months of peacekeeping duty in Kosovo beginning in November. She hadn't seen her son in eight months, since she had taken him to the airport after Christmas. The Kalinofskis had honored their son's wish and had not gone to see him graduate from Basic Training. Delores had so wanted to share in her son's accomplishment; she was confused by Gary Shane's refusal. Ski had tried to comfort her.

"He just wants to do this by himself, Delores," he had said, "and we should let him. We'll give him a little space and let him concentrate on himself. He'll gravitate back."

Meanwhile she had Cherish to take care of. When the seventh grader came home from school, she told her mother that most of her teachers were crying. Delores kept the TV turned off and did her best to calm her daughter.

"Nothing like this will happen here in Fayetteville," she assured Cherish. "We're safe." She kept her own worries to herself. Just before eleven in the evening, Ski called to say he was on his way home. Delores knew that at some point her husband would be going somewhere, she just didn't know where or when.

J ust after seven in the evening, with her children next to her in the wooden pew, Andrea Floyd covered her face with her hands and prayed. She knew she had much to be thankful for. She thanked God that Brandon's father, Art, was all right. He worked at the Pentagon and had been there when American Airlines Flight 77 crashed into the building that morning.

She thought back twelve hours, which now seemed so long ago. It was a beautiful Tuesday, one of those rare southern days in early September, marked by low humidity and sunshine cut with a breeze. The tranquillity of the morning was shattered with a phone call from a friend telling Andrea to turn on the TV. She tuned into the *Today* show just in time to see the second plane hit the Twin Towers. Stunned and horrified, she went through the motions of her daily routine.

Not wanting to be late for work, Andrea dropped the kids off at her friend's house and then headed to Dick's Sporting Goods, where she was helping prepare for the grand opening in October. She liked the job. She worked with nice people, and she got a sense of satisfaction from earning a paycheck once more. She hadn't felt like this since her Army days. She was smart; she had been raised to take care of herself. And now she felt important and smart again. Somewhere along the way she'd lost that. In high school she had always been determined to do well in academics and sports. She approached her new job the same way, giving it everything she had.

She usually savored the forty-five-minute drive into town. It was the only time she had each day to be alone, but this day her thoughts were consumed with what she had just seen on TV. Brandon was TDY—on temporary duty—again, exactly where she had no idea. Did he know what had happened? Was he a part of it somehow? Was he okay? What should she tell the kids? Her head began to throb as the radio droned on. Suddenly the announcer's voice brought her back to the present. An airliner had struck the Pentagon. Brandon's dad . . . *Brandon's Dad!* Andrea felt sick to her stomach. She pulled out her cell phone and called her mother and sisters. Had they heard anything? Did they have Art's work number? No, she didn't know where Brandon was.

And things had finally been coming together, Andrea thought. Maybe it was selfish to think that way, but she couldn't help it. She and Brandon had found a nice house on five acres of land in Stedman, a town southeast of Fayetteville with fewer than seven hundred people. They had already been through so much as a couple, it was nice to be excited about something they could do together.

But her mind kept coming back to the awful plane crashes. As soon as she got to work, she called Joanne.

"Joanne, did you see what happened? Quick, turn on the TV. The Pentagon got hit. Brandon's dad works at the Pentagon. We haven't heard anything. If you would, please call Cindy and start the prayer chain. We've got to pray, pray, pray."

As the morning's events began to sink in, Andrea was petrified. Brandon was deployed somewhere, and there was no way for her to reach him. All day she kept in touch with her friends and family, and by evening she had heard that her father-in-law was fine and Brandon was back at his unit. That night the church held a special service, and Andrea took the kids. Their church had been a saving grace for their marriage. Brandon had even talked to Mark Strickland about the seminary and asked him about taking correspondence classes.

"I feel like I may be led to the ministry after my military career," he had said.

Being involved in the church held them to a higher standard, and it made them accountable to each other. Now it provided a refuge and reassurance as Andrea prayed for all those killed.

Even people who never attended the church came that night. About 85 percent of the congregation was military families, and few men other than the pastor himself were in the building that evening. Many of the men were on lockdown at Bragg. Some wives hadn't heard from their husbands and didn't know where they were.

Like the others, Andrea was somber and worried. The events of 9/11 were the biggest acts of terrorism the country had ever experienced, and Brandon's unit specialized in counterterrorism. How could he not play a role? She knew, just like all the other Army wives sitting in pews around her, that life was about to change drastically for them.

On the morning of September 12, 2001, Rita sat in traffic and shielded her face from the sun. How was she ever going to get to class now? A month earlier, with the help of a Pell Grant, she had enrolled in classes at Fayetteville Technical Community College. She planned to finish her associate's degree and get a job as a pharmacy technician. At the moment, she couldn't figure out how she was going to get to her biology test in time.

Rita cocked her head to get a better view and saw nothing but cars ahead of her, bumper to bumper on Cliffdale Road. Subdivisions of affordable three-bedroom ranch homes sprouted off Cliffdale like tributaries off a river because of the street's proximity to post. They were popular among military families and bachelor lieutenants and their roommates. Morning rush hour, 5:30 to 6:30 A.M. in Fayetteville, was always a bear on roads like Cliffdale, but today it was gridlock.

Rita rolled down her window and lit a cigarette. Brian had left home at 3:00 A.M. to beat traffic. She stopped a driver about to pass her on the shoulder of the road and asked him how bad it looked ahead. When he told her he had been in traffic for four hours, Rita steered her Ford Escort onto the shoulder and followed him. She was determined to take that biology test, but deep down she knew the class was the least of her worries. Somehow the attacks on the Pentagon and the World Trade Center couldn't help having a direct impact on her family.

Yesterday, when news of the attacks spread through the barracks, Brian and the others in his unit had been getting ready for an inspection for their upcoming DRF-1 cycle. Under ordinary circumstances that meant three weeks in the hot seat. But now?

"Oh, my God, what are we going to do, Brian?" she asked him, when he got home last night at nine. "What's going to happen? Are you fixin' to go somewhere?"

"Rita, they're not telling me anything," Brian said. "We can probably watch CNN and find out as much as they're telling me."

If the shit hits the fan, Brian is gone, Rita thought. The thought made her stomach turn heavy. And coupled with the sights of yesterday's mass destruction, it was too much to absorb.

Rita had been to New York City on a ninth-grade field trip. She had sold Krispy Kreme doughnuts and snipped her grandpa's hair to raise money for the trip, and she remembered the way the tops of the Twin Towers were lost in clouds. Now her kids were asking, "Mama, why did they fly the planes into the buildings?" and "Why couldn't we get them out?"

Her friend Sherry didn't seem worried at all. A short, chubby, twenty-year-old with permed brown hair, Sherry was lighthearted and giggly, with brown eyes that disappeared into slits when she laughed. Brian and Sherry's husband, Charlie, were in the same unit, and the two women had become close friends in the spring. Friendships formed fast in the Army, and they were often over quickly, too, due to the frequent moves. Only truly special friendships spanned a twenty-year Army career.

From the moment Rita met Sherry that May, Sherry had constantly griped about her husband, whom she had married two months earlier. She complained of her husband's messiness and his habit of giving the TV more attention than he gave her. In many ways she was right. Charlie was a two-hundred-plus-pound dolt, who wound up on the Army's fat-boy program because he failed to make his tape measures. In the 82nd being placed on the program—a strict exercise regimen—was like having leprosy.

In Rita's view Charlie wasn't a bad guy, just a simpleton. Too many wives wanted their husbands to be something they weren't.

"You don't marry a project," she often counseled Sherry. "You marry him for what he is.

"Look, he's just come out of the barracks, where he's cussed, he's farted, and he's watched porn, and you expect him to come home and be refined? Why don't you try and make home a place your husband wants to come to? He should feel that here is somebody in the world who is glad to see me. Here is somebody who makes me feel right. My husband will run you over to get home."

But Sherry shrugged off her marriage, and now she shrugged off the seriousness of 9/11 the same way. Either she couldn't grasp the enormity of what had happened or she didn't want to.

Rita felt differently. A year at Fort Bragg had taught her that if trouble arises or plans change, you had to just roll with it. I've got to make the Army as much my life as it is Brian's, she thought. There's got to be some soldier in me, too.

At night, while they were in bed, Brian would draw out battle drills on a steno pad. It was Brian's way of unloading and Rita's way of taking it in. She tried hard to bring the Army into her fold, to embrace it like a family member. But the Army was a demanding relative. It could bring couples closer by making husbands and wives cling to each other for comfort and support, or it could rip relationships apart.

Rita worked at making sure she and Brian were in the first category. Gradually she shared with him some experiences of her own. In bits and pieces, over several months, she told Brian about her girls' night out the previous winter, occasionally adding tidbits she had earlier omitted. When

Brian raised a concern, Rita said, "What? I told you about that, sweet pea. You weren't mad about it then."

She finally made Brian realize that she couldn't be what he wanted her to be, a full-time mom and housewife.

"I don't know what I want to do, but this ain't it," she told him during one argument.

Brian had resisted, but Mandy, who was taking classes, kept encouraging her to go back to school. Rita researched scholarships and marketable degrees. Finally she told her husband, "I'm sorry. I've tried. I've tried, and I can't. I have to be stimulated up here," she said pointing to her head.

At last he gave in. Before long he was quizzing his wife with her generic and brand-name drug flash cards and taking care of the boys when she was studying. Still, Rita knew Brian didn't really get it. He'd support Rita's returning to school if that's what she wanted to do, but he didn't understand why she wanted to work so badly.

Rita looked at the cars stopped in all directions. Now they'd both have to adjust again, she thought, as the government decided what its response to the terror attacks would be. Rita gripped the steering wheel tightly. She thought back on the last twenty-four hours. Oh, God, this isn't happening. Well, Rita guessed, she'd just have to roll with it.

CHAPTER TWELVE

The phone rang in the middle of a chilly November night, and Rita sleepily groped to answer it. The voice on the other end asked for "Specialist Odom," and almost without thinking she handed the receiver to Brian.

"Red Corvette," she heard him repeat. She knew what was coming next. After he hung up, he'd kiss her, pull on his jump boots, and head to Bragg. She tried not to worry. It was a code for a recall; other nights there were green Corvette or blue Pinto exchanges.

The cryptic phrases are actually a more efficient way of doing business than saying, "Hey, we're jumping into Haiti tomorrow. Don't tell anyone because this is double top secret." And much more secure, too, if the enemy is listening.

I've crossed paths with some soldiers who thought "the enemy" could be the woman in bed next to them. To this day some veterans in Fayetteville blame wives for blabbing about the parachute assault into Panama in December 1989, which was one of the Army's worst-kept secrets. I've been told it was the State Department that did most of the damage, though, when Washington staffers warned colleagues in Panama of the upcoming invasion.

Most of the middle-of-the-night calls to the Odom home were to check the alert rosters, which were a calling chain with everyone's name and phone number; others were emergency deployment readiness exercises (EDREs). On those nights most of the soldiers didn't know until they arrived in formation if the recall was an exercise or a "real world mission."

Phone calls in the dead of the night are never good signs, but in the Army they take on new meaning, partly because of their frequency. If you are in a position of authority with a troop unit, the more calls you'll get, about everything from car accidents and fistfights requiring medical treatment to domestic violence and drunk driving. Whatever the problem, leaders up and down the chain of command will know about it before sunrise—and so will their wives.

The Odoms didn't receive those kinds of calls, but they did answer plenty of red Corvette alerts.

Rita had gotten to the point of being able to roll over and go back to sleep after the phone rang, just as she had learned to remain flexible with dinnertimes and weekend outings. It was all part of incorporating the Army into her life without allowing it to run her over. But she never got used to the idea she could lose Brian. It first hit her that something could go wrong when Brian called home one afternoon to tell her a soldier had been beheaded on a parachute jump.

"Ya know," she said, "I think I could have lived my whole life without you telling me that story."

Paratroopers jump out of planes moving at 130 knots, eight hundred feet off the ground. If all goes well the parachute opens in four seconds, and the soldier thumps on the ground in twenty to forty seconds. Occasionally a soldier breaks a leg or chips his tailbone, and there have been times when parachutes malfunction and a soldier plunges to his death.

Paratroopers take the danger seriously, but they also make light of it in an old song called "Blood Upon the Risers," sung to the melody of the "Battle Hymn of the Republic." The 82nd Airborne Division Chorus would boom out the verses at post events. The last time I heard it I was at a ball, as couples dressed in their finest thumped along with the rhythm:

There was blood upon the risers,
There were brains upon his 'chute.
Intestines were a'dangling from his paratrooper's boots.
They picked him up, still in his chute and poured him from his boots.
HE AIN'T GONNA JUMP NO MORE!

Then there's the rousing chorus:

GORY, GORY WHAT A HELLUVA WAY TO DIE!
GORY, GORY WHAT A HELLUVA WAY TO DIE!
GORY, GORY WHAT A HELLUVA WAY TO DIE!
HE AIN'T GONNA JUMP NO MORE!

When soldiers in the 82nd Airborne Division go eighty-two days without anyone getting killed, they are rewarded with a day off. A SAFETY-GRAM billboard on Gruber Road, leading into the division area, keeps track of the fatality-free days as an incentive to stay safe. Inevitably soldiers grumble when a paratrooper manages to die after the seventy-five-day mark and the billboard drops back to zero.

I've been around enough paratroopers to know that they, like ballplayers, are a superstitious lot. If you were wearing a certain pair of underwear the night you had a soft landing while your buddies all bounced like tumbleweeds, the same pair might just do the same the following month. Disrupt that routine, and you might get jinxed.

Before each parachute jump Rita would remind Brian, "Do your little mojo ritual."

"I know, I know," he'd tell her. Brian kept a picture from their wedding day tucked in the dome of his helmet. Before the plane's doors opened, Brian looked at the picture and kissed his wedding band. He wasn't religious, but he prayed anyway: "God, please keep everyone on the plane safe. I've got a wife and kids. They love and need me. I serve my country willingly. If it's your will, please get me home to my wife and kids."

On this autumn night she said, "Take care, sweet pea," as Brian tip-toed out. "Don't worry about us, we'll be fine." She knew he had worries of his own.

Brian Odom was serious about being a good paratrooper, and he wanted to rise in the Army ranks, but he was beginning to wonder if he would ever wear sergeant's stripes. Someone in Brian's unit had accused him of being a racist, and Fort Bragg didn't take such accusations lightly.

In 1997 two white supremacists, Sergeants James Burmeister and Malcolm Wright, received life sentences for murdering two black people for sport in downtown Fayetteville two years earlier. Since then, the Army has been diligent in screening soldiers for racist tattoos and scouring the barracks for white supremacist literature.

Although several years had passed, Brian served in the same battalion as Burmeister and Wright, and racism was an especially sensitive subject there. Brian thought he had a great relationship with his squad leader, who was black. As far as Brian was concerned, everyone in the Army was green. Some soldiers saw Brian differently, however. The Confederate stickers on his truck, his Alabama roots, and his shaved head didn't go over well in an Army that was a blend of ethnicities, races, and religions. In response to the charges, Brian's commander had opened a six-month investigation, which closed in October. The findings indicated there was no impropriety. All during that time Brian had been "flagged," meaning he was unable to rise in rank, go to Army schools, receive awards, or reenlist. Now, more than anything, Brian wanted to go before the board and get promoted.

Rita sometimes thought he cared more about the Army than their marriage. She felt the Army was another woman; heck, sometimes she felt as if *she* were the mistress. It drove her crazy. Why was everything so hard?

Again and again Brian told her that she didn't understand serving in a combat unit wasn't like a pogue Army desk job. ("Pogue" is a military slang term used to describe a useless air breather who does nothing but sit on his ass all day. The derisive term is also used to describe rear-echelon units, fat people, lazy staff officers, and slouches in general. It's a far cry from the adrenaline-rush atmosphere that reigns over most of Bragg, and which can take its own toll.) I've witnessed even the best soldiers in the fiercely proud 82nd succumb sometimes to the anxiety of being in a constant state of readiness for war. Since soldiers always have to have their "A" game on at work, the pressure-cooker environment can affect their health and relationships.

Brian once told me he was beginning to feel that his marriage was both blessed and cursed. He and Rita were still learning about each other. When things were good, they were really good, and when they were bad, the fights were horrible. He admitted he had an anger problem. The Army sent him to its anger-management classes when he punched a sergeant who Brian thought was treating him unfairly. Brian had received punishment called an Article 15, forfeited two weeks' pay, and spent two weeks after duty hours buffing floors and cleaning latrines. The Army liked aggression, but only on its own terms.

Brian tended to look at things in extremes. He was either depressed or elated, pissed off or happy. And he could get jealous. He wanted to be the one to answer the phone, which Rita interpreted as his not *wanting* her to be with or even have friends. Wasn't he enough? he'd ask her. All of Rita's friends, whether they were back in Alabama or here, seemed to be of questionable character to him. He disapproved of Rita's writing to a male friend who was in an Alabama prison. He felt that her friends in Fayetteville were hoochies, and he had never trusted Sherry from the moment he met her. Rita thought Sherry was friendly and bubbly. Brian considered her a flirt. He sure didn't need his wife hanging out with a friend who would attract men to both of them. His reactions made him seem territorial and possessive.

"You'd run me over if I let you," Rita told him during one argument, as she tried to explain her frustrations. "But I have enough strength to say uh-huh when I've had enough, and I've reached my limit." Still, something told her maybe she shouldn't have mentioned those escapades with the other wives or that a soldier in her class had asked her out.

One day that fall, during a cigarette break between classes, Rita sat at a picnic table with her classmate, Patti. Tall, thin, and tattooed, Patti was a retired Army master sergeant. She kept her hair clipped short and dyed red. She wore gobs of jewelry—expensive jewelry, Rita thought.

As the women smoked, Rita complained that Brian never took her advice about the promotion board. "Why won't he listen to me?" she said.

"Rita, shut the fuck up," Patti said, emphasizing each word by flicking her cigarette ashes and tapping her fake nails on the picnic table. "You need to understand you don't know shit about the Army. You're belittling him. He knows what he needs to do, and you don't. So you just shut your mouth."

Rita sat stunned as her fifty-year-old classmate put her cigarette to her lips and inhaled deeply, crinkling her eyes.

"What if Brian said, 'If you just do this on your chemistry test, you'll get an A'? What would you tell him?" Patti asked.

"I'd tell him he didn't know what he was talking about."

"Well, there you go. Don't tell him how to do his job."

Rita was still shell-shocked when she drove home after class. The "gospel According to Patti" woke her up. I'm not helping, she thought. Brian's dealing with crap at work, and I'm nagging the shit out of him at home. She knew she couldn't be selfish. A marriage can't all be about the soldier, but some aspects of it had to be. A soldier can't stop, Rita thought. He's gotta keep going. If the wife says stop, it will create distance between them. I don't know, she thought. I set out to be the best Army wife, and I'm failing miserably at it.

When Brian got home that night, she told him, "I'm going to be strong enough to stand up and say we have a problem."

"I don't have a problem, you have a problem," Brian shot back.

"No, we have a problem together, and we're gonna figure it out."

She suggested marriage counseling, and when Brian shot that idea down, she suggested he go to counseling alone.

"Rita, you can't go to counseling unless you want everybody to know about it. Why would I take the chance of things getting leaked around the company? I would be looked at as weak if the commander or the command sergeant major found out. It could stunt my career." He would never get promoted to sergeant.

"Counseling is kept confidential," Rita said.

"It's only confidential as long as the counselor deems it confidential," Brian answered back.

Brian was right. Though there is no shortage of counseling programs in the Army, few trust the system enough to take a chance on ruining their reputations. Soldiers are kept on such a tight leash during the duty day that it is impossible to see a counselor and expect to keep it private. And seeking help is considered a career ender, so most soldiers with troubles simply keep them to themselves. Officers and senior NCOs who want help, and can afford it, discreetly seek therapy off post. Psychiatrists and counselors in Fayetteville keep evening hours to accommodate their military clients.

For those seeking top-secret security clearances, the Department of Defense Personnel Security Investigations Medical Record asks on its questionnaire: "In the last seven years have you consulted a mental health professional (psychiatrist, psychologist, counselor etc.) or have you consulted with another health care provider about a mental health related condition?" If the answer is yes, the applicant has to explain the circumstances in writing. So much for confidentiality. From the Army's point of view, the question has to be asked. After all, who really wants someone with suicidal tendencies, anger problems, or self-esteem issues handling information that could put the nation at risk?

Rita wasn't about to let anything rock their marriage, even something as pervasive as the Army. You can't get married and then stop trying, she thought. That was why she'd stuck with her first husband so long. She didn't want Brian ever to stop looking at her the way he did when they were first married.

"Fuck the stripes!" Rita shouted. "I care about me and you and my emotional stability. So we're gonna keep talking about it and talking about it until we get through this. I'm gonna hurt your feelings, and you're gonna sit there, smile, and like it," she told her husband. They waited until the kids went to bed, then Brian and Rita would have their discussions.

"I'm stubborn," she said. "You're not getting away from me."

I've seen some couples deal with their marital problems in other ways—drinking, seeking companionship outside the marriage, or focusing on work or children. I've always been taken aback when I'd hear a deployed soldier say he missed his kids more than his wife. Not that he said it, exactly. He didn't have to; I could see and hear love when he talked about his kids. I usually had to ask about his wife.

One Army wife I know took drastic measures early in her marriage. When her husband constantly acted like a jerk, she'd pack up her things and leave when he was out in the field. He'd come home a few weeks later to an empty house and a note, no dinner, no sex. After a few notes he got the picture and changed his ways. They are now happily married with three children.

Other women leave and never come back. Still others, who believe they have already given their best years to their husbands and the Army, stay in the marriage. Though they may put up a united front with their spouses at official functions, some will complain in private about their husbands.

While she fought for her marriage, Rita wondered about herself. What kind of an Army wife she was anyway? She had been thinking about that since May, when she had attended Fort Bragg's Military Spouse Day. Rita had read about a car clinic there, and she showed up ready to get dirty and learn about car maintenance. She crossed her arms across her blue New Orleans souvenir T-shirt that spelled out "Bourbon Street" in now-half-gone glitter. It hung just above her jean cutoffs, which exposed her pale legs, the kind that never tanned. She didn't bother with makeup. Brian always told her she didn't need any.

As she waited for Mandy, Rita noticed a group of women off to the side, chatting. They were about thirty, wore coordinated tops and slacks with matching shoes, and their hair and makeup seemed a bit much for a parking lot on a Saturday morning.

Those women are immaculate, Rita thought, as she stared at one in pink pleated shorts, a matching sweater, and light pink flats with matching bows. The woman reminded Rita of a walking fluff of carnival cotton candy. Another woman was dressed like a Fourth of July picnic table. She had on a summer sweater with flags, red Keds and socks with flags, earrings, hair bow—all flags. Her white shorts were the only banner-free zone on her body.

Rita gave her ponytail a cinch and crossed her arms even tighter. "What's up with that?" she asked when Mandy walked over.

"Don't ya know? They're officers' wives. Your husband works for a living."

Until that moment Rita never had had any contact with officers' wives. She didn't realize they were any different. But now it was all making sense. She remembered driving past the Normandy housing area on Reilly Street and asking Brian, "Who lives there?" These were the senior officers' families quarters. Most of the women Rita knew lived across post or in boxlike apartments or trailers off Bragg.

One day as she and Brian were going through a checkpoint to get on post, she found out that officer and enlisted families had different registration stickers on their car windshields—officers blue and enlisted red.

"How come the guards know who to salute?" she had asked. Only officers got saluted. "They know because of the color of the registration stickers on the car," he told her. She pondered it for a bit and decided that it made sense. But then she wondered, Who thought of that? What kind of mind goes into such minutiae? Rita wished that whoever came up with that had been in charge of rations the time Brian and his buddies didn't get meals in the field because someone in charge forgot to tell someone else in charge that there was a group of soldiers out in the woods on Bragg in need of food.

As Rita waited for the car class to start, she overheard snippets of chatter about hair and daughters' ballet classes and caught some of the women glancing her way. She felt as if she were back in junior high. They're judging me, Rita thought. They think they're better than I am. *You're no better than I am, and furthermore you dress stupid!* That's what Rita wanted to shout.

When the women formed a half circle around a sedan, Rita stayed in the back. A soldier began explaining what was under the hood when one woman interrupted, "I need to know how to check my oil. How do you pull the thingy out?" Rita rolled her eyes. This was something so basic, like not knowing how to order off a menu.

He handed the dipstick to the cotton candy lady, and she held it like a Fourth of July sparkler. "Oh, you have to wipe it off," she said. She returned the dipstick to the soldier and looked at the grease on her fingers as if it were Martian dust. When another woman asked how to pop the hood of the car, Rita felt like walking away. This had been a total waste of time.

Over the next few months Rita had begun to notice other categories of Army wives within her own circle in the platoon. It's not hard to put the women in distinct groups based on their personalities and their identification with their husbands, but Rita's view of them was particularly colorful.

The "shit stirrers" irritated Rita the most. They were the gossipers. These were wives whose lives seemed so shallow and silly; they never volunteered for anything. They never cooked a hot dog or washed a car, but they never stopped talking crap about somebody or something. As far as Rita was concerned, gossip was a waste of time and emotion. These women just didn't have enough to occupy their days.

Neither did the drama queens, who embellished their sagas for the sake of attention: "I had to wait three hours to get my prescription filled at Womack, and I felt so ill I had to call my husband's platoon leader so he could have John come pick me up. The lieutenant called last night, because he was so worried about me."

The whiners always had to have something to bitch about. These women were so absorbed in their own woes they never stopped to think that all the wives were in the same fix. Didn't the whiners know that sergeant so-and-so was an equal-opportunity annoyer, and that chances were good their husbands weren't the only ones getting shit upon? There was no assuaging a whiner. If Rita tried to offer comfort, the whiner would always respond with the whiner's trademark, "*my* husband," as in "Things will only get better when *my* husband gets out of the field," as if *her* husband were the only grunt sucking it up in the Army.

The rank pullers were annoying women who loved to wear their husband's rank, as if they, too, had taken an oath to defend the Constitution. Rita overheard one rank puller tell a young private's wife at an FRG meeting, "My husband is your husband's squad leader, so you treat me accordingly." Rita was so angry she wanted to shout, *Ya know, I'm not in the Army and neither are you, so fuck off.*

The ass kissers weren't any better. They were usually married to ass-kissing men, and as an ass-kissing couple, they would smooch the hide of anyone who might get them ahead.

Finally, there were the shining happy people. The perky, cutesy shining happy people who had perky, cutesy marriages and perky, cutesy kids and always a perky, cutesy story to share. Those chicks drove Rita nuts.

Rita tried not to associate with any of these women more than she had to. She strived to be in the "I've-got-my-shit-together club." She wanted to be around women who could handle themselves and who had control over their house and their children. She wanted to be around women who made the best of it, who were stable and strong. That was the only category of wives Rita felt comfortable with.

And yet Rita was learning that it wasn't that easy to find the right balance for herself. Soldiers had to take matters at face value and follow orders, and the Army expected their wives to do the same.

Spouses who challenge the system are branded as troublemakers. You can't just call up the company first sergeant and ask, "How come my husband's not home yet?" Even though some wives do. Soldiers always loved telling me about those women. Every unit has some. You can't be too confrontational, either, but sometimes you just have to put your foot down.

One night, when Rita sat on the couch and rubbed Brian's back, she felt a lump on his spine.

"What is that?"

"I dunno, I've had it," he said.

Rita pleaded with Brian to get it checked out, but he refused.

"Baby, you need to go to sick call."

"No, I don't wanna be called a pussy for a week."

So Rita made the appointment herself, but Brian called her that morning and said he'd have to cancel. His squad leader wouldn't let him go. Rita was furious.

In the Army, pecking order is everything. Whoever has more stripes than you owns your life.

"I'll be there in a little bit," she told him. She dug a T-shirt out of her drawer with jagged lettering that coalesced into "motha fucka" if you stared at it long enough. She put it on and headed over to the barracks. When she found Brian and sergeant Clay, she stood with her arms crossed and stared at the sergeant, who was chubby and balding. *I'll knock him straight down if I have to.* She had discovered that men got uncomfortable when she looked them in the eye.

"He has an appointment," she said keeping her voice level. "He's going. I'm here to take him now."

Sergeant Clay eyed Rita back. "All right, go."

It turned out Brian would have to have surgery to remove two cysts. One more time Rita wondered which category of wife she was.

CHAPTER THIRTEEN

The Christmas season is a busy time in Fayetteville, not only for Army families but also for thieves who are as plentiful as the eggnog and white lights. The cops work longer shifts patrolling the area for thugs looking to steal presents from homes and cars or out of shoppers' hands. The problem is so prevalent that the Fayetteville Police Department has a "Holiday Safety Program," complete with mobile police stations set up in mall parking lots and other shopping centers along Skibo Road. It wouldn't be Fayettenam if there weren't some shadiness around the Christmas cheer.

In the middle of it all, Army wives go about readying themselves for the holiday. Veteran wives dig out their Czechoslovakian crystal, wooden German Christmas tree ornaments and nutcrackers, Korean red silk table runners, and Yuletide craft-show finds, all memories from a lifetime of Christmases spent elsewhere. Tastes honed abroad mean that commissaries everywhere line their shelves with European chocolates and sweets, and wives dig out their glühwein recipes. Wicker baskets in foyers or kitchens are jammed with Christmas cards, some in foreign languages, from old friends stationed around the world. Army wives learn never to write entries in ink in their address books. Army families are truly thankful for time together over the holidays. It can be rare. I had lunch the other day with two friends whose husbands are spending their second consecutive Christmas in Iraq.

Meanwhile officers' spouses shop wherever they like, while some "junior enlisted wives," the politically correct name for lower-enlisted wives, are almost entirely dependent on an Army Christmas food basket or a donated toy. Throughout the season, in town and on post, Army wives, who usually are socially separated by their varied ranks, and geographically by their neighborhoods, cross paths often, but their real stories are mostly hidden behind the Christmas garlands and holiday pleasantries.

In December 2001 Special Operations troops from Fort Bragg had been in Afghanistan for almost two months, and more were on the way. It's common to say what a difference a year can make, but it is especially true in the Army. This Christmas was unlike the previous one in ways Andrea Lynne, Rita, Delores, and Andrea could never have imagined, courtesy of Uncle Sam. They were following their individual paths, yet all were influenced by the military, which, like the weather, can be mercurial and unpredictable. In fact all four women would face new, unforeseen challenges in 2002. At that moment Andrea Lynne was marking her first Christmas as a widow; Rita, less naive about the Army, was nevertheless still finding her way; Delores's son was deployed to Kosovo; and Andrea, whose husband was in Afghanistan, was alone with a new house, a new job, new friends, and newfound independence.

Andrea found a spot next to Joanne's Suburban in the Bojangles parking lot in Spring Lake, and the women walked into the fast-food restaurant together. With them were Joanne's two youngest children, five-year-old Abbey and thirteen-month-old Luke. Bojangles was having its grand opening, and Andrea suggested they go for the fried chicken and biscuits. It was 11:00 A.M., and they were a few steps ahead of the rush, which started promptly at 11:30 A.M., when the post's forty-two thousand soldiers were released for lunch.

The women had caravanned from Joanne's house in Cameron. The town of Spring Lake, with a population of more than eight thousand, buffered Bragg to the north of the reservation and was a smaller version of Fayetteville—in a bratty kid brother sort of way. The main drag through town was a charmless strip of billboards, fast-food restaurants, car lots, gas stations, and Chinese buffet restaurants.

Andrea had spent the last two nights sleeping on the Stricklands' sectional couch. She'd rented out the house in Cameron but had only just finished moving boxes and furniture into the new house in Stedman, which they had recently bought.

The women ordered their food, and Andrea insisted on paying as a thank-you to Joanne for letting her stay at the house. It was rare that the women went out together for a meal. With eight children between them, they usually just ate at each other's house so the kids could play.

Now Joanne got a high chair, and Andrea found a free table near the front of the restaurant next to the trash cans. The place was already filling up. She took off her jacket—it was a cool morning—and sat down. She wore her hair loose and looked sharp in khakis and a white dress shirt.

After lunch she'd head straight to work. It was the first week of December, and the store was already busy with Christmas shoppers. It would grow only more hectic in the next few weeks.

"You heard from Brandon?" Joanne asked, as she fed Luke a spoonful of mashed potatoes and gravy. Joanne always worried about Brandon when he was away. "When is he coming home?"

"I have no idea," Andrea said between bites of dirty rice. Brandon had deployed to Afghanistan less than a week ago, just after Thanksgiving. Of all his assignments this would be the most dangerous. Andrea couldn't tell anyone he was leaving. She herself didn't know where he was going, but she had called Joanne the day before his departure.

"Do you want to talk to Brandon?" she had asked.

Joanne thought it was an odd question. She talked with Andrea every day, and she'd never asked if she wanted to talk with him. "Should I?"

"Trust me, you want to talk to him."

Brandon picked up the phone. "Hey, how you doin'?"

"I'm fine," Joanne said, almost quizzically.

"I'll be praying for you, and you be praying for me. Pray for our country, and our leaders and my dad."

"I will."

"I look forward to getting one of your home-cooked meals."

"Well, okay, you'll get another one, don't worry."

"Okay, I love you." Brandon always said that.

Brandon called Mark later that evening and repeated his prayer request. The next day Andrea called again. "Brandon's gone," she said.

"Is he where I think he's at?" Joanne asked.

"I don't know where he's at, but he had to leave." The kids took it hard. Harlee worried that her father would die.

The day Brandon left was the day the Floyds had planned to move. It was awful timing, but you had to expect that in Army life. Andrea had accepted that long ago. Thank goodness friends from church and Brandon's unit helped, and Andrea's two sisters came from Ohio, too. Lending a helping hand was also part of Army life. Her sisters took the three kids back to Ohio with them for a couple of months so Andrea could get settled in. With three little ones, a new job, a new house to fix up, and Brandon away, the arrangement made sense to Andrea, though Brandon wasn't thrilled with it.

At least Thanksgiving had been a chance to celebrate a holiday together as a family. Andrea had tried out her new turkey fryer, and Brandon showed up on the Stricklands' doorstep with a sample of the results.

By noon Fort Bragg soldiers and airmen from Pope Air Force Base had filled the restaurant, and a long line of cars waited in the take-out lane.

"How are the kids liking Ohio?" Joanne asked.

"They're doing okay," Andrea said. She was never one to give many details. Joanne's seven-year-old daughter, Brooke, was best friends with Andrea's daughter, Harlee, and the two girls missed each other terribly.

"Andrea, I know Harlee's okay, but she hated leaving her friends at school, and she misses Brooke."

"I know, but what else am I gonna do?"

"You've got to keep the kids in mind. Are you going home to see the kids, or is your mom coming down for Christmas?" Joanne asked.

"No, they're gonna stay up there. I might be able to get up to Ohio, but I don't know. I volunteered to work over the holidays. A lot of people want off, and we can use the extra money. And I need the time to get the house ready."

A $220,000 house with $1,800 monthly mortgage payments, along with all the remodeling they wanted to do on the twenty-year-old home, was more than the Floyds could really afford. Brandon's family had lent the couple $10,000 to show the bank they had enough equity to get the house loan, since they bought most things on credit.

"Well, you know you're welcome to spend Christmas with us," Joanne said.

"I know. Thank you, but I want to get the house ready for when Brandon gets back. There's so much to do. Between the store starting up, Christmas, and the house, it's crazy." She told Joanne about all her plans: taking down wallpaper, painting, installing ceramic tile in the kitchen, putting wood floors in the dining room, buying curtains and new furniture. "I haven't hardly unpacked any boxes yet, but I've started buying the kids stuff for Christmas." Her present for Brandon was a fifteen-hundred-dollar gun safe the size of a refrigerator. She knew he'd like it, and she got a discount on it through Dick's.

"Well, I wish I was closer to help you unpack," Joanne said. "Maybe one of these weekends I can help you."

The women stayed for an hour and a half, though Andrea mostly just picked at her chicken. She didn't eat much of her dirty rice or macaroni and cheese either. Joanne suggested she take it to work and have it for dinner. When they finally walked outside, Andrea carried Luke and waited by the Suburban as Joanne went back to get Luke's jacket, which she had forgotten.

"Have you decided what you're going to do about church?" Joanne asked, as she buckled Luke into his car seat. The new house was an hour's drive from Cameron. "Are you going to find a new one in Fayetteville?"

"You know we really want to try to keep coming to yours."

They hugged each other good-bye.

"Give me a call tonight when you get home," Joanne said, "and make sure you eat; you hardly touched your lunch."

Andrea got in her van and headed south down Bragg Boulevard. Tonight would be the first night in her new house. Alone. She wasn't used to this kind of freedom. Most of the time she was a mother and wife, on demand for everyone else. This would be a change.

Two nights before, she'd gone out with her coworkers to a nightclub and stayed until 1:00 A.M. They were a fun bunch, and when they had asked her to come along, Andrea said yes. She enjoyed their company. She had never really been one to go out or drink, but that night she did, and she came back to the Stricklands' a little tipsy.

"Did you get lost? Where've you been?" Joanne had asked when she finally walked in the door. The two women enjoyed joking with each other, but Joanne was serious this time. She had stayed up out of worry.

"No, we just went out for a bit, met lots of people," Andrea said, almost giddily. She smelled of smoke from the bar.

"Where'd you go?"

"We went to a nightclub. I'm real tired."

Andrea could sense her friend's disapproval. She was a preacher's wife, after all. "I just wanted to get acquainted with the people at work."

"You better be careful how much you get acquainted," Joanne said. "I don't mean to talk to you like you're a child, Andrea, but you're a Christian—and going to a place like that and being with people like that, they'll pull you down more than you can pull them up."

"I know," Andrea said. "I'll remember." Right now, though, she would concentrate on her job and the adventure of being on her own.

With Maddie's Christmas list in her purse, Andrea Lynne stood in line next to Roland in the checkout lane at Dick's. It was a few weeks before the holiday, and at Roland's suggestion, they had gone shopping. She knew Maddie would love the basketball sneakers. A helpful blond employee in khakis and a blue shirt brought their purchases to the register.

"I like your name," Andrea Lynne commented, noticing the woman's tag. "It's the same as mine. You don't run into too many Andreas."

Andrea Floyd had walked all over the store helping them pick out sports equipment and athletic shoes. It was the kind of assistance Andrea Lynne appreciated. After all those years as an Army wife, she understood the meaning of service, and since Rennie's death, she was especially sensitive to an act of kindness. She thanked the young woman several times.

Andrea had never been comfortable receiving compliments, and she shrugged off the praise. "Take care, and have a nice Christmas," she said cheerfully before she walked away.

"You, too. Thanks again." That woman has a caring spirit, Andrea Lynne thought, picking up some of Andrea's energy and beginning to be a bit more enthusiastic about the season.

Just the week before, Maddie, who still believed in Santa Claus, had presented her mother with her Christmas list. Andrea Lynne put it to one side without even looking at it. Later after Maddie went to bed, she talked about it with Roland, who had been coming by the house several times a week.

"What are you going to buy her?" he asked.

"I don't know. Maybe it's time she stopped believing in Santa." She took a sip of her Jack and Coke, Rennie's drink. It was the only way she could sleep at night. Andrea Lynne was in a bitter mood. With Rennie gone, she didn't feel like celebrating the holidays. "She probably knows the truth anyway, and I don't feel like playing anymore."

December is a busy social month on Army posts. The higher in rank your husband is, the more invitations you receive. There are Christmas formals, coffees, and lunches; platoon, company and battalion parties with Santa; and Christmas or New Year's Day receptions at the commander's quarters for officers and senior NCOs, where dress blues and cocktail dresses are required attire. Andrea Lynne always had a full holiday schedule.

She started to cry as she told Roland about family traditions—the shopping together, decorations, baking, parties, midnight mass. There were always toys for the poor and lots more for their own kids. Every Christmas Eve, she and Rennie were up till three or four in the morning wrapping presents. When the kids were young, he'd blow up a hundred red and green balloons and set them around the den with the toys, and Andrea Lynne would sprinkle a trail of "Santa dust" (foil stars and glitter) to each child's room. On Christmas morning, if their quarters had a fireplace, Rennie would light a fire, and they'd put on Christmas carols while the children opened the gifts. Turkey dinner was always at three, dessert around seven, sometimes with friends. The couple would end the day snuggling on the couch, often with Andrea Lynne falling asleep on Rennie's lap.

This year Andrea Lynne grudgingly got a tree, and she let the kids help her decorate it. She had been in the new house on Shawcroft Drive almost four months now. It was sunny and bright but nothing like the ivy-covered cottage and garden she'd always imagined having. She had each room painted a different color: yellow kitchen, burgundy dining room, green den—all fresh colors. She also bought new furniture and decorated in French provincial style with a bit of English country. After the holidays she was going to invite her friends over, open her garage and give away her hand-me-down antiques and thrift shop bargains. It was too painful to keep them.

Her bedroom was on the ground floor with a jetted tub in the bath and a private deck where the POW/MIA flag flew from the corner. At night she sometimes walked out, smoked a cigarette, and pictured Rennie walking toward her through the pines. Her closet was filled with black and white clothes on black and white hangers—"powmia outfits," the children called them, because they were the color of the POW/MIA flag.

The banquet-size dining room was her favorite room. She and Rennie had always entertained. Now she would do it on her own.

The Saturday after Thanksgiving she had invited forty people, including many of the guests from their Christmas party the year before, for a "house blessing." The ceremony was incredibly important to Andrea Lynne, who wanted to share a spiritual and emotional time with family and friends who had helped her. Father Matt, who had blessed Rennie's coffin in April, now blessed each room of the house with holy water. Andrea Lynne had him bless each cross, too. There was one on almost every wall in the house, since she had begun collecting them immediately after Rennie died.

Roland came to the party but left early, too shy to stay with the other visitors. He was becoming an indispensable part of Andrea Lynne's life, though. A confirmed bachelor, he was a big, attractive man of few words. Dark haired and dark skinned, Roland was broad and muscular, but different from Rennie. Roland was naturally strong; he never worked out. He and Rennie had met at Bragg's youth center when they were in middle school. Roland's father, now deceased, had been a soldier, too, and his mother, who still lived in Fayetteville and whom Roland looked after, was Japanese. Some people found him intimidating, but Andrea Lynne's kids were comfortable with him, and he seemed to know how to clean up, feed children, and help her out. She never had to ask; Roland just volunteered. And he showed concern about Andrea Lynne's diabetes, making sure she rested and ate. When she asked him about that, he said, "Rennie told me. He worried about you."

He had taken a week off work to help her get settled in the house. He organized the garage and picked up on little things Andrea Lynne needed, like a gate for the deck, or a cat door. He set up her entertainment center, moved her furniture, reversed the door on her refrigerator, and even came and unclogged a toilet. He taught the kids how to drive. Soon Andrea Lynne was relying on him for advice.

By Christmastime, Roland would come over two and three nights a week with fast food for the children. After the youngsters went to bed, he would stay and talk with Andrea Lynne over a whiskey or two in the kitchen.

She told him how helpless she felt, as though she couldn't do anything. She had been severed from her soul mate and life partner and was lost without him. There were things her well-intentioned friends and the Army couldn't fix. She needed Rennie. Roland never said much, but he was good company. And he reassured her about Rennie.

"Never doubt Rennie's love," he said. "I knew Rennie most of his life, and his future was clear from the moment you met. Look how fast he married you. You two were what I measured my own relationships by. Not just me, many of Rennie's friends . . . we're all unmarried to this day!" It made Andrea Lynne laugh.

The evening always ended with Andrea Lynne falling asleep on the couch as Roland covered her with a blanket and locked up before he left. One evening, though, just before Christmas, as she drifted off to sleep, Andrea Lynne found herself wondering, Does he care for me? Do I want him to?

Delores was still in her bathrobe in the early afternoon when the doorbell rang. It was a week before Christmas, and she had just taken another batch of chocolate chip cookies for Gary Shane out of the oven. She was never in her robe this late, but she'd been baking all day. The aroma in the house could attest to that.

As Ski answered the door, she darted upstairs to change. Thomas Capel, the command sergeant major for the 504th's 1st Battalion, and his wife Marissa, who was also in the Army, had come by to pick up the cookies. He was on his way to visit his soldiers from Delta Company in Kosovo, and he would be close enough to stop and see Gary Shane, who was now a SAW (Squad Automatic Weapon) gunner in Alpha Company 1st Battalion of the 32nd Infantry Regiment at Camp Magrath, thirty miles east of the provincial capital, Pristina. Capel was a good friend of the Kalinofskis. He had known their son since the boy was eleven.

"Wow, I never got cookies! This must be one special private," teased Capel, who always wore a smile, no matter the occasion.

Delores had come back downstairs and was packing Gary Shane's cookies in a large Christmas tin. She also put part of the batch into a huge coffee can for the other soldiers in the platoon.

"Oh, my gosh, well it's a good thing that I've got a bag of cookies just for you, for your plane ride," Delores said. "And, Thomas, if you don't mind, I have another package, too." Inside that one Delores had carefully packed items she and Ski had bought at Sears—thermal underwear, leather gloves and inserts, Chap Stick, hand lotion, toothbrush, floss, hand sanitizer, Kleenex, and several pairs of Wigwam socks that kept feet dry and warm in extreme temperatures. And as she did with every package, she tucked in sandwich bags filled with iced animal crackers, Gary Shane's favorite.

This wasn't Gary Shane's first Christmas package from her. Delores had already mailed a forty-pound box of toiletries, snacks, thick black boot socks, underwear, brown jockeys and 100 percent cotton T-shirts, a sleep shirt, Gore-Tex gloves, a fifty-dollar gift certificate to use in the PX, and a Christmas card.

Gary Shane had been in Kosovo since November, and the terrorist attacks remained fresh in everyone's minds on post, but Ski had still not heard if he himself was going anywhere. Although the 82nd had never been called up to help in New York, the Kalinofskis had had their own up-close look at the devastation there. On October 11 they had driven the 566 miles in a rented Cadillac to attend a memorial service for a thirty-eight-year-old police officer and former 82nd paratrooper. Ski was the division's representative at the memorial.

It was the Kalinofskis' first time to New York City, and they were struck not only by the city but also by the sadness all around them. Everywhere they noticed thousands of photos of missing loved ones, and during a VIP tour and briefing at Ground Zero, they saw lists of names posted on boards, folded flags to be given at memorials, weary-eyed workers, search dogs with bloodied paws, and bulldozers sifting for remains through rubble that still burned at one thousand degrees Fahrenheit. Delores knew that all the dust they were walking in—dust that made their nostrils dry and their eyes burn—was mixed with the ashes of human remains.

"Oh, no, Dad, Mom is crying again," Cherish had said as they toured Ground Zero in their hard hats.

"I'm just a weeping willow," Delores answered, still dabbing at her eyes, but she realized then just how blessed she was. It was an experience she would never forget.

In the early afternoon on a rainy Christmas Eve, before the Kalinofskis headed to five o'clock mass at Saint Patrick's Catholic Church, Gary Shane and Capel called from Kosovo.

Delores knew right away that her son wasn't well, though he didn't say a word about it. "Honey, are you sick?"

"Yeah, I've got a cold."

"Did you get anything from the doctor?"

"I'm okay, Mom."

"We love and miss you so much. I hope you enjoyed the package. I hope everything fit."

"They did. Command Sergeant Major Capel delivered everything in person." There was nothing quite like a familiar face when you were far from home.

The two talked for twenty minutes, then Capel came back on the phone. Finally, it was time to say good-bye to Gary Shane.

"I love you so much, son. Take care of your head cold. God bless you, angel. I love you, good-bye."

Capel, who had access to a phone in the unit's tactical operations center, took Gary Shane there again the following day to call home on Christmas. Delores was in her glory.

R ita had just turned on the Christmas lights when she heard Brian un-locking the front door. She rushed down the hallway and wrapped her arms around him. She had grown used to the hard bulkiness of her husband's lime green cast, the result of his flipping his buddy Charlie down on his right hand during hand-to-hand combatives instruction in November. It was now December 24, and Rita had already fed the boys a supper of hot dogs and fries. When Brian wasn't around, which seemed to be more and more often, she didn't cook a big meal.

Like last year, Brian was again on DRF-1, but September 11 had changed everything. Because of the heightened risk of a terrorist attack over Christmas, Brian's unit had been on lockdown at the barracks all week. Wives were allowed to drop off meals each night, and Rita went faithfully, bringing Brian's favorites, like fried chicken and collard greens or cube steak and potatoes. Commanders had given the soldiers Christmas Eve off, but Brian would have to return to Fort Bragg the following afternoon.

Meanwhile rumors continued to swirl around everyone on DRF-1. *I heard they were leaving next week. . . . Something's gonna come down to-day. . . . Oh, God, I'm gonna bring him dinner, and then he'll be gone. . . .* As long as he's here for Christmas, Rita kept telling herself.

Rita wanted to put all the stress of the last few months aside. She had a lot to be thankful for. She was doing well in school, and she and Brian were getting a handle on their finances. Every time Rita looked at families new to the unit, she remembered how much she and Brian had struggled the previous Christmas. This year they could even help other couples out. She gave John's car seat away; he now used a booster seat. She also gave two trash bags of baby clothes away to Jenna, who had a toddler. When Sherry told her about a young private's wife who couldn't afford to buy her baby anything, Rita bought the five-month-old girl formula and diapers and helped get the mother on WIC. Just because the couple wasn't good with money didn't mean the child should suffer.

Junior enlisted soldiers sometimes get into financial trouble because of their own irresponsibility, guzzling down their paychecks at Fat Daddy's or buying souped-up trucks with megawatt two-thousand-dollar stereo systems. Those with families try harder, but debts from their single days stick to them like camouflage face paint. Often a private's paycheck just doesn't stretch far enough with a wife and new baby.

Politicians and the Army brass never talk much about soldiers who rely on food stamps. It is somehow unpatriotic and un-American to have the fittest warriors in the world unable to afford baby formula. Usually company first sergeants take care of their own, holding canned-food drives in their motor pools, collecting dollars and spare change, and buying groceries over their lunch breaks, then discreetly delivering them to soldiers too proud to ask for a handout. It's hard to believe there are young couples scraping to make ends meet on the same post as the families at the other end of Bragg's economic ladder.

Yet that was brought home to me one winter afternoon when, as part of a story, I climbed a wobbly ceiling ladder up into the belfry of the church where I attend mass on post. The 82nd Airborne Division Memorial Chapel on the corner of Ardennes Street and Bastogne Drive has etched stained glass that commemorates Normandy, Nijmegen, Salerno, Sicily, and the Battle of the Bulge, the division's great battle campaigns. Though the parishioners at Sunday services do not know it, the chaplains stock the belfry from floor to ceiling with donated cans of soup, Spaghet-tiOs, green beans, Gerber applesauce, and boxes of Hamburger Helper to help families in a bind.

That day I found out that chapels all over post use the bell towers or fellowship halls as food lockers to help hundreds of families who access the pantries so often that they run bare five times a year, especially before the holidays. The food is donated from soldiers' canned-food drives and Army associations. Mostly young wives with kids trailing behind them like ducklings climb the ladder and take whatever they need to tide them over for the week.

Before I climbed back down, Chaplain Terry Austin insisted I take something for a snack despite my protests. He reached for a dented can of Chef Boyardee, took out his pen, and marked a cross on the label in black ink before handing the can to me. Food handouts and donated toys, holiday china and crystal. It was a reminder to me that Christmas on an Army post comes in many shades of Army green.

CHAPTER FOURTEEN

The telephone jostled Delores awake, and she dived across the California-king-size bed to answer it. It was 5:00 A.M., Monday, March 4. As in most Fort Bragg households, the phone was on her spouse's side of the bed.

"Hello?" she said sleepily.

"Honey, you'll never believe who I have on the phone; hang on." And with that Ski handed the phone to his son.

"Hi, Mom."

"Oh my gosh, Gary Shane! How are you, son?" It was the first time Delores had talked with him since his twenty-first birthday a month earlier. The connection was surprisingly clear.

"I'm doing fine, Mom; everything's great."

In the background Delores could hear men laughing and talking. Ski had arrived in Kosovo the day before. He and Colonel John Campbell would be there for a week, checking on the soldiers from Delta Company, 1st Battalion, 504th Parachute Infantry Regiment, who were deployed for six months in the village of Klokot. Ski had spent the morning looking at TCPs (traffic control points) in the area. Since Delta Company was only five miles away from Gary Shane at Camp Magrath, he'd come to see his son.

"Are you having a good time with your dad?" Delores asked.

"Yeah, we just came from the mess hall. Dad got here around eleven."

"I'm so happy you linked up. Did Dad give you your package?"

Delores had sent a padded envelope with a teddy bear card, snacks, and, of course, iced animal crackers. She had also tucked in a *Mad* magazine and a *Low Rider* issue, a belated birthday gift for Gary Shane from some friends.

"You're getting another one. I'll be sending a huge package in a few days. And an e-card on Saint Patrick's Day." Gary Shane got so many letters and packages from his mom that soldiers had begun calling mail call "Kali call."

"I wish moms could fly to Kosovo, too," Delores added. "I miss you *sooo* much."

They spoke for half an hour, with Gary Shane laughing and joking much of the time. After they hung up, Ski gave his son one of his sly smiles.

"You made her happy. You know how she is."

Ski had met his son for an early lunch. He hadn't seen his boy in more than a year, and the sight of him now in BDUs—the same uniform Ski was wearing—with the same last name KALINOFSKI stitched above the right breast pocket, startled the command sergeant major a bit. He was amazed and honored to see his son in this environment: He was a *soldier*. But he was still the same smiling little Gary. Though the boy had never worn braces, he had perfectly straight, bright white teeth. A million-dollar smile, Delores liked to say, that didn't cost a million.

Ski set down his tray of lasagna and salad and sat next to his son. Gary Shane had been through the mess hall line before his dad arrived and had just finished some pizza and a glass of lemonade.

"I've got something for ya," Ski said. From his pocket he pulled out a copper-colored coin slightly larger than a half dollar. On one side it read, "Presented by the Command Sergeant Major." On the other side it bore the 504th unit crest.

"This is something for you from your ol' dad. Keep it on you for coin checks."

The military-unit coin is a relatively new tradition. Started at Fort Bragg by Special Forces troops, it has become widely popular throughout the Armed Services. Commanders and senior NCOs hand out specially minted coins to soldiers for a job well done. Soldiers keep the coin in their wallets, and if they are asked by someone in a bar to show their coin, and they don't have it, they have to pay for a round of drinks. If they produce the coin, the challenger has to cover the round.

"Your mother told me you're getting out after two years, is that right?"

"Yep, in October."

"Let me see your ID card." Ski examined its expiration date. "What are you going to do when you get out?"

"My buddy and I are going to go to New York and work for GM; his mom can get us jobs there, and I want to enroll in school somewhere and take classes. I think I'd like New York with its music scene and all."

"Son, there's no General Motors in the city, but there's a plant in Newark. I think it's a good idea." Ski wanted to be encouraging. "You guys are interested in cars."

Ski was glad Gary Shane was getting out of the Army. The world was now more uncertain than ever for soldiers, and besides, he and Delores still wanted the boy to go to college.

"Now, just remember, if you want to come home for a while, that's fine, too. Your room is waiting. I was thinking of making it into an office, but you know your mom would never let me do that." That was classic Ski. "You sure you don't want to come home?"

"Yeah, I'm sure," Gary Shane said with a laugh.

"Hey, your mom gave me this camera and told me to take lots of pictures. Let's get some shots before we head out of here. It's not often you have two Kalinofskis in uniform."

Ski then took all the NCOs outside the mess hall and onto the porch in the frigid Balkan air for a pep talk and safety briefing. Gary Shane stood next to his father as Ski spoke.

"We're in the home stretch, guys. Watch over each other. Keep doing the right thing."

In the Army there is always paranoia about things going wrong near the end of a seamless deployment or field exercise. "Ol' Murphy" of Murphy's Law—if something can go wrong, it will—is one person soldiers never want to have around.

"You're doing a great job," Ski continued. "Take care of the soldiers. Don't let them do anything stupid. It's more important than ever to keep an eye on the men."

After the talk Ski and his son tried to call Delores, but Gary Shane's phone card wasn't working, so they headed for First Sergeant Tracy Long's office.

"I can't get through to my wife," Ski told Long. "Do you mind if we use your phone?"

"No problem, sergeant major."

As Gary Shane talked with Delores, Ski asked Long how Gary Shane was doing.

"He's doing great, sergeant major."

Ski asked the same question when he saw his son's squad outside on a foot patrol.

"Gary's doing great, we love him," came the response.

It was time for Ski to meet with the battalion command sergeant major. "I'll catch up with you later this afternoon," he told Gary Shane. "I'll be here for a couple more days. I love you."

"Love you, too, Dad." And with that father and son hugged each other good-bye.

In Fayetteville Delores finished up her coffee and dressed for Command and Staff. At 9:30 A.M. on the first Monday of every month, the division commander's wife presided over the meeting of senior wives at Fort Bragg's Watters Center, passing along information on post matters like health clinics, upcoming events, and updated rosters that the women would then take back to their coffee groups and FRGs. Delores had been attending the meetings for almost ten years, and she always looked forward to them. This morning her spirits were still high about the phone conversation with Ski and Gary Shane, and she was eager to share her news with the other women.

It was a clear morning, with the temperature in the thirties. Most wives wore slacks, skirts, or dresses, but Delores almost always went casual. She put on white sneakers, Lands' End blue jeans, a long-sleeve white T-shirt from L.L. Bean, and her favorite black shirt, which had "82nd Airborne Division," her name, and a rose all embroidered in red—a gift from Ski. She slipped her gold crucifix on last; she never left home without wearing it.

Cherish, who was now thirteen and out of school for a teacher workday, was coming with her. Delores made sure her daughter brought something to keep herself busy. "I'm going to be taking notes and listening to the head table," she said.

She was still beaming as she entered the Watters Center with Cherish, made her way into the auditorium, and sat down at the 504th table with ladies from her brigade.

"I heard from my two favorite guys this morning," Delores told two battalion commanders' wives. "Gary and Gary Shane called from Kosovo. You know, Gary's there for a week with Colonel Campbell."

"When is Gary Shane due home?" one of the women asked.

"He redeploys in mid-May to Fort Drum. We're going up there. I can't wait to see him. As soon as Gary gets back, I'll make reservations for the three of us."

Delores looked around as the meeting was called to order. It was odd that Ann Campbell, the wife of the brigade commander, wasn't in her seat. She had thought they might have lunch together after the meeting. Ann's books were on the table, and her coat was on the back of her chair. Something must be up with the unit, Delores thought.

Suddenly Ann appeared next to her. She was an ER nurse and had short dark hair and was always bubbly and optimistic, but now she seemed nervous, and her fair skin had turned the color of ash.

"Delores, could you and Cherish please come into the hall?" Ann said softly. Something was wrong. One of the soldiers in the brigade must have gotten hurt or into trouble.

Delores and her daughter followed Ann out. Across the hallway, standing in the entranceway to Room 124, stood Command Sergeant Major Thomas Capel. His soft brown eyes were red, as if he had been crying.

This has something to do with me, Delores realized. This is going to affect me in a way I do not want to hear. There has been a death. There has been a death. This is something I don't want to be hearing. All she wanted to do at that moment was grab Cherish and run out of the building.

"Please come with me, Delores," Capel said.

She started crying hard. Capel took her into a counseling room with a table and chairs. The space was filled with people, including the brigade chaplain, Major Jeff Watters, and the brigade surgeon, Major David

Doyle. Charlie Thorpe, the command sergeant major of the 82nd Airborne Division, and his wife, Willann, still in her white nurse's uniform, were sitting with all the others. All these people . . . this is not good, Delores thought. No one said a word until Delores broke the silence.

"Okay, what the hell are you going to tell me has happened to my husband in the short time since I spoke to him? That he has been killed?" Delores never used profanity. She looked over at Charlie Thorpe. She and Ski had been friends with him since before they were married.

Cherish, who was sitting in a wingback chair near the window, started to cry.

Thorpe was an old-school black sergeant major with a voice that sounded like a Humvee driving over gravel. "No, Dee, not big Gary—little Gary." He continued with the precision of a twenty-one-gun salute: "Gary Shane committed suicide in Kosovo at 1:13 P.M."

Delores froze, unable to move. She could barely speak. "No! Major mistake. No, not my baby! Not little Gary."

"Yes, Dee," the sergeant major said, his voice softening. Delores began to sob. She grabbed Thorpe and buried her head in his chest, coating his uniform with her tears.

"It's my husband that has been killed; Gary, my husband."

"No, Dee, it's Gary Shane," the sergeant major said again, gently.

Every Army wife, somewhere in the back of her mind, knows she can lose her husband, but a son? The thought was inconceivable to Delores. Gary Shane had just turned twenty-one.

She lifted her head up and looked at Thorpe. "Not my baby—not Gary Shane. Maybe it's a local or someone who resembled Gary Shane, but not my baby. Maybe he's just hurt somewhere? How do you know? Are you sure? This can't be true. I just spoke to Gary Shane and his dad this morning. I spoke to Gary Shane for thirty minutes. Tell me, please, how can this be true?"

She buried her head back in Thorpe's chest. If she could only go back in time an hour or so, to when her life was happy and normal. Maybe if she hadn't come to Command and Staff, this wouldn't have happened. Just get the keys, get back in the Camry, and get out of the building, she told herself. This cannot be happening.

Instead she found herself in a dark gray government van with an entourage of senior soldiers and wives taking her back to her house. Capel drove the Camry. Suddenly, in the midst of her grief, Delores had another sick feeling. She was an excellent housekeeper, but that morning she had left her kitchen table and countertop cluttered with fund-raising papers, envelopes, and brochures. What would the other wives think when they saw the mess?

It may seem strange to outsiders that having a house out of order would be such a pervasive and prevalent thought among Army wives in a moment of horror, but it is. Psychologists may have their own interpretations, but I think that Army culture and expectations within that culture have a lot to do with it. Army couples like to put their best foot forward at all times. A soldier's family and the neatness of his home are all reflections upon the soldier, who himself is expected to be orderly and disciplined. Army people never forget their dirty neighbors.

From the van Delores kept trying to call her next-door neighbor. The woman had a key to the house. Maybe she could go in and put things away. But Delores never got through.

She looked out the window, her eyes swollen and puffy. She desperately wanted to speak with her husband, to be in his arms. She had so many questions and no answers.

CHAPTER FIFTEEN

After father and son had said good-bye, Ski went to the battalion command sergeant major's office. He was there for a meeting, but he took the opportunity to ask the command sergeant major the same question he'd been asking everyone: "How's Gary doing?" And he got the same response he'd been getting since Gary Shane entered Basic Training: "He's doing great."

Ten minutes later First Sergeant Tracy Long came running into the office looking panicked. "Sergeant major, you gotta come with me." The sergeant major excused himself, leaving Ski in the office alone. He knew it must be an emergency of some sort. Something was obviously wrong. At least it ain't Gary, Ski reassured himself. He's with me. Something must have happened on a patrol.

A moment later the first sergeant and the sergeant major reappeared along with some other soldiers. The men stared at Ski with solemn faces. Some wouldn't meet his gaze. What in the world? Ski thought.

"I'm . . . I'm sorry," First Sergeant Long stuttered. "Gary's gone."

"What are you talking about, Gary's gone?" Ski was on his feet now, his hands on his hips, his jaw slightly dropped.

"Sergeant major, I'm sorry . . . he's dead . . . he's gone."

"What? It can't be. I was with him just ten minutes ago." Ski couldn't process what was being said. It felt like time had stopped. He could hear the distinctive chopping sound of helicopters behind the shouting and commotion outside.

"Are you sure? Come on . . ."

Gary Shane had been excused from a squad patrol because his father was visiting. He had gone back to his room, Conex #29, locked the door behind him, changed into his gray PT clothes, and neatly hung up his BDUs, placing them in the wall locker across from his bed.

The room was sparse—two bunks, two wall lockers, and a window air conditioner. His roommate was out with the squad. Gary Shane had secretly kept some ammunition from the arms room from an earlier patrol. Now he loaded it into his M249 SAW (Squad Automatic Weapon), a 5.56 millimeter light machine gun that can engage targets eight hundred meters away. At fifteen pounds it's a bulky weapon, and like a fat lady with skinny legs, the SAW's slender barrel seems out of proportion with its receiver. Gary Shane placed the cool round muzzle inside his mouth, pointing it upward. He pulled the trigger and fell facedown on the floor. Soldiers outside heard the gunfire. The smoke and sparks from the weapon set off the room's fire alarm. Soldiers had to get a master key to get into the room, but it was too late.

The day after Gary Shane's death, I was at work taking care of last-minute details for my trip to Vietnam when I opened an e-mail that had been sent from a public affairs office in Pristina. The subject line read: "Soldier dies in Kosovo."

I opened the e-mail. The writing was in another language, but the name "Pfc. Gary S. Kalinofski" stood out like blood on a white wall. In horror I scrolled down and found the English translation. Gary Shane had died from a gunshot wound "unrelated to engagement with hostile forces." It's a buzz phrase in news releases for either an accident or suicide. This couldn't be happening, I thought, tears streaming down my face. It must have been an accident. Maybe the soldiers were fooling around and something bad happened. Then I remembered, "Oh, God, Ski is over there."

I had run into Ski a few weeks earlier, before a parachute jump at Green Ramp on Pope Air Force Base. He was his usual upbeat self, eyes twinkling, arms crossed, and legs apart like an inverted V. He told me he was going to Kosovo and would get to see Gary Shane.

Now I insisted on being the one to write a story, and I began to track down Gary Shane's high school teachers and his friends at Fort Drum. The article never ran. Later in the day I was horrified to confirm through back channels that Gary Shane had committed suicide. My paper's policy on suicide was not to report it unless it was done in a very public way or involved a public official or other prominent person. I wrote a few short paragraphs citing statements from the press release.

Ski wasn't home yet. I planned to go over to the Kalinofskis' house that night but was told the family did not want visitors. It turned out that was never Delores's wish. She didn't know that a well-meaning relative was turning away people at her door.

That would change two days later. On Wednesday evening, March 6, Ski arrived home in Fayetteville. He and Colonel Campbell had accompanied Gary Shane's body on a C-130 cargo plane to Germany, where an autopsy was performed. At first Ski had been convinced there must have been foul play or that it was an accident, but the windows and door of Gary Shane's room were locked from the inside. It was clear that his son had taken his own life.

In front of the Kalinofski house, cars crowded the cul-de-sac. Inside casseroles, salads, sheet cakes, buckets of Kentucky Fried Chicken, coffeepots, and cartons of creamer covered the kitchen counter and table, along with boxes of tissues. Plants and flowers filled the family room, and neighbors, relatives, and friends from Bragg milled through the house.

Only later that night, behind closed doors in their bedroom, were Delores and Ski finally alone. She sat in her rocking chair while he knelt down beside her and cried.

"We've lost our boy. . . . We lost our baby. I don't know what happened," Ski said. "For the life of me, I don't know what happened."

All week neighbors and wives from the brigade filled the house with food. Ann Campbell had made sure of that. But the dishes had no taste to Delores, and she subsisted mostly on coffee and glasses of milk. The company of others comforted her during the day. At night, when everyone else was in bed, Delores would slip out of bed—quietly, so as not to wake

Ski—curl in her rocking chair, and cry. *Dear God give me the strength to let this broken heart and broken soul heal!*

She felt like a total failure. *How could my son speak to me for thirty minutes and ten minutes later commit suicide? Why didn't I sense something wrong with my son?* These thoughts consumed her. *What kind of a mom am I? What was his pain? Why couldn't he have told me?*

The night they made the funeral arrangements, Delores was again in her rocking chair. This time she was poring over photos of Gary Shane she planned to put together for a collage to be displayed at the funeral home. Ski came upstairs after everyone had left and put his head in her lap.

"He's gone. Our son is gone," he sobbed. "Oh, God, didn't he know that I loved him?"

Delores had never planned to tell her husband what Gary Shane had said before he left for Basic Training. She didn't want to hurt him further. But now she had to tell him.

"I don't know what he was thinking," she said. "Honey, honest to God, when he pulled that trigger, I don't know what he knew. He told me before he left for Basic that he thought you loved Cherish more than you loved him or me. I told him that wasn't true and he needed to talk to you about it."

Ski continued to sob as Delores stroked his head.

"We always showed him and told him we loved him," Ski said. "We never withheld our love from him. What made him do this?"

Delores was crying uncontrollably now, too. "Why didn't the love reach him? I want to know why my son took his life. I need an answer from heaven right now."

How on earth, she wondered, would they find the strength to bury their firstborn, their son?

On the following Monday evening, at 7:00, the Kalinofskis had a closed-casket wake at Rogers & Breece Funeral Home. By then Delores was in a fog. She was getting two or three hours of sleep each night and just barely holding up. The brigade surgeon had prescribed sleeping pills for her, but she refused to take any of them.

Delores had asked that her rosary be placed in Gary Shane's hands, and she had the mortician place a photo of her and Gary Shane together in her son's casket. It had been taken on the front lawn on Christmas morning 2000. He had just finished running and was wearing gray sweatpants and a gray Army sweatshirt. Delores had on a robe and ivory satin slippers, a Christmas gift from Gary Shane when he was fifteen. In the picture he was smiling and hugging his mother.

Now Delores wore a new black pants suit and stood beside her husband, touching her son's casket and greeting mourners. Hundreds of people came, including some the Kalinofskis had known from their early Army days. Delores's head ached, her throat was rough and scratchy, and her eyes were swollen from crying so much, but Gary Shane was all she could think of.

She had arrived at the funeral home fully intent on seeing her son's body. Thomas Capel, who was serving as the Kalinofskis' CAO, had told Delores that if she wanted to see Gary Shane's remains he would be right by her side. The damage had been massive, and everyone had gently suggested that it would be better to remember the boy as he had looked before. Delores knew that much of her son's face—his movie-star smile—was gone, but she still wanted to say a final good-bye and touch some part of him. As she leaned her head and arms on her son's casket and sobbed, she thought she would ask Capel to let her see Gary Shane.

Years before, when Delores wasn't quite ten years old, her brother, Richard, had burned himself over 95 percent of his body while playing with matches and kerosene on the farm. Delores's piano teacher had taken the girl to the hospital and had told her that her eleven-year-old brother wasn't hurt badly, that only his thumb had been burned. When Delores saw her brother wrapped like a mummy and in severe pain, she went hysterical. Ever since then, whenever anything happened, she did not want to be spared. Even now she wanted to imprint on her heart that her son was truly gone. If she could just see him.

When she looked up, her in-laws were surrounding her, and her mind suddenly was on other things. Later she would be thankful that she could remember her son as he had been.

Soon people filled the funeral home. Gary Shane's casket stood in the A-B parlor, the same place Rennie Cory's had been the previous April. How sad and tragic that had been, Delores thought. She and Ski had gone to the Corys' quarters to take food and help out. At Rennie's wake Delores prayed that she would never be in Andrea Lynne's shoes. This could have happened to any one of the wives. We're blessed, she remembered thinking. Our family is untouched by such a tragedy; how lucky we are. Life is short and precious.

Now Andrea Lynne came through the receiving line with tears in her eyes. This was the first wake she'd attended since her husband's death. Rennie had been in this same spot, she realized.

"My heart breaks for you," she told the Kalinofskis, trying to comfort them.

During the service they played Elvis Presley gospel songs Delores knew Gary Shane would have loved. She had learned about the soulful, bluesy gospel music as a child, from a wonderful black Christian lady named Althea who watched her while her grandparents worked. Delores would tell Althea to turn up the radio, and the two would sing and dance around the house as Althea cooked and mopped. The music soothed Delores's soul, and it gave her comfort now. But when Ski began to read aloud a three-page farewell letter to his son, and his voice cracked and broke, Delores's heart shattered all over again. To see any man cry, especially her husband, tore her to pieces.

The next day, following a ceremony at the Main Post Chapel, the Kalinofskis sat under a kelly green tent and saw their son's casket lowered into the fourteenth grave in the eleventh row at the Fort Bragg Cemetery. Delores wanted her son to be buried on post, because that's where her father's grave was, in the twenty-fifth row. Delores wore another new black pants suit. Both had been purchased for her at the PX. Under the jacket she wore a white shirt and red silk tie that belonged to Gary Shane, clothes he had worn at his parents' renewal of vows ceremony three years earlier.

Heavy rain had made the cemetery's thick grass soggy, and mourners in overcoats and carrying umbrellas gathered in close, as Delores placed a long-stemmed red rose on her son's casket. Its color seemed out of place against the still leafless trees and leaden sky.

At the end of March the Kalinofskis went to Fort Drum to pack up Gary Shane's belongings. In the parking lot outside the barracks, they saw his '96 teal green Chevrolet Cavalier coupe, which had a flat tire. Delores wanted to buy the car—it hadn't been paid off—and tow it home to North Carolina, but it had broken down so many times on Gary Shane it didn't seem worth it. Instead she sat in the driver's seat and cried. In the center compartment she found a short yellow pencil with no eraser, the kind used to buy lottery tickets. With tears in her eyes, she tucked it into her purse as a keepsake.

The Kalinofskis cleaned out their son's desk drawers, filled with his pens, pencils, and binders from high school, and his wall locker stacked with toilet paper, CDs, and the only new clothes he had bought since joining the Army—five shirts from the PX with the price tags still on, nineteen dollars apiece. They packed his possessions as lovingly as if he were coming home from college.

The Kalinofskis drove back to North Carolina with a stack of plastic containers holding their son's belongings in the back of their rented Ford. They had gone to Fort Drum hoping for clues that would help them piece together a life they once thought they understood. They were looking for answers, Ski would tell me later, but found none.

The Army was searching for answers, too. The week before the Kalinofskis made their trip north, Special Agent Justin Ryan, from Fort Bragg's CID (Criminal Investigation Division), paid the Kalinofskis a visit. Ryan arrived in civilian clothes: black slacks and black shoes, a white shirt and tie. His features were as nondescript as his attire. He was average-looking, with a medium build, no prominent features, and dark brown hair. He stood an inch shorter than Delores, and he was in his twenties—young enough to be her son.

As Delores led him into the kitchen, Ryan looked around the house. He's checking to see if we live like slobs, Ski thought. The agent placed a soda he had brought with him on the kitchen table along with a file, then set up his laptop.

The Army's CID "special agents" are junior-enlisted soldiers with an important-sounding title. I asked a lot of Army folks with years of experience about their dealings with and opinions of special agents. Down to a man, I received similar responses: There are good CID agents, but as a group, they are viewed by the rest of the Army as amateurs. The younger ones are kids with a badge and a gun, who get on-the-job training but frequently lack the ability to deal appropriately with victims or perpetrators. They also tend to believe that they are above the normal rules of military decorum and are almost always suspicious of senior officers and NCOs. They generally consider everyone they investigate guilty until proved innocent.

Ski had already been interviewed by CID in Kosovo.

"What could have happened?" he was asked repeatedly by agents there. His answer was always the same.

"Nothing happened. I just saw him." Ski went over the story again and again. "Everything was fine."

"Are you sure?"

"Yeah, I'm sure."

Now Ski answered the same questions one more time for Special Agent Ryan, recounting his last visit with his son.

Ryan asked about Gary Shane's childhood, his upbringing, how Ski disciplined him. He wanted to know if Ski treated Gary Shane like a soldier or a son. He kept referring back to the contents of the file as he asked his questions. Once, when Delores touched the file, Special Agent Ryan yanked it away.

"These are statements, but nothing you can officially see at this time," he said as he pulled the papers closer.

When Special Agent Ryan finally finished with Ski, the sergeant major read his statement, wrote "end," and initialed and signed it.

"I know you want to talk with Delores. It might be better if I'm not here," he said. "I'll go to bed."

Delores was sitting in her son's chair. She steeled herself for the questions she knew were coming.

Ryan weighed in with little introduction: "How do you perceive a padded mailer that was given to Pfc. Kalinofski by his father in Kosovo on

Monday, March 4, 2002, to be not on Pfc. Kalinofski's person at the crime scene?"

"I don't know," Delores said. "I was told that Gary Shane had forgotten it on the table in the DFAC (dining facility)."

Ryan kept asking about the envelope. The only things in it, Delores said, were the teddy bear card, two magazines, and some snacks and cookies.

"And why was it that none of the contents were found at the death scene?"

"I have no idea. I was told by several people that he left the envelope on the DFAC table in the tent after chow."

"Are you sure?"

"Yes, I'm sure. You've asked me this same question at least nine times now. How would I know how the envelope wasn't at the death scene or on my son's person at the time of his death?"

Delores wanted to shout, "Don't you know we just buried our son? Don't you know that Gary Shane was the most special and loved Pfc. of all? Don't you know that we are a Christian family and don't deserve to be grilled like this?" But she kept silent and endured Ryan's relentless questions.

"Your husband gave your son a coin. How come the coin also wasn't on Pfc. Kalinofski's person or at the scene at time of death?"

"I don't know."

"Are you sure?"

"Yes."

The agent asked the same question again and again, then finally moved on.

"Do you know or remember what you had written to Pfc. Kalinofski in your letters in that padded envelope?"

"It wasn't letters; it was one card. Yes, I clearly remember what I wrote to my son. I'm grieving—I haven't lost my senses."

"Please write it down." The agent pulled out a sheet of paper from his file. Delores remembered exactly what she had written—about loving him and missing him and seeing him soon—but it was grueling to rewrite it.

"Did you write Pfc. Kalinofski other letters?"

"Yes."

"Did you send packages?"

"Yes. Gary's Shane's last package from his dad and me was thirty-eight pounds."

A dozen times the agent asked her about their last conversation. "Did you argue on the phone?"

"No. Gary Shane was laughing out loud. Ask anyone who heard him speaking to me. Colonel Campbell said he heard everything Gary Shane was saying to me. He was as rational as always, happy-go-lucky—nothing out of the ordinary."

"Did you tell Pfc. Kalinofski that you loved him?"

"Yes."

"Did you hate your son?" Ryan asked.

"No, of course not!"

"Did you ever tell any of Pfc. Kalinofski's friends that you hated him?"

"Of course not."

"Did Pfc. Kalinofski hate you?

"*No!*" Delores was tired of being grilled. *What could I possibly know? When will this all be over?* The agent was way too young, she thought, to understand how much they had invested in their son, how much they loved him, how much they had lost.

"We loved Gary Shane," she said. "We can't understand why he chose to end his life. We love both of our children. And I know for a fact that Gary Shane loved us. I know, because I'm his mother. He hugged his father, and he told us that he loved us."

"Did you raise your son with morals and values?"

"Yes."

Special Agent Ryan asked his last question: "Were you a good mother to Pfc. Kalinofski?"

The words stung Delores to her core, and she began to cry, nearly as hard as the day she was told of Gary Shane's death.

"Yes, I was a good mother," she said. "No, I take that back. I was a *great* mother to Gary Shane. Ask anyone who knows me at Fort Bragg or in Fayetteville or at Saint Patrick's Catholic Church. My children were the first thing I ever talked about."

"Ma'am, I'm sorry to have upset you or to have made you cry. But I needed answers to these questions."

"I know you have a job to do," Delores said. "But I'm exhausted, and this has been excruciating. It's way past my bedtime. What more could you ask of me? I only loved my Gary Shane. Now he's gone. Can't we just wrap this up?"

It was two minutes before midnight when Delores signed her statement. As the agent packed up his laptop and took his file, he turned to Delores. "I want to come back and get a statement from your daughter. I need to see if Pfc. Kalinofski was a victim of child abuse when he lived at home."

Delores wanted to scream that the very idea was absurd. In the end the Kalinofskis said no, that they had had enough.

After Special Agent Ryan left, Delores let her poodle, Daisy, out in the backyard. Tears were flowing down her cheeks, and she had no strength left. She had been made to feel responsible for the suicide of her son.

CHAPTER SIXTEEN

Six months after 9/11, the United States was fully engaged in war against the Taliban and al-Qaeda, with troops hunting down the elusive Osama bin Laden. By March, Fayetteville had gotten a taste of what was to come. Fort Bragg and Pope Air Force Base suffered their first combat deaths in Afghanistan, Green Berets received medals for bravery, and in midmonth President Bush came to rally the troops. He told them the battle was far from over. His words were accurate. A year almost to the day after his visit to Fayetteville, the president declared war against Iraq.

At the end of March, following my trip to Vietnam, where I had spent much of the month confronting the ghosts of a different war, I drove back to Fayetteville. It was Palm Sunday, the beginning of Holy Week for Christians, who believe the week culminates with Jesus' resurrection on Easter Sunday. The holiday is rich in symbolism and often associated with the onset of spring, new life after death, darkness to light, forgiveness of sins. A second chance. For the Floyds, though, the season would be coldly cruel, as the promise of new beginnings faded.

Brandon was lying in bed, his bandaged leg propped up with pillows and a pair of crutches on the carpet next to the bed. On a tray next to him was an untouched plate of Hamburger Helper. A week earlier he had had knee surgery to repair ligaments he'd torn during a pickup game of basketball on post. He was still pissed at himself for getting hurt. It was the same knee he'd hurt years earlier in a ski accident. His stepmother was staying at the house and had been a big help, but Brandon hated being dependent on others. He flipped through the TV channels listlessly. He wasn't one to keep still, and the lack of mobility irritated him as much as the pain. He could hear the Labs barking outside. It irked him to know that he should be training them.

He'd be out of work for a while, and that ticked him off, too. Plus the leg hurt like hell, but he would never tell the guys in his unit that. No one talked about injuries or sickness. No one wanted to give the perception of weakness.

That's how it is in elite units as well as in the officer corps. One officer told me that the only way he would go to the doctor is if he were dead. Officers, sometimes to the detriment of their own health, believe they are setting an example for young troops, who are always going on sick call, by not seeking help themselves. I think it has as much to do with ego.

Brandon had been doing so well at his job, and now he faced months of physical therapy, though everyone expected a full recovery. The fact that he was injured hurt his pride more than anything. It was March, and he'd only been back from Afghanistan six weeks. With all that was going on in the Middle East, this was the worst time to be "broke"—the soldiers' expression for being hurt or injured. He didn't want his teammates doing missions without him.

It was late in the afternoon on Sunday, and Andrea came into the bedroom with an armful of her work clothes to iron. The new house had an oversize master bedroom, the kind that doesn't lend itself well to intimacy. Andrea plopped the clothes on an ironing board that was set up near the closet door.

"You didn't eat your dinner."

Her mother-in-law had been making dinners during the week while Andrea worked, but on Sunday she could do the cooking herself.

"Would it be too much to ask for you to cook something different for a change?" Brandon kept his eyes on the TV.

"The kids like it," Andrea said defensively, glaring at him. Cooking was not Andrea's thing. She didn't like it, though she had a knack for cooking deer meat, of all things, perfectly. And she did love baking, especially for the kids, things like banana-nut bread, muffins, and chocolate chip cookies.

Brandon sometimes joked about her cooking in front of friends. "Well, I guess we're having something out of the freezer tonight," he would say. Those kinds of comments didn't bother her when he was just playing around, but tonight was different. Andrea could tell he was in a bad mood. The same bad mood he'd been in since he got home from the hospital.

"Well, it tastes like crap," he said. "I'd rather eat fast food than eat your shit."

"Look, don't give me an attitude, Brandon," Andrea came back. "I've been busy, and I've been working weekends and buying things for the house, in case you haven't noticed."

"Yeah, I have noticed, and the house looks like crap, too. You need to be working extra shifts with all the money you've blown while I was away." Brandon blamed Andrea for spending the ten thousand dollars his family had loaned them.

"Like you're one to talk, Brandon." Andrea was now standing near the bed. Brandon was always wanting bigger, better, faster, stronger. It was part of his being a thrill seeker. "Don't you dare open your mouth to me about money. Maybe we can get out of debt if you sell the top-of-the-line eight-thousand-dollar four-wheeler you just had to have. Or what about your sixty-dollar running shorts? Could you part with a few of your guns? I can take back the gun safe. Or what about one of your registered dogs? While we're at it, did we really need a computerized washer and dryer on top of the eighteen-hundred-a-month house payments? You're all show. All you care about is what other people think."

The couple was deeply in debt, and, as it was for a lot of couples, it was a source of contention. As a Delta Force sergeant first class, Brandon made between $55,000 and $57,000 a year. Even that, coupled with Andrea's $30,000 salary, wasn't enough to cover their mounting expenses.

"With all the money you've blown, you'd think you could put up some decent curtains! These look like sheets on rods. Here we buy this beautiful house, and you manage to fuck it up."

Brandon's words stung Andrea, the kind of hurt that burns your chest. She had tried so hard to have the house ready for him when he came home from Afghanistan. She'd bought a beautiful cherry dining room set with a matching china cabinet and the leather club chairs Brandon liked. The promise of the house had been the one thing that united them, she thought. They had all the space and the land they could want. Brandon had his dogs and his dream job and the house he wanted. Why wasn't it enough?

Andrea posed the same question to herself. She loved her job and felt good about her success. She hadn't gone to college, and she'd been a stay-at-home mom for so long, she wondered what marketable skills she had when she first applied for the job. Now she was a supervisor. For the first time in her marriage, she'd made friends outside Brandon's circle. The marriage never had been an equal partnership in her eyes. Finally she was something more than Brandon's wife, or an Army wife for that matter, and she found it liberating.

Plenty of Army wives I know do it all. They raise families, have careers, and make brownies for FRG bake sales. They have friends both in and outside the confines of the Army and take an interest in their local communities. They are smart, well-rounded, organized women who have chosen a nontraditional path as an Army wife. The difference with Andrea was that her newfound self didn't include Brandon. In Andrea's eyes he wasn't around anyway, and when he was, he was a jerk. Army wives with strong, loving marriages can withstand the hardships that come with lengthy separations. They view themselves as part of a couple, a team. More and more, Andrea didn't want to be on Brandon's team.

As a young person she had never partied, drunk, or smoked, but she was having a great time now, going out with a group of friends from work to dance clubs like the Palomino and Mojo's. She hadn't looked this good in a long time. She'd lost twenty-five pounds since she started at Dick's—down to 138 pounds. She liked when people noticed, but she still wouldn't wear jeans. She didn't like the way she looked in them. Years ago Brandon had told her that they made her butt look big. That probably had something to do with it.

He was always telling her that she was too heavy and looked like a slob. No wonder she went on diets all the time. For a while she ate only bread with jelly and fruit. Another time she went on a watermelon diet. At Fort Campbell she'd get up and go running at 5:00 A.M., pushing her two babies in the stroller, while a friend of hers pedaled a bike and tried to keep up. It was nice to have other men notice her now and give her compliments, unlike Brandon, who was assailing her with his complaints.

"You know what else, Andrea, you're a shitty mom. You don't even keep the kids around when I'm gone, and when they're home, there's no discipline unless I'm here. Have you even had them to church since I've been gone?"

"Brandon, that's not fair! You know I've had to work a lot of Sundays." Andrea had one weekend off a month, and she worked alternate Saturdays and Sundays the other weekends.

Since they'd moved, Brandon had taken the kids to a few churches but still hadn't found one he liked. And it bothered him how much time the kids had spent in Ohio when he was deployed. He always insisted that as soon as he got home from a mission he'd go and get them. In February, when he returned from Afghanistan, he drove with his dad and picked the kids up.

Andrea argued that Brandon had no idea what it was like to take care of three small children, work full-time, move into a new house, and re-model, especially while your spouse is gone for who knows how long.

Brandon wasn't letting up now. "Did you go to work looking like that?"

"Like what?" Oh, God, here we go, Andrea thought.

"Like a slob, Andrea. Look in the mirror sometime. Did you bother to brush your hair this morning? Can't you at least try to be feminine? Women wear makeup, Andrea. Would some eye shadow and nail polish kill you? I didn't know I married a man."

He was throwing his full arsenal at her now. She had put on mascara and a dab of lip gloss that morning and, yes, she needed to wash her hair, but she had other things to do. She had never been one to care much about her appearance. Brandon was constantly comparing her with her two beautiful sisters and talking about how they did their hair and makeup. To please him she had recently started going to the salon to get artificial nails and highlights in her hair. When Brandon said he didn't like the way her eyebrows looked in last year's family portrait, she had her eyebrows waxed, too. None of that seemed to matter.

"You cook for crap, you clean for crap, you don't care for the kids, you look like crap—"

"Shut the fuck up, Brandon. Leave me alone!"

She was fed up with his sarcasm and carping. Other people didn't treat her like this; why did he? If she didn't want to wear eye shadow, she shouldn't have to.

Suddenly she had had enough from Brandon. Andrea could be sharp-tongued, too, and now she lashed back, matching him hurtful word for hurtful word.

"You treat your goddamn dogs better than you treat me. You know what your problem is? You're a control freak. Nothing's ever good enough for you. Whenever I'm successful, you put your thumb down. You can't stand it!

"Ya know what else? People think you're so outgoing and friendly, always ready to tell a joke, always the life of the party. But that's because they don't know you like I do. You're an asshole, always have been. Stop taking your frustration out on me because you went and busted your goddamn knee!"

"You're a bitch!" Brandon countered. "I can't understand why Dick's would want you around. You're worthless."

Worthless. The summer before, Brandon had been so proud of her for getting a manager's job, he had taken her out to dinner while Joanne watched the kids. On the weekends when she was in training, he'd pile the kids in his truck and drive the fifty-five miles to Cary so they could have lunch with their mom. Now he called her worthless.

"Well, fuck you!" and with that Andrea walked out of the room and slammed the door behind her.

It had come to this. After eight years of marriage and three children, they had resorted to shouting matches and ugly put-downs. They never used to swear at each other. Now door slamming and yelling was routine, even in front of the kids. Thank God, they were outside playing this time, Andrea thought, as she grabbed her coat and the cordless phone and went out on her front porch. She sat in a rocking chair and dialed her mother's phone number. This was Andrea's favorite part of the house, the place where she felt most at home.

"Mom, it's me."

"Hi, what's wrong?" Penny Flitcraft knew by the tone of her daughter's voice that something wasn't right.

"Brandon and I just had a huge fight. Really ugly. I'm just so tired of him putting me down."

"There's no reason for you to put up with that," Penny told her daughter. "It's been going on too long. You need to make a decision. It's not good for the kids, and it's not good for you."

"I know. I'm considering a divorce. For sure this time."

Only Andrea and Brandon knew the depths of the troubles they were going through. She was never one to draw her friends into her marital woes, and few of them knew how bad things were.

I learned that Delta has a chaplain and psychologists in the unit, and they have an open-door policy for counseling, too. Delta is a small community, and word might get around. Even more than conventional Army soldiers, Delta operators don't want their home problems to be seen as a reflection of their professional abilities. The Floyds had never sought that help, and Brandon was never around for long enough anyway.

Once a few years back, at Fort Campbell after a blow out with Brandon, Andrea had called another Army wife, a woman to whom she was close, and told her she was leaving Brandon.

"It's over; we're getting divorced," Andrea had said. "I don't know what I'm going to do, but I'm thinking of going home. Can I stay at your place for a night?"

"Whatever you want," her friend said. She didn't ask what had happened. She didn't want to pry. The following day Andrea had called back and said everything was okay, that they had worked it out.

It was always like that after a bad fight. Andrea would threaten to leave, and Brandon would promise to change. What had just happened upstairs seemed different, though.

Love wasn't supposed to hurt, she thought. Brandon used to tell everyone about his beautiful wife and wonderful kids. What happened to the man who used to kiss her forehead and dote on her? So many of their friends thought they made a beautiful couple, Barbie and Ken, they called them. Friends could see how similar they were—independent and strong willed, athletically competitive but supportive of each other. They both loved the outdoors, country music, and NASCAR. They liked to drive to

Charlotte for the Sunday races, and they rooted for Dale Earnhardt. When he died in a crash, they were so devastated that they missed church that Sunday night. Now they weren't even going to church.

"This is it, Mom. I'm done. I'm not going to live like this. When he gets better, I'm getting a divorce. If he doesn't move out, I'm coming home."

They talked for an hour. When Andrea hung up, she stayed on the porch. It was dark now and much cooler. The kids were inside.

She tried to think back to better times, like the Special Forces winter formal they'd gone to at Fort Campbell a few years before. That night she wore a low-cut green velvet dress. Her hair was short and spiky, like Faith Hill's. Brandon loved that country music star and thought Andrea resembled her. When Faith cut her hair, Brandon asked Andrea to do the same. Brandon had been the only enlisted soldier on his team wearing dress blues to the dance; the rest were in their greens. His buddies joked with Brandon about being all show. They didn't want to buy the expensive formal uniform. But there was no doubt about it, Brandon looked sharp.

And she had been so proud to be there with him. She watched him talk with Special Forces living legends, officers like retired Colonel Aaron Bank and retired Lieutenant General William Yarborough. Brandon chatted easily with the elderly men as if he knew them, and Andrea could only watch admiringly.

What had happened to the husband she looked up to?

Later that night Andrea went upstairs and crawled into bed. It took every bit of willpower she had to get in next to Brandon. Like two wounded animals, they lay there in the dark. Neither spoke. And although her presence was an olive branch, her body was rigid.

She had made up her mind. She was leaving Brandon.

PART THREE

✦ ✦ ✦

RESOLUTION
SUMMER 2002

CHAPTER SEVENTEEN

B y May 2002 spring was fading fast, like the dying jonquils that blanketed Fayetteville's flower beds. Summer always came too early in Fayetteville, and the coming months would be particularly brutal, with a punishing drought. There would be other surprises, too.

Even as *Time* magazine put Saddam Hussein on its cover, with the tag line "The Sinister World of Saddam," I was busy reporting on an upcoming summer deployment of three thousand 82nd Airborne Division soldiers to Afghanistan. Leaders were telling soldiers to stay "mission focused," to be mentally and physically ready for whatever might come. Not an easy thing if your kid is having trouble in school, your spouse is grumbling about not enough quality time with you, your car needs three thousand dollars in repairs, and your in-laws are coming for a week. Everyone has a life outside the mission, and tensions typically rise before a major deployment. Soldiers have told me the worst part is waiting to leave, without knowing the exact date of departure or how long they will be gone.

Lengthy deployments were always big news, but looking back, I see that I had no idea of the future events that would put a chill on the Fayetteville heat. At Fort Bragg, May started off routinely enough. It was the season of endings and the anticipation of new beginnings as tours wound down and families geared up for PCS (permanent change of station) moves to new Army posts. Their life—now memories in transit—would be packed off on moving trucks alongside the dining room set and the

Corning Ware. But not everything can be tidily packed up and shipped off; the human condition is a more fragile thing.

For Andrea Lynne her refrain, "Home is where the Army sends us," no longer applied, but the Army still echoed in everything she did. Delores wondered if she could ever return to her old Army life, which seemed meaningless now, and Rita would deal with the biggest curveball the Army had thrown her yet. By May these three women were each coming to grips with their own predicaments, trying to resolve their crises within the institution that defined their lives in so many ways. Would they cut ties? Or forge forward "as the Army goes rolling along." The fourth wife, Andrea, had already made up her mind to set herself apart. She was planning to leave her husband. Of all the wives, she was distancing herself the most from the Army's orbit, defiantly at times. Ironically the Army would have the strongest impact on her fate.

More than a year after her husband's death, Andrea Lynne was still subject to the scrutiny and expectations that confront every Army wife, and officers' spouses in particular. From kitchen cleanliness to wardrobes to relationships with others, what these women do reflects on their husbands, and therefore on the Army itself. That Rennie Cory was no longer a visible presence at Bragg was irrelevant when it came to his widow, who could only draw on inner strength and fortitude when it came time to defining her future.

At Terry Sandford High, students streamed out the main doors of the school and into the afternoon May sunlight. Andrea Lynne left her motor running as she waited behind a line of cars, all parents picking up their kids. Her mind was on a difficult conversation she was going to have to have with little Rennie.

Her seventeen-year-old son seemed to be having trouble adjusting. He played sad music constantly, especially the CDs his father had loved. He wore his father's clothes and shoes, and when Andrea Lynne was depressed, he cried with her. He was also spending a lot of time at Bragg with his friends, staying overnight in their quarters in Normandy or working at his job at the golf course there. Andrea Lynne thought the time in his old environment would help her son heal, but that wasn't the way everyone saw it.

One general's wife had been questioning little Rennie's presence on post. And according to a rumor going around the PTA, Andrea Lynne was soon to be married. *Don't feel sorry for her. She's already engaged,* one wife who served on the board told others. Andrea Lynne heard about it the way she heard about everything: through the wives' network. And a friend had recently informed Andrea Lynne that a colonel was spreading rumors about her and Roland: *She doesn't miss Rennie. She's got a live-in lover,* the officer had told Andrea Lynne's friend. That was why little Rennie was so upset. The colonel had said he'd reprimand her himself.

It was too much for Andrea Lynne. For someone to question her son and criticize Roland infuriated her. She knew that it didn't take much to start the rumor mill at Bragg, and she was an easy target.

She'd had suitors since Rennie's death, including a married officer, an out-of-town newspaper photographer, an artist in Raleigh, even one of Rennie's former lieutenants in the battalion, a thirty-year-old who was now a Special Forces captain.

She'd run into the captain one Saturday evening the previous fall when her college roommate was visiting. Andrea Lynne had been feeling low, and to cheer her up they went out to Cross Creek Brewery and then on to a dance club, It'z. The captain pursued her, and he was so physically attractive that the thought of actually going out with a captain caught her off guard. It was daring and inappropriate—but tempting.

They'd kissed, but the courtship ended before it ever got started, with the captain's phone call on Monday afternoon.

"I can't date you," he told her.

"Oh," Andrea Lynne responded, rather shocked. "Okay. Well, I suppose I should ask you what changed your mind?"

He went through a litany of reasons: marriage, children, age. All things that hadn't come up two days earlier.

Then he got to the real reason: "Andrea, you know a lot of important people. If they decide that it's not right for you to be dating me, then it might hurt my career."

"What?" she said.

"Well, you are good friends with a lot of people—everyone, in fact—on Bragg. I don't know what I was thinking."

"Well, I don't know what you are thinking now," Andrea Lynne said. "It doesn't matter anyway. This is a silly conversation. We are not going to go out, but even if we did, who would care?"

"Look, I was talking to friends today," the captain said, "and people already know that we were at It'z. They know who you are, and the word is not to go near you. Don't you know that?"

"Who said that?"

"Nobody said anything. I just think I should think about my future. I'm sorry. But it's better this way."

Andrea Lynne paused for a second, baffled by the turnaround but determined not to let it faze her. "Absolutely. I hope you do well. Goodbye." And she hung up.

She was a grown woman. It bothered her that the Bragg mafia would try to control her personal life. All because she wasn't "behaving" as an Army widow should, that her life wasn't what people would expect. As Mrs. Rennie M. Cory Jr., she had been the wife, mother, friend, homemaker, and, as she saw it, coleader with her husband in the military. As Rennie Cory's widow, she could have been expected—before Rennie died, she, too, would have expected herself—to do volunteer work and be content with Rennie's memory.

She could have continued to pursue all the things that gave her joy, cultivating her garden, caring for her children, painting and listening to music, captivating her secret admirers. Yes, she still wanted admiration, she admitted that. What she never counted on, what no one outside could have known, was that Rennie had become so much a part of her that when he died, a lot of her went into the earth with him. She had found out over the last few months that she needed some other men to get through the days, to figure herself out, to understand her relationship with Rennie, and to determine how she would go on from here.

"Know yourself, know who you are"—hadn't she always told her young Army wives that? Now she had to apply her advice to her own shattered life. Once she was the perfectly dressed and made-up woman, with manicured nails, freshly glossed lips, and hair expertly arranged, the one who helped all the others, who e-mailed and called them and sent the little card or gift. That was no longer who she was. She chafed at being "expected" to play any role. No matter what people thought.

L ittle Rennie got into the car. Halfway home Andrea Lynne gingerly raised what was on her mind.

"You know, Rennie, we're still a family. And a family protects each other. What happens within the walls of our home is private. It belongs to us." Her son remained silent.

"Believe it or not, Rennie, some people are going to think badly of me no matter what I do. It doesn't matter that I'm a widow. If I wear black, they'll say, 'Oh, she's taking it too hard.' If I wear bright clothes, they'll say, 'She must not remember what happened to her husband.' If I work, they'll say, 'She needs to be with her kids.' If I don't, they'll say, 'She needs to get on with her own life.' If they see me with anyone, they'll say, 'Oh, she's dating already!' even if I'm just friends with that person. If they see me laugh or having dinner out, they'll assume I am not grieving anymore."

She looked over at her son as they waited at a stoplight on Ramsey Street. "Rennie, has anyone said anything to you about me?"

"No, ma'am," he said, looking straight ahead.

Andrea Lynne knew he would never tell her, never hurt her. Little Rennie constantly reminded her of his father. Her love for her son was almost painful.

"Rennie, do you understand who Roland is?"

"He's a friend of Dad's," he said, acting bored.

"And mine," Andrea Lynne chimed in. "But do you understand who he is? Roland knew your dad a very long time. Daddy and Roland were like you and Andrew—boyhood friends. Like brothers. Better than brothers because they held on to a bond without a family connecting them. They lived together in college, and Roland adored your father.

"When Daddy got orders for Vietnam, Roland almost lost his life in a head-on collision that same month. He didn't tell anyone. Not even his mother. For six months he recovered by himself. When he finally called, Daddy was already gone to Vietnam. Later he said that there must have been some reason he survived. You know, Roland has very few friends. He never had children of his own. Dad had us, a family that needed him.

Roland came to help us for Dad." Andrea Lynne paused. "But he stayed to help us for us."

She pulled into the driveway and looked over at her son again. "That's who Roland is."

They walked inside, and Andrea Lynne followed her son upstairs into his room. "Is there anything else?" she asked.

"No," he blurted out, visibly upset, "but you can never marry." Little Rennie broke down in tears.

"I don't want to be anyone else's wife," she said. "I was Daddy's wife. No one can take your dad's place. You know that." She pulled him close to her again.

"Now listen to me. You have a girlfriend, right?"

"Yeah," he mumbled.

"Do you spend time with her on the weekends after work?"

"Sometimes."

"Okay," she said. "Do you like to hold her hand?"

"*Mom,*" he whined.

"Hold on—and maybe you might want to kiss her once in a while—"

"*Mom!*" he said again, pulling away.

"Okay, well, you just want to spend time with her, to have fun, to feel better, maybe, and that's it, right? Well, that's how I feel about Roland."

Rennie looked at her, and she knew they understood each other.

"Now, I need to ask you something. Did anyone ever ask you about my relationship with Roland?"

"No," he said hesitantly.

"Well, anyone who does is not my friend and not yours either. Because whatever impression they may have is wrong. It's none of their business, and they should not be discussing it with my children."

He nodded, with his eyes locked on her.

"I'm going to remind you, what happens within this family is private. Even the simplest things. You would be surprised at what people make of the most innocent scenarios. If I weren't a widow, no one would think twice. But I'm just learning!"

As Andrea Lynne walked down the stairs she couldn't help running the conversation over and over in her mind. She had never explained her relationship with Roland to anyone, not even her girlfriends. She didn't really understand it herself.

During the winter Roland had played a big role in her survival. He seemed different from other men she'd met. He didn't compliment her on her physical beauty or flirt with her. She knew he was looking out for her, and a part of her wondered if their friendship could or should develop into something more. She was not looking for another Rennie. What he had done for her only Rennie could do, and she didn't need that anymore. She had new wounds, blanks spaces that were gouged out from grief and heartache, and she needed someone who could fill those.

On an evening when Andrea Lynne had been especially depressed, she asked Roland if they could talk. "But not in the kitchen tonight," she said. "On the couch."

She wanted to sit down and relax. Her legs hurt from standing, and she didn't want to perch on a stool. She turned the lights off in the kitchen and carried a candle into the family room. They had never sat on the couch together before. She put in a Leon Russell CD, music Rennie had liked. Andrea Lynne sat with her legs crossed, a cup of hot tea, laced with Jack Daniels and honey, in her hand. Roland said nothing, till she broke the silence.

"I'm depending far too much on you, Roland. I call you over every decision that I make, and it's bothering me. You're going to get tired of that."

"No, I won't. I'm not here out of friendship for Rennie," he said. "Oh, in the beginning, I came because of Rennie, but I wouldn't have stayed this long if it weren't for you. As long as I can help you, I will. I'm your friend."

Andrea Lynne nodded, though she didn't really understand the words. Men don't befriend women. They just don't. And if Roland could, then what's wrong with me? Am I unattractive? It just didn't make sense to her.

She was so tired. It seemed she never slept. She looked terrible.

Andrea Lynne was wearing black pajama sweatpants and a black tank. No bra, no panties. She had showered but had no makeup on, and her hair had dried into ringlets. Her eyes felt papery from crying too much. She sat back and listened to the music. She found herself edging toward Roland but quickly stopped.

"It's odd that I have so much difficulty sleeping," she said, "and yet, whenever you drive me anywhere, I sleep in your car. Even for fifteen minutes I can fall fast asleep."

They were quiet again. After a minute she asked, "Roland, would you mind if I leaned against you?"

She placed her head against his arm. "If I could just stay by you for a little while, I might be better. . . ." Her voice trailed off. They stayed like that, listening to the CD. Then she said, "I just want you to know how much your friendship has meant to me." She sat up and slowly moved her face closer to his. Most people found Roland intimidating, but she wasn't afraid of him. He had a big heart.

Andrea Lynne wanted to tell him something, but she didn't know what. She was operating by instinct now, and she almost panicked. But Roland came closer, too. He closed his eyes, and their lips met. His hands came from somewhere, reached under her arms, and pulled her on top of him. He kissed her more forcefully now, although his lips were softer than she would have guessed.

She never kissed anyone like this before. He was so patient, tender, and unassuming. She wanted to kiss him all night. When she finally moved back, he pulled her to him again and held her close. His hands caressed her back under her clothes. He felt her waist and rib cage as though he were measuring her. As Roland kissed her again, she hesitated. He stopped and looked at her. "I will never leave you," he said in a clear voice.

Andrea Lynne's chin dropped, and he lifted it with his right hand. "Listen to me, I am not going anywhere. I am staying with you. I will not leave you."

I will not leave you. The words brought her up short and echoed in her head. They were the same words Rennie had always used, the very ones she had repeated when she first heard the news of his death: "Rennie would never leave me."

CHAPTER EIGHTEEN

By June soldiers were popping their malaria pills, buying extra gear, and tooling around Fayetteville wearing their newly issued tan desert uniforms and matching boots, a sure sign of upcoming six-month deployments to Afghanistan. But Special Forces soldiers, who often grew beards and wore the traditional garb of the Afghans, had been quietly coming and going for months. At the beginning of the second week of June, a Green Beret came home without his team to work out some marital issues. Instead, he shot his wife in the head and then turned the gun on himself. Few details were reported, and the murder-suicide received minimal publicity, partly because no one wanted to talk about the case—not the family, not the police, especially not the Special Forces. What I have learned since has never been reported and makes this tragedy a cautionary tale. Gossip spreads quickly in the compact neighborhoods on Army posts. This time it may have been deadly.

Sergeant First Class Rigoberto Nieves, of the 3rd Special Forces Group, had been in Afghanistan when he asked his superiors if he could return home for a few days to deal with his marital problems. He wasn't busy anyway, he griped, just sweating in the hundred-plus-degree heat, sitting around and feeling depressed. His wife, Teresa, wanted a separation, and Rigoberto was eager to confront her with a rumor he'd heard.

Teresa was a pretty, petite, twenty-eight-year-old nursing student. Of Mexican descent, she had long, highlighted brown hair, pretty skin, and big brown eyes. She was quiet and a good mother to the couple's six-year-old daughter, Brianna, certainly not one to go out with a group of friends, though one woman from their old neighborhood used to come by the house uninvited. Teresa didn't care much for her or her visits.

The couple had lived on post until May 1, when they bought a four-bedroom house for $157,500 in the northern part of Fayetteville, east of Fort Bragg. Since Rigoberto was deployed, Teresa's family helped her get settled in. The Green Beret felt bad about not being there.

Rigoberto's parents were Puerto Rican, and he had grown up in the Bronx. He was tall, 6 feet 1 inches, and well built, with dark brown eyes under full bushy eyebrows, and a thin, pointed nose. At eighteen he had joined the Army and now, at age thirty-two, planned to make it a career. In six years he'd be eligible for retirement.

Serious and strict by nature—with a strong work ethic that stemmed from delivering newspapers and cleaning offices as a kid—he was well liked by his Special Forces A team. After an assignment to Germany, Rigoberto was stationed in Fayetteville in the summer of 1994, where he met and married Teresa. Her dad had retired from the Army, so she was no stranger to Army life.

Rigoberto got his leave. He arrived home from Afghanistan on Sunday, June 9, while Teresa's sisters and some other relatives were visiting. On Tuesday he went out shopping and bought some T-shirts, met a few of his new neighbors, and then went back to post to pick up some clothes that friends had kept for him. He left Brianna playing with her cousins.

I learned that while he was on Bragg, he bumped into the woman Teresa had never liked, who told Rigoberto his wife had been fooling around. By the time he got home, Teresa was back from nursing school, too. He went upstairs to see her and never came back down. Around 11:00 P.M. Brianna wanted to go to bed, but her parents' bedroom door was locked. Concerned, one of Teresa's sisters tried calling her on her cell phone, but there was no answer. When the police arrived, they found both bodies in the master bathroom. Three hours earlier Rigoberto had shot Teresa in the head with a .40-caliber gun, then put a bullet in his own head as well.

The news had hit the papers, then quietly faded away.

Several weeks later, on a Friday morning in early July, Andrea Floyd had been on the road several hours when she turned her van around and headed back to Stedman. She was taking the kids to Ohio to her mom's for three weeks of summer vacation. Ever since Andrea had told Brandon she wanted a divorce earlier that week, it had been unbearably tense between them. Brandon had to leave early in the week for Washington, D.C., so Andrea was driving the kids to Ohio by herself. Three hours into her trip, Brandon called her on the cell phone and insisted she come back to get him.

"Let's use the trip as a chance to talk things out," he told her. "Plus I've hardly had any time with the kids; now I'm going away again for a couple weeks. I'm not gonna get to see the kids. . . . Please. I don't want to leave without us talking about this. If you care about me at all, you'll come back."

Partly out of guilt, Andrea turned around. She *had* just asked him for a divorce, and she knew how much he meant to the children. But she also realized he knew just how to play her. Isn't that why she had stayed around for this long? Her twelve-hour trip was now extended by several more hours, and she was in a foul mood.

Andrea used the cell phone to call her older sister, Angie. "I'm gonna be later than planned," she said. "Brandon decided he wanted to come, so I'm getting a slower start. And he insisted on bringing the dog." Brandon had a new young Lab. Even though her mom already had a house full of pets, he didn't want to leave the puppy behind. Andrea didn't want to say too much in front of the kids.

"What the hell are you thinking, going back to get him?" Angie asked, irritated. Andrea was supposed to get in at 6:00 P.M. Now she wouldn't arrive until midnight. "That's so typical of him being an ass. There's no way in hell I'd turn around," Angie said.

"I know. He wanted to come so we could talk things out. But I'm still going to go through with everything."

"I'll believe it when I see it," Angie said. Andrea had told her sister she was leaving Brandon many times before, but every time she went back to him. Sometimes she'd joke, "I wish he would just cheat on me, then I could leave."

Two weeks earlier Andrea had talked to her sister, who'd been through a divorce herself, about what she should ask for in a settlement. "What do you think is fair?"

"Anything that pertains to you and the children."

"Should I ask for the computer?"

"Does Harlee use it to do her homework?"

"Yes."

"Then you should take it. You'll get child support for the kids, but you'll need to figure out what you need to set up a home."

Angie wondered if Andrea would really go through with it. Each time Andrea had threatened to walk out, Brandon would ask for forgiveness. It had been up and down like that for years. In 1996, when Andrea had actually filed for divorce, she told her sister, "I can't take it anymore; I'm done." Then once again Brandon promised he would change, and Andrea called it off.

"Ya know, he promised he would treat me better," she'd said to Angie that time. A friend of Brandon's had taken him aside and told him, "You've got a great wife here; you need to get your act together." And he did. Brandon seemed to realize he had crossed some line, that Andrea was truly fed up. Frustrated, scared, and worried that he might lose her, he came to a defining time in their marriage, and did whatever he could to win her back. Shortly after they decided to stay together, Andrea became pregnant with BJ, their middle child.

Now, she was sitting next to Brandon in silence, back on the road to Ohio. Andrea kept the radio on to fill the void. "A Fort Bragg soldier has been charged with murder, after firefighters found the burned body of his wife dead in the bedroom of her Rim Road home Tuesday. . . ."

Andrea listened closely. Like a schoolteacher, coach, or police officer, a soldier caught in a scandal was always big news. The disgrace caught people's attention. Plus the part about a burned body made it sound especially horrific. It was a heinous crime, even worse because it was the second murder Andrea had heard about in a few weeks.

Still on the road, Andrea pulled out her cell phone and called her mother. "Mom, I'm going to be later than usual," she said in a tongue-in-cheek sort of way. "Brandon decided he wanted to see the family."

Brandon's knee was still fragile, but he wasn't about to tell that to any-one. As long as he could perform his duties and was competitive, that's all that mattered. After being at home for a couple of months, he had gotten so stir crazy that he would put on his leg brace and drive his four-wheeler around the property. Finally he had gone back to work in May and was away for much of the month.

Andrea had hurt her ankle playing softball in April and had to wear a leg brace herself. Her friends teased her that she "had to keep up with Bran-don." At home it was no joking matter. When she had asked Brandon to take her to the hospital, Brandon reminded her how she had blamed him for hurting his knee. "Drive yourself there, bitch," he told her. "You did it to yourself, take yourself." He wasn't happy that she was on the team in the first place. She had enough to do.

They arrived in Alliance after dark, the atmosphere between them so tense it was immediately obvious to Andrea's mother. Although they were exhausted, the couple stayed for just two hours, kissed the children good-bye, then headed back to North Carolina so Brandon could leave the next day. They hardly spoke the entire way. Andrea was preoccupied, thinking back to the previous weekend.

Brandon had been gone again. When Andrea had to work late and close the store, she asked Joanne if she would watch the kids overnight. As the athletic footwear manager, Andrea was also an assistant manager for the store. That meant she often closed the store at nine-thirty in the eve-ning and left at ten. She'd seen the Stricklands only three times since mov-ing to Stedman. When the couple were in town, they'd drop by the store to say hello.

That Sunday Andrea drove back to Cameron and met Joanne and the kids at church. It felt good to be back, but odd, too. So much had hap-pened since they'd moved away from the town. Things seemed simpler then, purer. She listened as Mark Strickland finished his sermon. "Now I'd like to extend an invitation for anybody who wants to pray to come forward to invite Christ into your heart. If you already know the Lord and are burdened and need help, come forward."

Andrea and several others stood up and walked to the front. Mark asked if anyone would like him to join in prayer, and Andrea, who was kneeling, nodded yes.

"I feel like I'm not as close to the Lord as I once was," she said.

Andrea hardly ever cried, but now the tears streamed down her face. "I had a relationship with the Lord," she went on, "and I need to rededicate my life to Christ. I haven't been in church like I should be; I'm not happy that the kids haven't been going. Since I left here I haven't found a church where I fit in. I'm under a lot of stress. Pray that I can find peace."

Mark leaned over her and prayed for her to recommit to the Lord. Andrea felt better and gave Mark a hug.

"I appreciate it," she said. "You'll always be my pastor."

After church Joanne and Andrea went to Food Lion for groceries. Since Joanne had watched the kids, Andrea paid for the pork chops. She tried hard to be peppy.

But as they waited in line Joanne couldn't help asking, "Is everything okay?"

"Yeah, everything's okay."

Joanne didn't push it. Andrea and the kids stayed for dinner, then left as the Stricklands were getting ready for Sunday-night prayer service.

That was a week ago. Now on the way back to Stedman, she blocked out Brandon sitting next to her. Andrea kept her eyes on the road, but her mind was elsewhere.

She'd met another man.

CHAPTER NINETEEN

Every Fourth of July thirty thousand people gather on Fort Bragg's Main Post Parade Field for a day of relaxation and fun. In 2002, the FBI wanted to make sure the explosions remained the fireworks variety. The bureau had warned local and state law enforcement officials throughout the country of possible terrorist attacks. Fort Bragg took its own precautions, inspecting vehicles entering post and randomly searching bags and coolers along the parade field. The summer's drought made Fayetteville feel like a preheated oven, and by 1:00 P.M. the temperature had hit ninety degrees. It would climb another five as the afternoon progressed.

Army wife Marilyn Styles-Griffin spent the long holiday moving into the fifteen-thousand-dollar trailer she had rented. It was a first step for the thirty-two-year-old-woman, who was starting a new life apart from her estranged husband, Sergeant Cedric Griffin. Less than a week later, Marilyn was dead, and her new home had been swallowed up in flames. Soon after her husband was charged with her murder.

Ever since I first heard the details of the attack, I've wondered what could have caused such violence. Was it rage? Madness? What could possibly lead to such a brutal act? New details that I have uncovered make clear that the attack was even more vicious than had first been reported.

Marilyn, an attractive black woman, had separated from her twenty-eight-year-old husband in May. It was the third time during their eight-year marriage that she had tried to break away. Her two daughters, six-year-old Breaunna and two-year-old Kiana, were the children of other men with whom she had had relationships while the couple was separated.

By the time Marilyn had moved into her trailer, things were finally coming together for her: She had recently gotten a job as a security guard, working at a chicken-processing plant in the next county. And now she had her own place. It wasn't much, but it was hers, one that she hoped her estranged husband wouldn't find.

Cedric Griffin, a cook with the 37th Engineer Battalion, worked at the post commissary preparing ready-made meals. Marilyn had threatened to tell his supervisors that he had gotten a female subordinate pregnant. On Monday evening, July 8, he stopped by for a visit.

Marilyn opened the door. She stood five feet eight inches tall, 164 pounds, her feet were bare with toenails painted bright red, the same color she had painted her daughters'. She wore her hair in a ponytail and had on a T-shirt and shorts. A heart-shaped tattoo with the name "Dale" was visible on her right outer calf.

Cedric walked in, and three hours later Marilyn was dead. She had been stabbed with a kitchen knife more than seventy times, and her body set on fire. Many of her wounds were shallow half-inch punctures. But deeper gashes had punctured her liver, aorta, and jugular vein and fractured some ribs. She eventually died of internal bleeding, but I learned she had been alive for a short while after she was set on fire. Firefighters found her charred body under a pile of bed sheets, which had been lit. Part of a blue plastic milk crate had melted into her hair.

Investigators told me there easily could have been three murders that night. When Cedric Griffin ran from the trailer, Marilyn's two little girls were asleep in the bedroom they shared at the opposite end of the trailer. Marilyn had taught her oldest what to do if she ever heard the smoke alarm go off: Grab your sister and run for help. When Breaunna heard the blaring noise at 2:00 A.M., she got up and sped down the hall to her mother's bedroom. The door to the bedroom was shut and too hot for her to open, so she ran back to her bedroom, took her two-year-old sister by the hand, and went next door to a neighbor's.

By Tuesday evening Cedric Griffin was in handcuffs, charged with first-degree murder, two counts of attempted first-degree murder, and first-degree arson. He hung his head and shuffled his lanky frame past the TV cameras as homicide detectives from the sheriff's department brought him before the magistrate in the basement of the Cumberland County Law Enforcement Center. Soldiers all over Fayetteville cringed when they saw what Griffin was wearing—a gray PT T-shirt with the word ARMY in three-inch black letters stamped across the front.

Just a few days earlier, in Carolina heat unparalleled for its humidity, thousands of people were moving along Fort Bragg's Main Post Parade Field like ants over a slice of Wonder Bread. They had gathered for the post's annual Fourth of July celebration, which was topped off each year at precisely 9:45 in the evening with fireworks and the 1812 Overture with enough cannon blasts, compliments of the corps artillery, to rattle the general's bedroom windows. The festivities started at three o'clock with live bands, carnival games, kiddy rides, and food stands selling everything from bratwurst and beer to funnel cakes and fluorescent glow-in-the-dark necklaces. Some families staked out their turf with a blanket when the grass was still cool with morning dew, but the lucky ones could watch the festivities from their front porches.

The Odoms had arrived an hour ago. As they maneuvered their way through the throngs of people, Brian's cell phone rang. (They could finally afford one.) He knew before he answered who the caller would be and what he would have to say. Brian had told Rita a few days ago that she should be prepared for him to deploy to Afghanistan on short notice. What he didn't tell her was that his bags had been packed for weeks. He didn't want to break any rules, but as the deployment window drew closer, he didn't want to catch his wife off guard either. Instead it was Brian who was caught off guard. He had thought the call would come after the holiday weekend.

"We're leaving tomorrow," his squad leader said. "Make sure you have everything. Be ready to leave in the morning." Brian put the cell phone back in his pocket and looked into Rita's eyes.

"I'm leaving tomorrow. Do you want to stay or go?" Brian watched the color drain from his wife's face. It was as if all the sounds around them had been muted.

"I'm not in the mood to stay," was all Rita could say. Even before the Army had entered her world, Rita knew that life wasn't fair. "Play with the hand you are dealt" was her motto. If life gives you lemons, squirt someone with juice. And she had learned what every Army wife knew to be true: Believe it when you see it. For Rita that meant not when signed orders arrived or a phone call came, but when her husband was back in her arms, or left.

She believed it now. The moment she had been dreading for almost two years had arrived. At least Brian had been there to celebrate their second wedding anniversary the day before. The Odoms headed home. Instead of watching the fireworks at Bragg, the couple lit sparklers for the boys in their front yard.

The next morning Rita stood near Gela Street, where the 1st Battalion of the 505th Parachute Infantry Regiment had five sets of three-story beige concrete barracks, and watched Brian and the other soldiers lay out their weapons and rucksacks on the rocks.

The "rocks" is the name given to what looks like a huge oblong sandbox, filled with stones, where soldiers line up for formation. The barracks and the battalion headquarters have a good location, across from the 82nd's parade field on Ardennes Street. The disadvantage is that the path from the Division headquarters to Ardennes Street cuts through the battalion area. Every morning, the 82nd's commanding general and his command group jog by and see what is happening. Some days that can be a positive thing, others not, but the battalion got a lot of visibility just by coincidence.

Brian wore his desert camouflage uniform and his rank of sergeant, which he had finally pinned on the previous January. The promotion meant more responsibility and $163 a month more in pay.

Suddenly the platoon sergeant announced, "We're not going today, we're going tomorrow." The soldiers let out a collective groan.

Departure times and dates are notorious for getting scratched, delayed, rescheduled, and then changed again, due to everything from bad weather to maintenance problems. Such changes rattle the soldiers and their families. It is like waiting for your execution, then having a couple hours' reprieve.

Brian had already said good-bye to Rita and the boys and sent them on their way. He would have to call Rita's school and have someone track her down so she could pick him up.

When she arrived, he wasn't sure what to say. Finally he mumbled a less-than-convincing, "All right, the hard part is out of the way. It won't be as bad the second time."

That night Rita and Brian lay in bed, naked under a sheet, as was their nightly habit. Instead of making love, they held each other and cried. Rita just wanted to soak in as much of her husband's physical being as she could. What if he didn't come home? When he was gone, she wanted to be able to close her eyes and see him and smell him. They never did sleep that night, just lay in the dark whispering and holding each other and focusing on their favorite memory.

"Do you remember the night we met, Brian?" Rita said, her arms circling her husband's waist. "It was a night that seemed like nothing. But it was the moment that defined our lives. Look how far we've come. Who knew that a few years later we'd be holding each other like this?"

The following morning, a Saturday, Brian again laid out his equipment on the rocks and again said good-bye. And again the soldiers were told they weren't leaving for another day. Brian and Rita were at Taco Bell when his cell phone rang this time. His squad leader told him to come back. They were leaving that afternoon.

Back at the barracks one more time, Rita looked around at all the families grouped together near the picnic tables behind the flat-roofed buildings. Children ran after one another, and soldiers lined up their equipment and bags on the rocks.

Rita stood near Sherry, who was holding Tiffany's new baby. It was the first time Rita had seen Tiffany since she had flashed her backside at the guy at the Waffle House. Mandy had moved during the summer, and she had met Jenna only a few times at FRG meetings. The women started to catch up, but when the cattle cars lumbered to a stop and lined up on Ardennes, they broke off their conversations. They stared at the drivers as if they were ferrymen who had come to take their husbands across the river Styx. The cattle cars resembled windowless metal boxcars on wheels. Inside, soldiers burdened with rucksacks and rifles sat on wooden benches against the skin of the truck while others packed into the aisle. The trucks were an easy, albeit uncomfortable, way to transport large numbers of paratroopers wearing full battle rattle.

"Okay, the cattle cars are here," Rita said, sighing deeply. This time Brian really was leaving. Rita now knew what a soldier meant when he says, "The sooner I leave, the sooner I can come home." Three good-byes in two days had left her as emotionally dried up as her tears. Rita rounded up her sons and made her way over to Brian.

Brian looked down at the boys and gave each a hug. "Help your mama. Stay strong. You guys have to be the little men of the house. Don't be fixin' to get a free ride 'cause I'm not here," he added. "Your mama's softer than I am, but I'm coming back."

"Go kill the bad guys," said Johnathan, who was now four. He had been telling everyone he came in contact with, from store clerks to his day-care teachers, that his daddy was going to kill bad guys.

The chaplain had coached soldiers in what to say to their kids. Brian explained he was leaving so he could help their family and other families feel safe, and that it wasn't their fault he was going away. Rita showed the boys on the calendar how long their father would be away. "It's going to be a long time," she said.

"If daddy just comes home for my birthday," Johnathan piped up.

Brian turned to Rita. All their problems seemed trivial now. He wouldn't see her again until the following winter.

"Thank you for sticking by me and putting up with me," he said. It was one of those awkward moments where no words seemed to be the right ones.

"Stay safe and keep your head down," she said, her arms forming a wreath around his neck.

"Rita, we've been training a long time for something like this—"

"I know. Just be safe and come home to me."

"I will. Let's go to the car now, Rita. It's time to go."

The news crews were arriving, and Brian could tell that his superiors were antsy to have the families gone and their soldiers refocused.

"Rita, it's time."

Brian walked Rita and the kids to the car on Gela. Rita had parked in the B Lane, the yellow-lined middle strip of road designated for military vehicles. She had written Brian love notes and hidden them in his duf-fel bag.

"Look through your bag, but don't find them all at once," she told him.

Rita got in the car and rolled the window down and kissed Brian again.

"Can you call my mom and let her know I got off?" he asked. "Write me and send me pictures and don't forget to crank my truck once in a while."

Yes, she would do all those things.

"Be sweet, but not too sweet," Brian said. He always told Rita that. It was his pet saying, a way of telling her to be tough when she had to be.

"I'll be here when you get home," Rita said. Brian had told her a lot of the guys were worried about Jody moving in once they moved out.

"Are you sure you're going to be okay?" Brian asked.

"No, I'm not going to be okay, but nobody's gonna know I'm not okay."

How could you be when you were losing your right arm? Rita thought. As she watched Brian walk away, she realized how much she had come to rely on her husband. It took a certain level of trust to be depen-dent on somebody else. She had let Brian in, and it had taken away some of her personal power. I'm gonna have to get back in touch with the chick who didn't need anybody, she told herself.

Brian picked up his gear and headed for the cattle cars. He had wanted to join the Army ever since he watched the GI Joe cartoon as a kid. He never missed an episode. Now after five years in the Army, this was the moment he had been waiting for. It was like a surgeon practicing on cadavers for five years, then finally getting a chance to operate.

As much as he wanted to stay with Rita, he was excited to go on a real mission. All the guys in his platoon were ecstatic, euphoric almost. Like Brian, most of them came from rough backgrounds, and they took pride in the fact that they weren't preppy boys with Polo shirts and BMWs in high school. While a few had joined the Army for college money, most just wanted to be soldiers and go to war. And this mission, on the heels of 9/11, was a significant one.

Rita sat behind the wheel with tears leaving wet trails on her cheeks. He's gone. She started up her Ford Escort. We're going to get through this and come out the other side better. I won't fail. I'm not going to be weak.

Brian's going to come back to the same wife he left and to the life he left. Rita would make sure of that. He was going to be gone for seven months in a foreign country. Rita didn't want him coming home to another strange land.

As she turned onto Gruber Road she looked at her boys in her rearview mirror. "Okay, guys, now we start off on our big adventure."

Life didn't stop. Rita had to take an exam that afternoon. Soon she'd start her new job in the pharmacy at Highsmith-Rainey Memorial Hospital downtown. That night, after she put the boys to bed, she slipped one of Brian's T-shirts over his pillow and placed her own head against it. She was experiencing what she had been so afraid of for the past two years, utter aloneness. In the middle of the night, Rita got up to check on the kids and found Johnathan asleep with his blanket and teddy bear next to the front door. She knew how he felt.

One day before class, a few days after Brian left, Rita found herself doing what she usually did, leaning over her classmate Patti's shoulder to look at the newspaper. Reading the paper before class was Patti's ritual, and she hated it when Rita read along over her shoulder. She good-naturedly swatted her friend away, but Rita kept reading about the stabbing death of a Fort Bragg Army wife. Hadn't another Army wife died the previous month, also at the hands of her husband?

Rita began to worry, not that Brian would one day snap and kill them all, but about what the guy next door might do. If a GI could kill the woman whom he had pledged before God and family to love, honor, and cherish, then what was to stop him from turning on a neighbor he barely knew? She found herself a little more wary of her surroundings, eyeing the soldiers that were everywhere in Fayetteville and wondering, Is he a killer? . . . I wonder what it would take to make him break and kill someone close to him? . . . He doesn't look like he has it in him. . . . Did those dead women think the same thing about their husbands?

The newspaper accounts also made Rita realize how glad she was that she had ended her earlier marriage. That man never served in the military, but there were many emotional firestorms. It didn't take much to set off a furious quarrel with him: not having his dinner ready on time, refusing to have sex with him, hugging her friends, or, once, smiling too much at a child's birthday party. She grew to dread the hour when he would come home from work.

Yet soldiers are trained to kill their enemy. What might they do, Rita wondered, if they suddenly felt, for whatever reason, that their *wives* were their enemies? Get a divorce? Punch the wall? Get drunk? Forgive? Move on? Or kill? Soldiers are not told that it is okay to have a problem. In fact, when it came to teaching soldiers how to live outside the Army, Rita believed the United States military was sorely lacking.

I have my own thoughts on these matters. Why blame the Army for every marital problem in the military? Sure, the Army affects every aspect of the lives of soldiers and their families, but there's still a reasonable expectation that people are responsible for their own actions. Although the Army has room for improvement when it comes to helping its men and women deal with life outside the Army—including how to interact with loved ones—recently the Army has done more than most civilian corporations to help its people and their families cope with personal problems and crises. The gesture is not altruistic, though. The Army wants its soldiers mission focused, and spouses and families can get in the way of that. The best way to insure that a soldier's attention isn't diverted is to help him have a happy, peaceful home life. Do that, and the Army benefits with an undistracted, productive soldier—or so the theory goes.

The first time this was explained to me, I was shocked by the coldness of it all. I had thought all the outreach programs and resources were there for benevolent reasons. When I questioned it, I got this response from an officer: "This isn't the Salvation Army, Tanya. This is the U.S. Army. We train soldiers to fight our nation's wars and accomplish our nation's missions."

The Army has another stake in domestic affairs. Soldiers are extremely expensive to train. To cash in on the investment, it pays to take care of families. The Army has an internal saying: "The Army enlists soldiers, but reenlists families." Most soldiers are single when they join the Army. They marry and start families along the way. To get a soldier to continue serving past his initial enlistment, the family has to be on board, too.

Rita didn't know the murdered wives. She certainly didn't know if the couples were having problems. It wasn't uncommon for difficulties to arise if a husband was gone. She had seen for herself that some wives turn to the arms of another while their husbands are away. Hell, she thought, some wives turn to the arms of another while their husbands are still home. Her friends cheated because their husbands weren't around or they were emotionally unavailable or just because there were so many horny men to choose from in Fayetteville—or over the Internet.

A few weeks after Brian and Charlie left for Afghanistan, Rita's friend Sherry met someone in an Internet chat room called Hot or Not. His name was Jeff, and he lived in Atlanta, Sherry's hometown. She told him she was a single soldier at Fort Bragg and passed off a picture of a Russian mail-order-catalog bride as herself. Sherry was just having fun, she insisted, and she enjoyed the attention. She never thought it would go anywhere, but Rita could see it turning into something more. One night, as she prepared cubed steak, she gave Sherry a call.

"Hey, I'm cookin' with some grease tonight. Come over."

"I can't, Rita. Jeff is supposed to call." Sometimes when Rita telephoned in the middle of the day, Sherry would be asleep because she had been up all night online chatting with Jeff. When she did come over to Rita's, Sherry spent the time instant-messaging on Rita's computer or talking on her cell phone with Jeff.

One day Rita suggested that she and Sherry send their husbands care packages. Rita knew Charlie wasn't getting anything from his wife. As Rita sat on the floor in Sherry's apartment and placed Starbursts, Combos, Pringles, beef jerky, and bourbon-flavored cans of Copenhagen in a box, Sherry seemed to think Charlie had become a nuisance. Instead she called Jeff. When Rita encouraged Sherry to put a letter in the package, Sherry merely replied, "Why do I care if Brian's the one who gets all the mail?" Rita wrote Brian every day.

Rita realized her friend was hurt and lonely with Charlie gone, but an Internet fantasy affair was no way to deal with it.

Why couldn't Sherry be a strong enough woman to be okay? Rita wondered. Sure, Charlie was a bit dim, but no husband deserved this.

She persisted. "You're not being fair to Charlie. He's over there fighting. He could die. All you do is complain about him. Why did you even marry him?"

"We had so much potential," Sherry said. "I don't know what went wrong."

"Honey, nothing was ever right. You wanted him to be something he's not. What have I always told you? You can't marry a project. You don't go to Lowe's or Sears and go to the do-it-yourself section and pick out a husband. Why don't you get a divorce?"

Sherry always gave the same answer: "No."

Being married to Charlie took Sherry to where she wanted to go. She didn't have to work, she liked the Army lifestyle, and Charlie's family had money, at least enough to suit her needs. When the couple needed cash, her father-in-law wired money into their account. When Sherry got tired of lugging her laundry up steps, Charlie's family bought her a washer and dryer.

Women like Sherry are notorious in the barracks, where seasoned sergeants warn junior enlisted soldiers about gold-digging women out to deplete their bank accounts. Of course, twenty-year-old privates don't have much in their bank accounts to begin with, but that is beside the point. The moral is: Don't get suckered by the first piece of ass that comes along.

Meanwhile, six thousand miles away in Afghanistan, Brian and the guys in his platoon gathered outside around the burn barrel, the soldiers' version of the office watercooler. Wood was always burning in the fifty-five-gallon drum, and the men were supposed to burn all their mail so names and addresses wouldn't find their way into the hands of the Taliban, who could then send envelopes of anthrax to their loved ones. That was the Army's thinking, anyway. Brian didn't want to disobey an order, but he wasn't about to burn any of Rita's letters, so he kept them in a locked metal box.

Some guys' letters belonged in the burn barrel. Brian could always see it coming. Joe would be smoking and dragging his head.

"Man, what happened?" Brian and the other soldiers would ask.

His girlfriend, fiancée, wife—fill in the blank—had just dumped him.

And each soldier around the burn barrel would shake his head and take another drag on his cigarette. Damn females.

Oh, God, am I gonna get one of those letters? Brian worried to himself. What if she waits until I get home to dump me because she feels sorry for me being over here?

Stories about the home front spread through the platoon like dysentery. One wife in the platoon showed up to an FRG meeting in her pajamas, high on methamphetamines. Another contracted herpes, and a third was busy racking up three thousand dollars of debt. Another would come home to a wife three months pregnant.

Of course there is another side to all this—the wife's version of events, and it doesn't always mesh with the burn barrel brigade's. Sometimes a husband or boyfriend deploys after he's been a perpetual asshole. Back home, the wife or girlfriend thinks, Ya know, I'm not gonna put up with this shit anymore. And she writes a letter.

Sherry finally admitted to Rita that she loved Jeff, and she made plans to meet him at a bookstore and fess up—partly. She planned to tell Jeff she was married, but that picture she sent him, the one that didn't look all that much like her—well, that was because she had broken her nose and had surgery. Meanwhile she told Charlie she'd be visiting a gay cousin and flew out to Atlanta.

Once more Rita was torn between being loyal to her best friend and confiding in her husband. Charlie was one of Brian's soldiers, after all. The affair was weighing on her, and she couldn't keep secrets from her husband. I like Sherry, Rita thought, but I don't want to be associated with this.

One night when Brian called, she told him all that had happened. "What am I going to do?" she asked him. "I've avoided people like this. How am I supposed to be best friends with her?"

As disappointed as Rita was in Sherry, she was even more annoyed with herself for being a bad judge of character. "I can't believe she was weak enough to let the Army get to her," Rita said. "She behaved like everybody else."

"Just stay out of it," Brian counseled.

He was pissed, but he wasn't going to tell Charlie. What good would it do to let him know that his wife was a cheat when he was so far from home?

While Rita tried to distance herself from Sherry, she got acquainted with a woman named Ginger whose son went to Johnathan's day-care center and whose husband was stationed overseas for a year. The two boys were friends, and the mothers instantly hit it off. One afternoon Rita and Ginger exchanged phone numbers and made a date to take their boys out for lunch and a day of shopping at the Cross Creek Mall.

That weekend over pizza at the mall's food court, Rita decided to find out how Ginger felt about what some wives do when their husbands are away. Brian was so big into guilt by association.

"I have a boyfriend," Ginger said matter-of-factly.

"Oh, really? What about your husband?"

"Well, he's been gone all year."

"Oh, okay." Rita realized how naive she still was. She looked at her boys, who were laughing and playing with their food. She no longer felt like shopping. "Well, we need to go. Hurry up, guys. Finish eating. Mama's got things to do."

She never got together with Ginger again.

If Rita had wanted to cheat, she had lots of chances. One day when she was eating lunch and watching CNN in the hospital cafeteria, she commented about the news to a soldier in uniform who was sitting near her. The soldier responded by asking her out.

"Thanks, but I'm married," Rita said.

"Well, so am I. You're married, I'm married, so doesn't that kind of make us married?"

"That's original."

Everyone at work knew Brian was deployed, and every day a greasy-looking custodian gave Rita a Tootsie Roll. Once she asked him why. He told her, "I'm weaseling my way in, so when your husband comes back you won't want him."

"The only thing you're doing is weaseling your way into a hole. My husband would kill you," Rita shot back.

She had come a long way to reach this point, and she wasn't going to allow some sleazeball to shoot her down.

Since the Army wife murders, I have been asked a lot if I thought infidelity was higher in the military than among civilians. I doubt it, but I once had a conversation with a very candid retired Green Beret, who had done and seen quite a bit in that department. He didn't think infidelity was more prevalent in the military, but he made a valid point: Because of the lengthy separations, the Army provides plenty of opportunity for those with cheating on their minds.

CHAPTER TWENTY

Andrea Floyd had met Danny Wilson through a coworker at Dick's a month before, when she was out at the Palomino Club, a lively country-and-western dance club on Owen Drive. Danny shared Brandon's Southern accent and good-old-boy nature, but otherwise he couldn't have been more different from her husband. He was thirty, a year older than Andrea, and ran two low-end convenience stores. At six foot two, Danny weighed two hundred pounds, but had a slender build and a gentle manner. Brandon was meticulous in his appearance and exacting in attitude; Danny wore shell necklaces and had more of a Joe Six-pack outlook on life. Andrea found it refreshing. (Of course he never told her about his repeated run-ins with the law. He allegedly attempted credit-card fraud, made "unauthorized use of a conveyance," and "tampered with a motor vehicle.")

Andrea hadn't set out to meet someone else. It just happened. Perhaps now that she had actually decided to leave Brandon, she was more open and aware of the people—particularly the men—around her. Danny was so much fun, so sweet to her, and nice looking, too. It was easy for her to fall for him. She told him she was unhappy in her marriage. In fact she told him all about Brandon and her family. She liked being with him. She even liked helping him with his business. And she loved it when he handed her a wad of bills to pay for store items at Sam's Club.

Everyone thought they were just friends. In the beginning, that's all it was. She'd see him out at clubs or talk with him at company softball games. Soon she was going over to his house and crashing on his couch. After a while they were in each other's beds. They'd had sex for the first time earlier in the week.

The previous night they'd gone to the Palomino for Dollar Beer Night and met up with her coworkers, many of them from her softball team. The Palomino was a popular place to sit back with a beer and watch the social action. The club could have come right out of Nashville. On most nights of the week, the Palomino was filled with couples, some in matching outfits, two-stepping to the songs of Garth Brooks and Toby Keith. On Wednesdays the specials drew more than the usual cowboys, as soldiers who generally preferred heavy metal or hip-hop packed the place for the cheap longnecks. By the time Andrea and Danny arrived, the parking lot was already jammed with pickup trucks. Harleys lined the curb near the club's entrance. Inside near the front door, in the corner, soldiers tried their luck riding the mechanical bull at two bucks a shot. Women rode the bull, too, but usually at the lowest speed, so their movements resembled a sex act. That always drew a big crowd.

I've always thought of the Palomino as the kind of place where you leave your troubles at the glass doors. The windowless club and the country tunes provide a haven for people who needed a break from reality. Perhaps that is why Andrea allowed another man to come into her life.

Andrea enjoyed two-stepping. By her second Long Island iced tea, she and Danny were gliding along the dance floor, which was shaped like a wooden racetrack. Above them, a rhinestone saddle turned and twinkled like a disco ball. At the bar young men wearing Stetsons, boots, and plaid shirts tucked into tight, starched Wranglers stood in packs of five or more, holding longneck bottles and ogling every female who walked by.

Soldiers, especially those in the combat arms, like to call women "females," said in such a distinct way that "alien" could be easily substituted. Whenever I called or waited at Bragg to talk with someone, I was often referred to as the female on the phone or in the lobby, and in my interviews soldiers always referred to women other than their wives or mothers as females. Once on the phone, I overheard the soldier who took my call tell his boss, "Sir, there's a female lady on the phone for you." I took it as a compliment.

I remember one evening at the Palomino seeing a visibly pregnant female out on the dance floor holding a cigarette and swiveling her hips. The girl was having a grand time, and so were the two soldiers dancing with her. "Some guys go for pregnant females," a young GI standing near me told me, as matter-of-factly as if he were talking about redheads or blonds.

I was well aware of the saying soldiers had about the women in Fayetteville: "Females are either brought here or left here." In Andrea's case she may have been brought here, but she certainly wasn't going to be dumped here or treated like trash either.

Andrea downed her third Long Island iced tea. She had never been a drinker, and the alcohol went straight to her head. She had to be helped out of the club by Danny and a friend. She spent the night on Danny's couch, then early in the morning went into his room and woke him up to make love.

Although people at Dick's, including her boss, knew she planned on leaving Brandon as soon as he returned, no one knew about the affair, and the secret weighed on Andrea. God, what would the Stricklands think? She could never tell them, or her family.

Andrea had to admit she was troubled by what she was doing. She knew right from wrong. Her husband was away serving his country, and here she was with another man. That didn't look good. But, she'd ask herself, how could it be wrong or selfish for her to be happy? She had spent her whole married life appeasing her husband, trying to please him. Now it was her turn; she was ready to leave Brandon and the Army behind and start a new life.

She was tired of pretending everything was okay when it wasn't. She was never going to have a figure like Barbie or be the June Cleaver kind of mom and housewife her husband wanted her to be. With Brandon gone so much, she was finding out how much more she enjoyed life without him and his put-downs. She didn't need his shit. She could make it on her own. The new house had been her last attempt to make the marriage work. She was ready to give that up, too.

It was now the third Thursday in July, and Brandon was due home from Washington in four days. The kids were still in Ohio. Yesterday she had called her mother to make arrangements to pick them up. She would leave on Friday after work and drive all night. That's the way Andrea liked to travel. She'd arrive early Saturday morning, catch a few hours of sleep, then stay for the weekend. She could leave with the kids Sunday night and be back in Stedman before Brandon got home on Monday.

The conversation with her mother had put her in a good mood. She told Penny she was thinking of coming home for good.

"I'm going to see if I can get a transfer through Dick's. I still have to look into that. I'm going to have to give up the house."

"We'll make arrangements so you and the kids can stay with us," Penny said, talking on her cell phone from her city truck. She was a code-enforcement official and zoning inspector in Alliance. "Is everything else okay? How are you holding up?"

"I'm fine. Things are good."

"Just remember, verbal abuse is as bad as physical abuse, Andrea."

"I don't need a counselor, Mom. When he gets back from Washington, we're going to start the divorce proceedings."

"Okay, I'll see you when you get here. Be careful. Have a safe trip. I love you."

"I love you, too."

In truth, Andrea was torn. She loved her job in Fayetteville and didn't really want to leave it. Plus she wanted to see where her relationship with Danny would go. She had to take advantage of the time they had.

Thursday was her day off, and she spent it with him. She and Danny and his roommate went out four-wheeling in the afternoon. At 7:30 P.M. they were getting ready to watch TV when her cell phone rang. It was Brandon.

"Hey, it's me. I'm back. We got in earlier today; I've been trying to reach you. Where have you been?"

"Are you at the house?"

"You sound really thrilled. I've been here all day mowing the lawn. It's hot as hell." Mowing had taken much of the afternoon. It was a way for Brandon to channel his frustration and give himself time to think. "I want us to drive up and get the kids on Sunday."

Andrea answered him coolly. "I'm going up to get them Saturday and drive back Sunday."

"I can't go up Saturday, I've got to go in to work."

"Well that's too bad, I'm driving up Saturday. It's already set."

"Andrea, that's bullshit. I want to go up for them. It'll give us a chance to talk."

"Too bad."

Brandon was irate now. It was 7:30 in the evening; where *was* she anyway? "I know you're not still at work, so where the hell have you been?"

"Look, Brandon, I told you this is it—"

"Give me a chance to work this out." Brandon immediately tempered his anger. "We'll get counseling. Give me a chance, Andrea. This is all I've been thinking about since I've been gone."

"No, Brandon. When I get home, we're gonna pack your stuff up, and you're going."

"I'm serious. We're going to talk about this," Brandon said. "What can we do to make things work?"

"Look, Brandon," Andrea said calmly. "You can pack yourself or I'll pack my stuff—but one of us is leaving tonight."

"What can we do to make things work? I don't want a divorce—"

"Brandon, my mind is made up."

Andrea hung up abruptly and looked over at Danny.

"He's back. I guess you gathered that."

"What are you going to do?"

She looked intently into Danny's blue eyes. "Maybe I'll tell him I'm in love with you."

"You better not," Danny said, not sure if she was joking.

"No, I would never do that. I'd never put you at risk."

One night a few weeks ago, while Danny and his roommate were over at Andrea's house, he had asked: "What would your husband do if he came home right now?"

"He'd kill all three of us," she had told him matter-of-factly. "He's a very possessive man, and he's been trained to kill by the military."

Now Andrea gave Danny a hug and gathered her purse and keys. She still had on the white T-shirt and tan shorts she'd been wearing all day.

"I'll either call you later, or if things don't go well tonight, I'll be back."

As she left Danny's house and pulled out onto the road, she felt confident and determined in a way she never had before. She'd gotten a

231

big dose of what life was like without Brandon, and she liked it. He was gone so much, it was as if they had already separated, she reasoned.

As she turned into her driveway and parked next to Brandon's truck, she took a deep breath. It was just past eight o'clock. This is it, she thought. He better budge, because I'm not going to. What I want is worth something, too. She purposely left her car keys in the van and got out.

She couldn't help being relieved, though, that she'd cleaned the house. At least Brandon couldn't give her shit about that. Then she remembered she hadn't finished vacuuming the upstairs, and that she'd left the vacuum in the hallway outside the spare bedroom. Well, it was too late now. It annoyed her that she was still wearing the press-on nails Brandon liked and she hated. That didn't really matter right this moment. She needed a good night's sleep. She had to work the next day, and then she'd be driving all night.

How events unfolded next, what exactly was said—or shouted—only Andrea and Brandon would ever know. Based on crime-scene evidence, though, investigators were able to reconstruct what probably happened on the night of July 18. Andrea entered the house through the side door that led into the kitchen. She set her purse down on the counter and soon came face-to-face with her husband. Brandon had two days' worth of stubble on his face, and his normally shaved chest hair was growing back in, too. Their words became an argument, turning to taunts that rose in volume until even the next-door neighbors could hear the shouting. Then suddenly it was quiet.

Brandon went to bed in a spare bedroom, then got up, walked into the master bedroom. He was shirtless and wearing only his gray boxers. Andrea was in her closet, beginning to pack for her trip. He picked up the argument once again.

What could she have said to him? Did Andrea insist she was leaving? Did she compare him with her new lover? Brandon had worked hard his whole life to be strong and sure and confident, to be a man whose actions spoke for him. More than anything he wanted to command respect. That's all he'd ever wanted. He served his country in ways others couldn't or didn't want to do. Did the mother of his three children strip away his armor, transforming his vulnerability to venom?

By now Andrea was lying crossways on the bed near the pillows when

Brandon climbed off her. Her black bra, which snapped open in front, was open under her T-shirt, and her tan panties dangled around her right ankle.

Andrea grabbed the edge of the blue-checked bedsheet and pulled it up to cover her genitals. She crossed her arms over her chest, like a mummy—the classic victim's posture—then turned her head toward the pillows, which were stacked against the headboard.

Brandon walked across the room to his chest of drawers and opened the right door. There on a shelf was the Bryco .380, a semiautomatic handgun. It was a cheap pistol, the one he had bought for Andrea when they first married. He walked to the right side of the bed, the side he slept on. His sunglasses and cell phone and a glass of water rested on the nightstand. Andrea was still facing the pillows, her arms still crossed, her panties still wrapped around her ankle. Investigators believe she had no idea Brandon was still in the room.

Brandon peered down at his wife's head. Methodically, as if he were finishing off one of his wounded bucks, he leaned over the bed and angled the gun downward. He put the muzzle above and behind Andrea's right ear and pulled the trigger, execution style. The bullet passed through her left temple, severing her brain stem and killing her instantly.

A new bullet automatically rechambered. Brandon raised the muzzle to the center of his forehead and squeezed the trigger. By the time his body slumped on top of Andrea's, he was dead.

CHAPTER TWENTY-ONE

It was now July 26, Friday afternoon, exactly one week since Master Sergeant Bill Wright had led detectives to where he had buried his wife, Jennifer, and since the bodies of Sergeant First Class Brandon and Andrea Floyd had been discovered. For the last few days, I had been putting together a story about those two dead wives and Teresa Nieves and Marilyn Styles-Griffin, raising questions over whether hardships of military life were a factor in their deaths, if the military did enough to help families cope, and what would happen now.

My story ran that morning. Within hours a media frenzy had erupted. It took me a while to fully grasp what my story had unleashed. News crews and writers flew in from New York City and LA, and over the weekend crews from London, Tokyo, Toronto, and Frankfurt would arrive. Journalists couldn't resist this one: Four soldiers—three of whom had served in Afghanistan—kill their wives, two then commit suicide, all in one summer in one Army town. In the weeks to come, magazine, newspaper, and TV reporters would swarm over the story like moths on a back porch light. Attention-getting headlines were everywhere:

RASH OF WIFE KILLINGS STUNS FORT BRAGG; DEATH AT FORT BRAGG; FORT BRAGG KILLINGS RAISE ALARM AND STRESS; FOUR MURDERS IN SIX WEEKS AT FORT BRAGG.

The national media seemed particularly interested in the Wright case, partly because the husband was still alive. Bill Wright was sitting in a cell at the Cumberland County jail, the last place those who knew him would have expected this former Green Beret to end up. Over time I learned why. Bill had enlisted in the Army right out of high school and during his eighteen years in uniform he had served all over the world as a Green Beret in the 3rd Special Forces Group. Bill was now a master sergeant in the 96th Civil Affairs Battalion. As in his Special Forces days, he was deployed for long stretches of time throughout the year. But his wife, thirty-two-year-old Jennifer, had grown weary of the long separations.

At five feet eight inches, Jennifer was a bit taller than her husband, slender and attractive, with long, dark brown hair. The pair had met in Mason, Ohio, in high school, and as soon as Jennifer had graduated, they got married. They had three boys—Ben, thirteen, Jacob, nine, and John, six. Bill was bright and articulate, a good father and husband, and he loved to take his sons fishing at the lakes on Fort Bragg when he was around. The family spent Wednesday evenings and Sundays at church. Jennifer sang in the choir at Aaron Lake Baptist, which was near the modest three-bedroom house they had bought the previous May.

There were problems. Jennifer told friends she was tired of Army life, and the deployments seemed to have changed Bill's demeanor and personality, too. There were rumors flying around the battalion among soldiers and their wives that Jennifer had been with other men, including someone from her church choir and a man she'd met at the airport after dropping Bill off there. Some of the talk eventually got back to her husband.

When confronted, Jennifer denied the stories as preposterous, but she did want a different life and was ready to move on. Bill was desperate to save his marriage and keep his family intact. In mid-May he requested leave to come home from Afghanistan to work out his marital problems. He'd been deployed two months. By then Jennifer had told people she was already divorced, and that Bill moved into the barracks on post at her request.

On that last Saturday morning in June, at the first sign of daylight, Bill, now living in the barracks, had returned home and found Jennifer—wearing a red T-shirt, leopard-print bikini panties, and a black bra—still in bed. As they yelled at each other behind closed bedroom doors, the fight escalated till Jennifer threw a coffee mug at her husband. When one of the boys came to see if everything was okay, his father reassured him. But things weren't okay. Bill felt as if his world was crumbling, as if his life and everything he defined himself to be—a loving spouse and father, a good NCO—was about to disappear.

Though he had never been violent toward his wife before, Bill took a baseball bat and swung it hard at Jennifer's face, shattering the right side of her jaw. She tried to defend herself, but she was no match for her husband's rage. Next Bill reached for a black sports bra and used it to strangle Jennifer to death. He put her body in a black garbage bag, tied it with a knot, and placed it inside a canvas parachute kit bag. Later he put it in the back of his pickup truck and buried her body in the woods. He went on to the construction job he worked to earn extra money. The next day, a Sunday, he took his sons fishing.

For three weeks Wright had been able to keep up the pretense that his wife was missing, then he crumbled and confessed. He was now awaiting trial.

As I continued to pursue my story, I came to know Lieutenant Sam Pennica. Weekends were now workdays for him. His phone was ringing constantly with calls from reporters, his detectives, and victims' relatives. As many as eight of his men were on the wife-murder cases, following up leads, gathering evidence, waiting for forensic results and autopsy reports, and interviewing neighbors, friends, and soldiers who knew the Army couples. There were also older homicide cases that needed attention. Bragg's CID had been calling for updates, too. The two offices didn't work side by side, because all the wife murders had happened off post, in the jurisdiction of either the sheriff's department or the city police department. Still, CID was helpful in gathering most information the cops asked for, including records of deployment schedules and names of soldiers and friends for interviews.

None of the wife murders were premeditated; investigators had already established that. A rape-kit procedure had been performed on Andrea Floyd, and authorities needed to find out if the semen found on her body was her husband's or someone else's. The semen had no sperm, meaning the man had had a vasectomy. The Army had stalled on handing over Brandon Floyd's medical records, eventually saying they had been "lost." No one in the sheriff's department bought that one. Investigators later confirmed Brandon's vasectomy through a close relative.

To Pennica a murder had always been a murder, but recently his attitude had changed. Now, when the phone rang in the middle of the night about a homicide, his first question to the deputy was, "Did a soldier do it?" It wasn't that he thought soldiers were more likely to kill, it was just that he didn't want to be involved with the media circus surrounding the case.

"If we have one more soldier involved with a murder, CNN is gonna land its helicopter on top of the jail," Pennica told his boss, Sheriff Earl "Moose" Butler, a large beefy man with white hair and a drawl as deep as well water. For twenty minutes one hot July night, the men stood outside in front of the sheriff's department, their pockets filled with paper towels to wipe the drip off their faces, as they waited to be interviewed live by Connie Chung. Another time police had to strike the fear of God into one national news crew that tried to break into the Nieves house to get footage. A neighbor had called authorities.

For my part, as I drove up Bragg Boulevard to a press conference Fort Bragg had hastily arranged the day my story broke, I couldn't help thinking about how a relationship could go from love to violence to death. I'd seen it before. More than 50 percent of all homicides in the county were domestic. People never think they'd be capable of killing a loved one, but then few people have ever been pushed to their emotional limit.

Inside the car I reached for my sunglasses and cranked up the air conditioner. It had reached ninety-one degrees outside. I don't know why I bothered with makeup anymore—it just melted off my face. To make things worse, that summer the county, along with more than fifty others in the state, was experiencing the worst drought in North Carolina since the 1930s. Cotton and corn withered in fields, and the Cape Fear River dipped lower with each passing day. Mandatory water restrictions in town helped with conservation, but the result was dirty cars, wilted flowers, and grass that had turned a matted yellowish brown that crackled underfoot.

I parked my car and walked into Mulligan's, the clubhouse at Stryker Golf Course, for the press briefing. All day phones had been ringing incessantly in the public affairs offices at Bragg. If the Army hated operating on the defensive in combat, it hardly enjoyed being backed into a corner on *Dateline NBC* and *20/20*. In the aftermath of 9/11 and with the war in Afghanistan, the spectacle of uniformed men in disgrace was made for prime time, and the post dug in for a spin-control battle on the home front. I entered a back room overlooking the golf course; it was crammed with reporters and producers who had just arrived in town.

TV cameras on tripods, lights, and wires formed an arc around Colonel Tad Davis, Fort Bragg's garrison commander. Soon reporters shot out their questions: "Is this a trend?" "Did these couples ever seek counseling?" "Is this combat-stress related?" "Did the units know there were problems?" "What made these men do it?"

The room got stuffier as the barrage of questions continued. Davis was forty-five and a West Point grad with a masters in Public Administration from Harvard. He had been in the Army twenty-four years. With each question Davis squinted his deep-set eyes, which were set under a prominent brow. He knew Bragg well; it was one of the many posts he lived on as a child. He couldn't say whether the killings were related to the soldiers' duties and missions in Afghanistan, and he didn't know if any of the couples had sought help from their unit or post counseling programs. Each case, he said, would be closely examined.

"We will be looking at the duty performance of the soldiers," Davis said. "Were they good soldiers? What was the relationship? What was going on in the family? What was going on in that household? We will look at all of those issues together to see what we can put together as a total picture as to what was going on in that family."

I liked Colonel Davis. He was a good-hearted man and expressed genuine concern over what had happened. He promised to seek answers, improve the system, and strengthen ties between the post and the community.

Days passed and frustrations grew, as reporters felt the post was trying to shape their stories by controlling the information flow. Only a few officials were allowed to give interviews. Several reporters called me voicing their frustrations and seeking help with sources. My phone rang constantly, and it got to the point where my boss, Mike Adams, forbade me to answer it until I had met my own deadlines.

It was a difficult story to cover. News hacks who wanted to put some meat on their stories and go beyond talking with the people Bragg paraded in front of the cameras, with their perfunctory responses—family-oriented program directors and official post spokesmen—found they were largely shut out. Requests to interview leaders in Special Operations, where three of the four soldiers had served, were denied, as was access to individuals in the soldiers' units and to the FRG groups. Bragg never did admit that Brandon Floyd was a member of Delta.

As the Army saw it, the reporters covering the murders were a distraction to the investigations and a disruption from operations and training. The media saw it as something else—stonewalling.

Everyone wanted to know why these men did it. The scandal and dishonor, the scrutiny and the gossip, swirled outside in the heat like a swarm of mosquitoes. Outside Fayetteville, people who knew nothing about the military squawked on about "trained killers," while many career soldiers and their spouses were saddened to see the Army dragged into the debacle.

Blaming the Army outright for what these men did was ludicrous and too easy. Yes, the Army can make a bad marriage worse, but I don't believe Army training played any role in the murders. Soldiers are not robots programmed to "kill" like some *Bourne Identity* assassin. The reason soldiers kill in combat isn't for God, glory, and country but for self-preservation and for their buddies to the right and left of them. Ask any combat vet.

Meanwhile the debates raged all over Fayetteville. I heard a variety of commentary and snatches of conversation that summer. At one of Bragg's mess halls, single soldiers sitting down at a square table to a meal of "chili mac," a chow hall favorite, talked as the TV screen anchored near the ceiling, above a wall of fake plants, reported on the wife murders.

"Those women got what they deserved," one soldier said. Soldiers always liked talking that kind of "smack." "That's what happens when you're a cheat."

"Yeah," chimed in another. In the soldiers' minds, the women must have committed adultery, the only thing that could have set an otherwise rational man over the edge.

"I don't care what those women did or didn't do; they didn't deserve to die over it," weighed in a third. "Look at the poor kids involved. No kid deserves to lose his mom. Some of them don't have a mom *or* a dad now." Young soldiers always had soft spots for children.

"Ya know what? If I had a wife and she cheated on me, I'd walk away and divorce her ass. If I knocked her off, I'd just be ruining my own life. I wouldn't give her the satisfaction. I'm not gonna rot in jail over her. But I'd bust up the guy she was with."

Outside, in a park on the post, three Army wives sat on a blanket in the shade, watched their children play on the swings, and discussed the murders.

"Do you think your husband could get mad enough to do something like that to you?" one of them asked.

"No way. My husband won't even kill a spider in the house. Those men were probably genetically inclined to such a thing."

"Well, I don't know about that," another said, as she swatted at flies. "My husband loves me, but if I ever betrayed him and rubbed it in his face—girl, he'd go nuts. There's no telling what a man would do in that situation. Men have a lot of pride, especially military guys. He'd definitely hunt down and kill the guy, though."

"But it's such a double standard," the third one said. "On my husband's old team, one of the guys basically started a second family in Colombia when they were deployed down there, and here was his real wife stuck back at Bragg. Everybody in the unit knew about it but her. And when my husband's buddy was in Bosnia, he was the only married guy on his team not cheating. His team captain, who was single, even warned everybody not to cheat."

"Have your relatives called y'all yet? My mom telephoned wanting to know what's going on down here. She wondered if I knew any of the women. I was, like, Mom, it's a huge post. She wanted to know if deployments or Lariam [the antimalarial drug the Army gives soldiers in countries where there is a malaria risk] had anything to do with it. That's what's been on the news."

"Well, if you're gonna cheat, a deployment sure does give you the opportunity."

"That's not what I mean. I think a deployment plays with the guys' minds. You know, the stress, the shitty environment they're stuck in."

"Well, every time my husband has been away like that, he's just happy to be home with us. Sure there's some adjustment afterward, but that's normal. Soldiers aren't robots—and no, I don't think Lariam had anything to do with it either."

"Well, I don't think it should be the Army's responsibility to get involved in soldiers' marriages."

"Why not? The Army gets involved in everything else."

There was a lot of speculation. One of the biggest questions involved Lariam; I began receiving anonymous calls from soldiers telling me to look into Lariam as a possible factor in the crimes. Studies had shown that a small percentage of people who take the drug experience paranoia, aggression, depression, psychotic actions, hallucinations, and suicidal tendencies.

Some of the men who had been in Afghanistan had indeed taken Lariam. And though I never believed Lariam had anything to do with the crimes, I couldn't say that at the time. I wanted to remain open-minded and explore every possibility.

The side effects of Lariam were well known in the Army. I had heard soldiers joking about the drug for years. Whenever anyone was in a bad mood or lost his temper on deployment, the comment was always, "It must be the Lariam." Soldiers often took their dosage on a designated day, "Mad Mondays," for example.

The Lariam connection hit the airwaves with a vengeance, and I found myself talking about it on CNN and *Good Morning America*. Millions of Americans going abroad had been prescribed Lariam without incident. I had taken Lariam myself several months earlier when I went to Vietnam. My experience with the drug wasn't a great one, it made me so sick to my stomach that I never took my last dosage upon returning to the States, not a smart thing when you consider the alternative, which is getting malaria.

Meanwhile, Lariam hysteria swept through the housing areas, as wives with husbands on their way to Afghanistan asked, "Are you going to have to take that?"

"Probably," was the reply.

On Bragg some wives confided in their friends, "What if it makes them go crazy when they come home?" Others treated it as a big joke. "My husband's been back from Afghanistan for three weeks, and I'm still alive."

Lariam was never a real issue with the cops or the DA, nor, as it would turn out later, with the Army. As the speculation rose to a frenzy over what had led the men to murder—deployment stress, Army training, and now Lariam—detectives like Pennica, who had dealt with homicide cases for years, wanted to jump up and yell, "Bullshit!" The Army wives died because serious domestic issues resulted in violence, and in the detectives' minds the Army had nothing to do with it. For me the questions remained: Did aspects of military life contribute to or exacerbate marriages already in trouble? And if so, could those be fixed? Congressmen on the House Armed Services Committee were planning to come down to find out for themselves, and the Pentagon was sending an epidemiology team of its own to investigate.

On post something else was happening: Chaplains and FRG leaders were getting calls from wives, some of them abused women, worried about problems in their own marriages and asking for help. I got my own share of calls, and before long my coverage had sprouted another branch, domestic violence in the military.

It had turned out to be quite a fourth week of July in Fayetteville. Aside from the dead wives and the reporters crawling all over town, it was still hotter than heck. And a few other scandals livened the local news. Police issued a citation to the chamber of commerce president, who was caught in a prostitution sting (he denied the charges, which were later dropped), then Fayetteville's beauty queen, who had gone on to be crowned Miss North Carolina, abruptly resigned after an ex-boyfriend allegedly told pageant officials he had topless photos of her. Fayettenam was back like a bad aftertaste. Could it get worse?

I got my answer when news came that a Fort Bragg officer's wife had been charged with murdering her husband.

In the early morning of Tuesday, July 23, Major David Shannon had been shot in the head and chest as he slept. The Shannons lived in a rented, sixties-era, three-bedroom ranch home in Cottonade, a large subdivision just outside post, filled with mostly military families and retirees. Major Shannon, forty, was a fifteen-year veteran and worked in the U.S. Army Special Operations Command headquarters. His thirty-five-year-old wife, Joan, told police she saw an intruder. The couple had been married eleven years.

After the murder Joan had been comforted by an Army chaplain and families from her husband's office. Her coworkers at the Fort Bragg Federal Credit Union, where she worked as a secretary, raised five hundred dollars for the family. A week after the killing, on July 30, police charged Joan with first-degree murder and conspiracy to commit murder. She has denied the charges. The motive was insurance money, police believe. Joan's fifteen-year-old daughter, Elizabeth, David Shannon's stepdaughter, was charged with the same offenses and would later admit to actually pulling the trigger. The girl said her mother had been bugging her to do it.

Joan Shannon claimed that she had a good marriage, though according to police records she said she had a boyfriend, who had been introduced to her by her husband. She also told police that in their free time she and her husband engaged in group sex and partner swaps with local couples they met over the Internet. I had learned about that from sources in the early days of the investigation, though that information wouldn't come out publicly until much later.

Bragg now had its fifth Army domestic slaying of the summer. One local news station actually inquired at Fort Bragg whether the post thought the weather had made people go mad. It was the one question regarding the murders Bragg could give a definitive answer to: No.

In early August, over sweet tea at a monthly officers' wives gathering I attended, the conversation quickly turned to Joan Shannon's unkempt appearance. Footage of the officer's wife had played repeatedly on Fayetteville news. There she was, shuffling along before the television cameras, hunched over in her bulky orange jumpsuit, her hands cuffed across her abdomen. Long strands of brown greasy hair hung in her sullen face. She wore no makeup, just oversize glasses. This was not a look sanctioned in the Officers' Wives' Handbook.

A major's wife no less. . . . How embarrassing. . . . She looked godawful. . . . Couldn't she have washed that hair? . . . What a sight. . . . The women winced just talking about it.

CHAPTER TWENTY-TWO

The deaths of four Fort Bragg Army wives continued to receive attention throughout the month of August as talk of toppling Saddam and invading Iraq made headlines. At that point the threat of invasion of Iraq was a sleeping beast for military wives. Amid the swirl of a chaotic and deadly summer in Fayetteville, Army wives far from the spotlight soldiered on.

For three Fort Bragg women, Delores, Andrea Lynne, and Rita, that meant standing strong on some days and trying not to show their weakness on others, faking for their children's sake. Meanwhile a fourth wife, Andrea Floyd, was buried on the last Saturday in July near a huge old oak in a cemetery along a country road in her hometown.

By the end of the month in Fayetteville, after days of temperatures in the triple digits and months of aridity, rain poured down like liquid sheets soaking thirsty soil and flooding some streets. As a retired colonel would later tell me, life's blessings are always mixed.

Delores sat in her Camry in the Watters Center parking lot, crying and wondering why she had come. There was no way she could go back into that building. It's too soon. I'll just go home. No one will know the difference. Rain pelted her windshield. She had been there for thirty minutes, parked in the same spot in which she had parked the morning her life changed on March 4. She purposely wore the same clothes she had worn that day, hoping now they might give her strength and courage: jeans, white sneakers, a long-sleeved white T-shirt, and the black 82nd shirt with her name and a rose embroidered on it. It was 10:00 A.M., on the first Monday in August, and one hundred senior Bragg wives were half an hour into their monthly Command and Staff meeting.

Delores had stayed away from wives' meetings and committees for months; she gave up her cleaning jobs and put her substitute-teaching plans on hold. She had always seen herself as an Army wife working behind the scenes, serving selflessly with dignity and style. Now she was on an extended leave of absence. She focused solely on her home life and her daughter. She knew some people might consider her overprotective, but after having lost one child, she couldn't bear to have anything happen to Cherish. She put all her energy into her family, which was more important than any meeting.

On several mornings Delores had woken up to the sound of Cherish crying. The girl had been greatly affected by her brother's death. She had a small bulletin board in her room, covered with pictures, that she called her Gary Shane Angel Board. On the sole of her right sneaker she had written in permanent black marker, My Angel Gary Shane. Once she asked Delores, "Mom, did Gary Shane die because he thought I got all the attention because I was the baby?"

Delores tried to reassure her. "No, sweetie, no one is to blame except for Gary Shane. It was just a major mistake. He should have talked to me, or Dad, or a chaplain . . . or someone. What his pain was we'll never know, but none of us are to blame for what he did. Only Gary Shane." She wiped her daughter's tears. "God holds Gary Shane now. He is free from his pain at last."

But the pain had now taken hold of his family. The heartache was so great that Delores and Ski couldn't really talk about it. Instead they talked around it. Delores wanted to hear, over and over, what had happened that day in Kosovo. Patiently Ski would go over it with her again, and if his wording changed ever so slightly, she would break in, "But I thought you said—" He knew Delores was looking for answers, hoping that maybe he had forgotten some crucial, revealing detail.

"Did you make him call me?" Delores asked.

"He wanted to."

"What did he say when you got off the phone?"

"Delores, we've been over this so many times."

"Are you sure something else didn't happen?"

"Wouldn't I have told you by now?" Ski felt tremendous anxiety. He was the one who had seen Gary Shane last. After all these years, Ski thought he could sense when something wasn't right with a soldier. *What did I miss? What should I have seen that would have prevented this from happening? Was there anything I could have done? I thought he was so grounded, but maybe he needed to tell me things.*

For her part Delores felt like a failure as a mother. She couldn't avoid every Army function, and she often found herself chatting with people she had never met. With so much coming and going on the post, there constantly were new people to be introduced to, and those first conversations always pulled from the same reservoir of questions: *What unit is your husband in? Do you live on or off post? Where are you from originally? How long have you been here?* And the one Delores didn't know how to respond to: *Do you have children?*

The topic of children invariably came up. Sometimes Delores would say they had lost a son in Kosovo, and if someone asked how, she would answer, "to suicide." She was neither ashamed nor embarrassed over the way Gary Shane died, but the *S* word abruptly ended the chitchat.

Sometimes Delores would run into wives at the commissary or the PX. "Delores, how are you doing?" the women would ask. "Check your calendar. Let's do lunch." There were dozens of lunches and conversations that allowed Delores to focus on memories of her son.

So many people at Bragg had helped the family through their grief. Wives sent her cards and letters; friends passed along books on suicide and grieving. People would never know how much their support had meant to her and her family.

But there was a dark side, too, a contagion of whispers and innuendos from some of the same people who offered their friendship. Army life is fishbowl living, and unfortunately the Kalinofskis, who were experiencing their worst nightmare, were not spared speculation and gossip: *Delores is too fragile. You know, she's not Gary Shane's biological mother. Command Sergeant Major Kalinofski's finished. He'll retire. He forced his son to join the Army. They had a terrible fight in Kosovo, didn't you hear?* I heard all those fabrications and gossip, but I also know that those who truly cared about the Kalinofskis gave them loyalty and love.

Ski expected people to think that he and his son had had an awful argument, that he must have said *something* to push Gary Shane over the edge. In truth his visit with his son had been one of their best. The bigger question for him was whether to return to work. He wasn't concerned with what other people thought, but he needed to know if he could function in the military world again. He had his doubts.

"Delores," he had said soon after he came back from Kosovo, "I don't think I can lead young soldiers anywhere. I'm old enough to be their father. What do you think I see in these young faces? I see my own son."

"Gary, you've got to pick yourself up and dust yourself off," she said. Delores knew her husband, and she knew that being with soldiers would be the best medicine for him. "Go back to work. You must go back. You cannot end your Army career. You have to bounce back. I will be fine."

Ski knew she was right. Not only did he have obligations—a family to take care of—he had to think of himself: If I don't get off my ass, I'll be lost, he decided. It was the old Ski talking.

He had returned to his job at the end of March, and within a few weeks he had realized he could make it as long as he stayed busy. The PT routine helped immensely. There was something about running down Ardennes Street on a summer morning, when the coolness of the previous night merged with the rising sun's humidity. Ski thrived on the 0630 reveille, and the formation runs or calisthenics—the jumping jacks called side-straddle hops and the "leaning rests," or push-ups. He loved "hitting the street" with some of the most physically fit people in the Army.

At one point, when Ski felt as though everything was being handled for him, he sat his battalion command sergeants major down and told them, "You guys have your battalions, let me run this brigade." Things were back to normal after that.

He still had questions and anger, and Ski felt guilty over the times he had missed with his son. He blamed himself for not balancing the Army with his personal life. He realized he should have insisted that Gary Shane spend more time on family activities, too. He knew Delores had been both mom and dad much of the time. That was true in many military families.

How many times, summer after summer, have I heard a commander give a farewell speech to his unit and thank his wife, often sitting in the first row with a dozen red roses cradled in her arms, for raising their children.

"You can't let the Army consume you," Ski counseled other NCOs. "If you do, your children will be raised and gone."

The first few weeks back, Ski called Delores every hour. He worried about his family, and he made sure people were around his wife. When he suggested she see a counselor, Delores responded, "Gary, my primary question is 'Why?' And I've worn that question out completely. Is a counselor going to be able to answer it any more than we can?"

The Command and Staff meeting had now been in progress forty-five minutes, and Delores was still inside her car, a pile of crumpled tissues next to her. The last thing she wanted to do was to walk into a room full of women and be labeled as the wife whose son committed suicide. There was so much more to who she was, to who *Gary Shane* was.

Delores had always known how precious and short life was. She believed that her story had been written by God long before she was ever born, and that all the things she endured as a child had prepared her for the death of Gary Shane. It comforted her to know that he was in God's hands. But could she now walk into the building where she had heard the worst news of her life?

She regained her composure, dried her eyes, checked her mascara, and got out of the car. She walked into the building and down the hallway, pausing for a while at the closed double doors leading into the auditorium. Through the glass she could see the 504th table, where Ann Campbell sat with the other wives. Her old seat was still there with her name card—Delores Kalinofski—and her blue folder.

Delores took a deep breath, forced a smile, and strode in carrying the small binder that held a yellow legal pad and pen, the one she had always carried. As she sat down, Ann Campbell reached across the table and touched her arm.

"Delores, I'm so proud of you," Ann said. "I'm glad you're back." Both women's eyes welled with tears, as the other women at the table welcomed her. Delores couldn't speak, but she made herself smile. She couldn't help thinking of Gary Shane and that awful March day. But she had returned; she had made it back.

On a Saturday in August, Andrea Lynne gazed at her garden and noted the changes in the landscaping, the passage of time. The front yard was mostly finished, with gardenias and boxwoods and a few annuals like white impatiens. She had only white flowers, no color, except to mark a few occasions. She had put in three red tulips in the spring for her anniversary and two huge orange chrysanthemums for fall. She looked forward to their cool-season blooms after the relentless heat and a summer of drought, which had taken a toll on everyone's lawn and flowers. Eventually she wanted a Zen garden in the backyard, with a gazebo, a spot for the birds, a fishpond with Japanese koi, and memorials for her father and Rennie. And she envisioned a huge signpost with hand-painted arrows and the names of all the places she'd ever been and the mileage to them, marking how far she'd gone, and how far she had returned.

Originally she hadn't planned to keep the house for long, but she could see that the children liked it, that they wanted a place to call home. Perhaps they were too young to understand what all Army wives have learned—that home is less a physical space than a place where you're loved. She just wanted her children to be happy again, to know what she once knew.

She was comfortable there, too. She knew most of the local storekeepers by name, and she herself was recognized in the neighborhood. They called her the "pretty widow" on Shawcroft. When people asked about her husband and she told them he died in Vietnam, they said she was far too young to have had a husband die in that war.

Andrea Lynne still grieved for Rennie, but she no longer lived in the painful past. She avoided old acquaintances and trips onto the post. They were all too much of a reminder of what she had lost.

The Army is like the bottom of the sea. What is there is soon gone. People move on, they retire, get promoted, or head to different posts. And in a world after 9/11 the Army had had massive disruptions with back-to-back deployments, war duty, and more widows.

Andrea Lynne felt as if she was no longer even a small concern in this huge machine, just a number in a file at the mercy of bureaucrats. Her military health benefits and Rennie's paychecks and retirement pay, all things she thought would be secure for life, weren't, and she had just enough to scrape by. She had no rank or status. She was a widow—a fact overlooked by the Army, which sent her letter after letter recalling Rennie to active duty.

Is this what the Army really had in store for me? For Rennie's family? she wondered. Andrea Lynne thought about every soldier who packed his rucksack and kissed his sleeping wife and children good-bye. Is this what they would want in return for their sacrifice?

When news of the Army wife murders hit, implicating the Army to some degree, Andrea Lynne felt sad but numb. After the shock of Rennie's death, nothing affected her in the same way. She could not be shocked, only more disillusioned.

She never discussed the murders with anyone. Rennie was gone, and his was the only opinion that would have mattered. Talking about the news or world issues was something she used to do with her husband over coffee or as a way of keeping each other up to date while they were apart. Now anything she saw, heard, or read in the newspaper just felt like more of the same.

But when she let herself think about the wives, it was stress that she blamed for the outburst of violence, stress from being apart under terrible circumstances, stress—and jealousy—over not being able to comfort your spouse and thinking that perhaps someone else would.

Rennie sometimes visited her in her dreams. He was still in her view, just a little more distant. It was Roland who was closer now. Through the love they both had for Rennie, they had come to love each other. Her feelings for Roland were different from anything she'd ever experienced, more resonant, more shaped by loss. She couldn't help but wonder if Rennie had something to do with Roland's appearance in her life. She remembered how she had met the two men on the same day so long ago. It was an egotistical thought, she knew, but maybe, just maybe she was destined to be the woman for both of them.

Roland insisted that she had been meant for Rennie, and that never once did he imagine himself with her. Not even after Rennie died. Yet now he couldn't imagine his life without her.

Still, it was Rennie who had shaped her, who was responsible for the person and Army wife she had become. He was her history, the father of her children. As she contemplated her garden, looking out through the window, she realized that Rennie was right: She *was* good. She *was* strong. She *was* the heart of this family. And she would always try to manage her life, *their* life, as he would have wanted. In a way, he never did leave her.

When she had started school the year before, Rita had hung a sign above her computer at home. YOUR GOAL: 4.0 YOU CAN MAKE IT! She looked at it every time she was tired, or whenever she felt frustrated or didn't understand how to do something, or whenever she had to sit with Jay for hours on end getting his homework done, while she felt like quitting school herself. In the end she was the only person in her class to graduate with highest honors. Rita had the highest GPA in her class, a 4.0, and she got the one job all her classmates wanted: the only hospital pharmacy position available with Long-Term Acute Care, a new facility that treated seriously ill patients.

She wished Brian were there to share in her accomplishment, but it felt great to know that, with her husband in Afghanistan, she could feed, bathe, and clothe her three rambunctious boys, get them to school and day care on time, and still hold down a full-time, busy, balls-to-the-wall job that required constant diligence and attention to detail. Rita was proud that she could do all those things without her husband there to help. I'm contributing to the welfare of my family, not just depending on Brian to take care of us, she thought.

At night, after Rita put the kids to bed, other feelings took over. She tried everything to thwart the silence of the house. She watched late-night TV, surfed the Internet, and shampooed her carpets. Her house never looked better, and Brian wasn't even there to see it. She kept up their private rituals. At 8:00 P.M. each night, no matter where she was, Rita looked outside at the night sky and at the same time Brian peered into an early morning sky. They had done this ever since Rita pointed out Orion to Brian on the Christmas Eve when they first met. It was something they could say they did together even though they were physically apart.

As time dragged on, it got increasingly difficult for Rita to get through the daylight hours, too. Her grandmother and uncle died, her mother was sick, and Rita got gastritis. The little things that Brian used to do—taking out the garbage, gassing up the cars, and wiping the boys' pee off the toilet seat—were getting to her. Rita tried not to complain. It didn't do any good to tell Brian how she felt. Instead she cried into her pillow or cussed at the tree in her front yard, which did about as much good as complaining to the first sergeant. She never wanted Brian to have to say he was sorry for something he had no control over, but Rita felt she couldn't get by anymore without him. When her Ford Escort broke down, it was the last straw.

It took two weeks to get the car fixed. Rita didn't trust Brian's truck to get her around, so she had to get rides to and from work. Then the owner of the auto body shop wouldn't accept her seven-hundred-dollar check. He was retired military, that's why Rita and Brian had chosen him. As far as the owner was concerned, when it came to bounced checks, that connection didn't mean a damn. Rita and Brian purposely kept their credit limit low so they wouldn't spend much. Rita had to get her boss to pay the owner, and then write her boss a check. It was humiliating.

That night Brian called as Rita was getting ready for bed.

"Hey, sweetie, it's me."

"Hey, sweet pea," Rita said as she walked out with her cell phone into the driveway and sat in Brian's truck. It made her feel closer to him. She had grown accustomed to the delay of the crackling and beeping telephone line.

"Hey, guess what, Rita? I got to name a mountain after you."

"You what?"

"Yeah, it's called Mount Rita."

The platoon occupied a firebase on the border of Pakistan and Afghanistan at a three-thousand-foot elevation. Their platoon leader, Lieutenant Truitt, a boyish-looking twenty-four-year-old who wore his hair in a high-and-tight (shaved on the sides and short on top) like his men, sent them up another three thousand feet to look for caves and do counterreconnaissance.

"I'm gonna break y'all," Brian told his squad. "I'm gonna go straight up and not stop."

"You're not gonna do it," one of his buddies countered. Brian was far from the biggest guy in the platoon.

"Watch me."

Halfway up the mountain, it began to rain, then hail, though the region rarely had precipitation.

"Odom, ya gotta slow it down," Brian could hear Lieutenant Truitt's voice behind him. The soldiers had a lot of respect for Lieutenant Truitt, even if he was a privileged college boy. If the soldiers were digging holes, Truitt would grab a shovel and dig along with them. Brian gave him credit for that. Truitt couldn't help where he came from.

When Brian reached the top, he bent over and put his hands on his knees and breathed heavily. He could look straight into the barren wasteland of Pakistan.

"All right, Odom. You were the first one up. Name it," Lieutenant Truitt said.

Brian took out his knife, walked over to a smooth slab of rock, and in one-foot letters carved out MOUNT RITA.

Hearing that, Rita smiled, for the first time in a long time. It made her miss Brian even more, and she started to cry.

"What's wrong, Rita? I didn't tell you that to make you cry."

"I just can't handle this anymore," she said. "I'm sick, and I'm exhausted. I feel like I'm failing. I'm not strong enough. I need you to come home."

"Rita, look, you gotta hang in there. You're not a failure. I can see that from six thousand miles away. Rita, you know I'd hug you if my arms reached that far," Brian said. "We train all the time. We're supposed to be the toughest men on earth, but Rita, you're the toughest person I ever met. You put up with my sorry butt and take care of me."

It was all Rita needed to hear.

Across town on a Saturday afternoon in late summer, a young woman is about to be brought into the Army fold. Shaded from the sun by a covered walkway of stucco stone and an orange cobbled roof, wedding guests gather and wait with their cameras for the traditional ritual of every military wedding. Six young officers, friends of the groom, in dress blues and white gloves, with sabers at their sides, form two lines, three men on each side, and turn to face each other. Suddenly the doors of Fort Bragg's Main Post Chapel swing open, and down the steps comes a smiling officer, also in dress blues, with his bride on his arm. They have just said their vows.

The members of the saber guard draw their swords and form a steely arch for the newlyweds to walk beneath. They don't get very far. As they pass under the second set of swords, two sabers are lowered and crossed in front of them. Only after the secret password—a kiss—can they proceed. The sabers rise again, and the couple continues. There's one last step. As the bride comes through the final arch, the last officer lowers his sword and slaps her on the backside with it, bellowing: *"Welcome to the Army!"*

During the summer of 2002 I wrote twenty-six stories—many of them picked up by media far beyond Fayetteville—covering the Army wives' deaths at Fort Bragg. It was important to me to look beyond the specific crimes, and throughout my coverage of the murders, I underlined the broader issues of how the military's culture and perceptions and its stress and deployments affected Army marriages already in serious trouble. I also examined how the Army dealt with domestic violence by means of prevention and intervention. My reporting fostered discussion and debate, and the repercussions of the crimes echoed throughout the Army in many ways.

On September 30, 2002, five members of the House Armed Services Committee visited Fayetteville and Fort Bragg and promised to work for changes in the way the Department of Defense handled abuse in military families. Then, in November, the Pentagon released a forty-one-page report that found marital problems were a "major" factor in the murders, and that the stress from Fort Bragg's high operational pace contributed to marital discord in marriages that were already experiencing problems. The report went on to say that the Army's behavioral health services were flawed, since they discouraged early identification and therapy for marital troubles while problems were potentially solvable. It emphasized that families needed earlier and more accessible therapy and counseling that did not jeopardize careers. The report said Lariam was not likely to have contributed to the killings.

Congress authorized $5 million for domestic violence programs in the military, and on December 2, 2002, President Bush signed into law an act that makes state domestic violence protective orders enforceable on military installations.

The murders of 2002 raised enough concern for the Army to take a hard look at itself. Among other things, the tragedies, coupled with the war on terrorism, prompted the military to redefine its attitudes about the crucial role wives and families play. With back-to-back deployments to Iraq, ongoing war in Afghanistan, and no end in sight, it's none too soon. Military families are venturing into uncharted territory. Andrea Lynne is no longer alone in her young widowhood, scores of parents are burying sons Gary Shane's age who died in far-off places, and much as Rita did, wives are juggling jobs and kids while husbands are abroad.

Meanwhile strides have been made in providing care, counseling, and treatment for individuals and couples in need throughout the armed forces. Yet, in a culture that values not only physical but also emotional strength and stability, the stigma of reaching out for help will be difficult to remove.

Since three of the soldiers who killed their wives served in Afghanistan before the murders, the Army began having its soldiers deployed there fill out psychological-screening questionnaires before coming home. The fifty-five-point checklist, called a "Pre-Redeployment Screening," asked about feelings of depression, anxiety, and hostility. Some soldiers nicknamed it the "Don't Kill Your Wife Questionnaire" and thought the whole thing was not only ineffective but also a joke. After all, who would put down something negative that would end up in his file? Others saw the questionnaire as nothing more than "finger drilling" (going through the motions), an attempt by the Army to show it was doing something. Nevertheless, if a soldier did use the questionnaire to cry out for help, he or she would receive counseling both before and after coming home. Commanders have also been encouraged to look for such symptoms of distress as depression and anxiety.

Fort Bragg has altered its domestic violence policies, held domestic violence workshops, leadership seminars, and candlelight vigils, and mailed brochures with family-help contact numbers to thousands of

Army spouses. Many commanders on post now want to be immediately informed of domestic abuse involving soldiers in their units.

Although Armywide redeployment and reunion briefings have long been mandatory for soldiers and also offered to spouses, they have generally been taken more seriously since the murders. Depending on the unit and the attitude of those involved, these briefings can be meaningful or just a check-the-box exercise. The talks emphasize examining expectations and putting yourself in your spouse's shoes. The men are told not to assume everything will be just as it was when they left home. After all, their kids have grown, and their wives, who have had to be both mother and father, might not want to relinquish their newfound independence. Husbands have to realize they are coming back to a family unit that has adjusted to life without them, and now has to adjust once again.

The women are counseled about expectations, too. They hear that their husbands may not welcome candlelit dinners at home or big nights out. Instead they might be withdrawn and want to sleep day and night. The men may be emotionally and physically exhausted and may not want to talk about their experiences. Wives are told not to take it personally and advised to keep things low-key for a while. In the past the recommendation was to maintain the status quo, which some leaders took to an extreme, admonishing wives not to cut their hair or rearrange the family-room furniture. More recent briefings take into account that life does move on during a six-month or yearlong deployment. As for sex, that's covered, too, with husbands and wives urged to communicate with each other before jumping in the sack.

Most Army units today in Iraq and Afghanistan have also incorporated a transitional week or two of "light duty" when soldiers return and before they take their standard two weeks of leave. Going to classes and physical training, and cleaning and inventorying weapons, help maintain routine and counteract the reverse culture shock of coming home.

Fort Bragg continues to be a busy place. Before the September 11, 2001, attacks, the post had more than five thousand soldiers deployed to thirty countries. With the war in Afghanistan, the number of deployed troops tripled. Since the war in Iraq began, half of Fort Bragg's soldiers have been deployed at one time.

The exact causes of the Fort Bragg slayings will, of course, never be known. In the end we can only surmise. We can't talk to the dead. Some military and law-enforcement officials have said the only link among the murders was troubled marriages, and surely a strong case can be made to prove that point. I tend to agree with the Pentagon report, which points to a combination of existing marital problems compounded by the stress of hectic training schedules for combat units and lengthy deployment separations. As Rita Odom said, Army life will either pull you apart as a couple or bind you closer together.

My premise here has been that the soldiers who committed murder saw they were about to lose something to which they were emotionally attached, and it triggered a wrath they never knew they had. I am still puzzled by the demonic reactions of otherwise rational people, and I find myself asking questions that have no definitive answers: Does every man have a breaking point? And if so, how does it manifest itself?

It's too easy and too much of a generalization to say, "He just snapped" or "He was wired that way," though that's what I heard about the Bragg murderers. I believe it's more complicated, that it has less to do with decent people losing it and everything to do with emotion—something soldiers are expected to keep in check. I have asked Army guys, married and single, if they could ever envision themselves getting enraged enough to kill a spouse. I got all kinds of answers, from "No, I'd walk away," to "Maybe when I was younger" and "If I was mad enough." The answer that struck me as the most revealing was: "I don't know."

As the war in Iraq kicked off, many people told me to mark their words, we hadn't seen anything yet. They were sure there would be more spouse murders to come. Their prediction was borne out on July 22, 2004, at Fort Hood, Texas. Sergeant William Edwards shot and killed his estranged wife, Sergeant Erin Edwards, on her front porch. He then went across the street to a parking lot and killed himself. The couple had returned from Iraq a few months earlier, where both served with the 4th Infantry Division. The Edwards, who had two young children, had a history of domestic problems.

In the second case on May 21, 2005, in a bizarre twist, a Fort Bragg soldier, Ronna Valentine, returned from Iraq for two weeks of leave, but within hours her husband, James Valentine, had killed her with a 12-gauge shotgun before killing himself. It was Armed Forces Day. This couple, too, had problems in their past.

Meanwhile the subjects of this book have continued on with their lives:

Andrea Lynne still loves and grieves for Rennie. She says that her pain and loss have sharpened and shaped every aspect of her life, including her happiness. She has found new love with Roland, who remains her comfort and shelter. The Corys' oldest daughter, Natalie, graduated from Baylor University in May 2004 and was married in November 2004. Caroline is a junior at the University of North Carolina at Chapel Hill, and their son, Rennie, is a freshman at his parents' alma mater, Appalachian State University. Their youngest, Madelyn, is a high school freshman.

Rita is still employed at Highsmith-Rainey Memorial Hospital. Her husband, Sergeant Brian Odom, returned from Afghanistan on January 15, 2003, three days before Johnathan's fifth birthday. Brian got out of the Army on December 12, 2003, just before his unit left for a six-month deployment to Iraq. He is currently studying to be a forensic technician at Fayetteville Technical Community College. When Brian graduates in 2006, Rita plans to go back to school to obtain a doctorate in pharmacy. Jay, Alan, and Johnathan are all in elementary school.

Delores is considering part-time or volunteer work and would like to be on a suicide prevention hotline. Her son's memory is with her daily. She plans on taking a few classes at Fayetteville Technical Community College and is interested in studying piano and voice. Command Sergeant Major Gary Kalinofski deployed to Afghanistan on January 4, 2003, and returned home July 12, 2003. After thirty years of active duty, he retired from the Army on July 9, 2004. He is now the vice president for military affairs for a military housing company at Fort Bragg. Cherish is a high school sophomore.

The three children of Sergeant First Class Brandon and Andrea Floyd are being raised by Andrea's mother, Penny Flitcraft, in Andrea's hometown, Alliance, Ohio. Penny and the children visit Andrea's grave often. She says the ache of losing her daughter never goes away, and the family continues to miss and honor her.

Master Sergeant Bill Wright hanged himself in his jail cell on March 23, 2003, as he awaited trial. The Wrights' three sons now live with Jennifer's sister in Springboro, Ohio.

In March 2005 Sergeant Cedric Griffin pleaded guilty to murdering his wife, Marilyn, and setting her home on fire. He is serving a life sentence at Central Prison in Raleigh, North Carolina. Marilyn's two daughters live with relatives in Georgia.

On August 31, 2005, a Fayetteville jury convicted Joan Shannon of first-degree murder, conspiracy to commit murder, and accessory after the fact to murder for the death of her husband, Major David Shannon. The judge sentenced her to life without parole; her attorney said she plans to appeal. Joan Shannon's daughter, Elizabeth, pleaded guilty in June 2004 to second-degree murder in the death of her stepfather. In exchange for testifying against her mother, Elizabeth will serve a twenty-five to thirty-year sentence.

The daughter of Sergeant First Class Rigoberto and Teresa Nieves lives with Teresa's mother in California.

Lieutenant Sam Pennica of the Cumberland County Sheriff's Department was promoted to the rank of major, and his homicide detective, Sergeant Charlie Disponzio, was promoted to lieutenant.

As for me, I met a Fort Bragg officer on a blind date in August 2002. We got engaged seven months later in Kuwait, and I left the newspaper shortly after. We married in June 2004, a few months after his return from Iraq.

ACKNOWLEDGMENTS

As a writer and Army brat it has been an honor, a privilege—and a great responsibility—to write this book. Telling the story of U.S. Army wives and the culture that surrounds them was something I didn't do lightly, and I hope I've done this cloistered, unknown world justice.

I first want to thank the women who shared their stories. I learned much from each of them, and I appreciate their candidness, honesty, and their faith in me to neither distort nor sensationalize their lives. In the case of Andrea Floyd, I am grateful to her family and friends.

A special thank-you to my agent, Rafe Sagalyn, for introducing me to the world of book publishing and for encouraging me to think big. Thanks also to his assistant, Jennifer Graham, for her early encouragement.

I am grateful to Diane Reverand, my editor at St. Martin's Press, who believed in and supported this project from the beginning. Her assistant, Regina Scarpa, also made this whole process a more pleasant one. My appreciation to the copyeditor, Sue Llewellyn, for her astute observations.

It has been an honor to work with Joan Tapper, my editor, confidante, and friend in Santa Barbara, California. Joan helped make my transition from newspapers to books enjoyable. Her editing and organizational skills are reflected throughout these pages.

Many thanks to Major Sam Pennica of the Cumberland County Sheriff's Department. His assistance and professionalism were truly valuable.

Among my friends I especially thank Patti Kogan, Harvey and Anne Oliver, and Dougald and Tori MacMillan for their love and support.

Special thanks to my husband, Michael, and my sister, Maria, who gave me love and encouragement from afar. Both were serving in Iraq while I was writing much of this book.

Finally, I thank my parents, Sam and Pat, whose forty-plus years of love for each other was the greatest gift to their children. Their lives confirm that love, commitment, and the Army can go together quite nicely.